WOMEN'S AUTONOMY AND REPRODUCTIVE BEHAVIOUR

WOMEN'S AUTONOMY AND REPRODUCTIVE BEHAVIOUR

S. Gunasekaran

KALPAZ

Women's Autonomy and Reproductive Behaviour

Rs. 885

ISBN: 978-81-7835-804-8

Published in 2010 in India by
Kalpaz Publications
C-30, Satyawati Nagar,
Delhi-110052
E-mail: kalpaz@hotmail.com
Phone : 9212729499

Laser Type Setting by: Rudra Computer Graphics, Delhi
Printed at : Chawla Offset Printers, Delhi

Contents

List of Tables

List of Figures

List of Abbreviations

BC	-	Backward Caste
CEB	-	Children Ever Born
DACF	-	Decision about Contraception and Fertility
EDHS	-	Egyptian Demographic and Health Survey
FC	-	Freedom of Choice
FGDs	-	Focus Group Discussions
FINM	-	Financial Management
FM	-	Freedom of Movement
GDI	-	Gender Development Index
HD	-	Household Decisions
HDI	-	Human Development Index
MBC	-	Most Backward Caste
MDG	-	Millennium Development Goal
NFHS	-	National Family Health Survey
PSPA	-	Participation in social and political activities
PSUs	-	Primary Sampling Units
RH	-	Reproductive Health
SC/ST	-	Scheduled Caste / Scheduled Tribe
SD	-	Standard Deviation
SHG	-	Self Help Group
SLI	-	Standard of Living Index
SNNPR	-	Southern Nations, Nationalities and People's Region of Ethiopia

SPSS	-	Statistical Package for Social Sciences
SSI	-	Sex Segregated Interaction
TA	-	Total Autonomy
UN	-	United Nations
VAW	-	Violence Against Women

GANDHIGRAM RURAL UNIVERSITY
(Estd.u/s 3 of the UGC Act. 1956 vide Notification No. F.9-1/76-U.3/3.8.1976 of GoI)
GANDHIGRAM - 624302,
DINDIGUL DISTRICT, TAMILNADU, INDIA
Phone : Off : 0451 - 2452305/2453845 Res : 0451 - 2452345
Mob : 94421 05116 Fax : 0451 - 2454535

Foreword

The women folk have all along been struggling for their existence, recognition, rights, freedom, decision making etc. since time immemorial. Society, Be it literate or illiterate, culturally evolved or primitive, rural or urban, poor or wealthy, the women folk in general have been kept in green room and neither their merits were weighed nor their rights were reserved. In certain segments of the society even they had no freedom to own a child of their own gender choice and the society has been cruel to the extent of even female infanticide. This scenario, though has however started showin.g signs of change in the recent years, yet we are to go a long way and the women folk are to enjoy full rights and also fortified in the realm of the society.

In this back drop, Dr. S.Gunasekaran has carried out a unique study to understand multivariate issues related to women autonomy. He has carried out rigorous statistical modeling taking, large number of samples both from the rural and urban regions of three districts of Tamilnadu and collecting data on different variables such as socio economic, demography, fertility behaviour, knowledge on family planning, freedom of movement, freedom of participation in social and political activities etc. Through this, he has made a hierarchy of note worthy observations and salient amongst them are that the women with more children have less autonomy, educated women, have freedom of movement, freedom of participation in societal and political activities are generally less, but little more with educated women involved less in the decision making etc. He has embedded the findings with lucid explanations and adequate exhibits in his book "*Women's Autonomy and Reproductive Behaviour*".

I am confident that this book will of immense help not only to the academic and researc community but to the planners and administrators as well.

(S.M. RAMASAMY)

Preface

The International Conference on Population and Development (ICPD), Cario (1994) and the fourth International Conference on Women, Beijing (1995) recognised the need for the empowerment of women for a sustainable development. While taking into consideration of the contemporary campaign for 'women empowerment' especially after the passage of the Resolution adopted by the ICPD in 1994 and with the advent of emphatic assertion of women's right to control all aspects of their health, in particular, their own fertility, this book on Women's Autonomy and Reproductive Behaviour is highly relevant now. Ability to obtain information, and its use for the purpose of decision-making pertinent to one's exclusive private domain are two functional components of 'autonomy'. Unfortunately Indian women enjoy very little 'autonomy' in respect of selection of life partners, kinship relationships and finances etc. Studies suggest that improvement in the status of women particularly in these fields have positive influence upon the family size through the adoption of family planning methods. The right to plan and regulate family size is admittedly a basic human right; women as human being must be assured of this right. In both developed and developing countries, women should decide the family size by way of child birth as well as spacing of child birth.

The autonomy of women may be operationalised by introducing two interrelated expressions: 'freedom from' and 'freedom to'. 'Freedom from' refers to relaxation or absence from men's control and assertion of women's right to decision-making. 'Freedom to' espouses interaction with the outside world including freedom of movement. Like in many other societies, in Tamilnadu as well married women do remain under the 'control' of husband and mother-in-law and enjoy very little autonomy even in regard to reproductive behaviour.

The present book based on the findings of a large scale survey conducted on a sample of 2400 currently married women aged 15-29 years selected from both the rural and urban areas of three districts of Tamil Nadu focuses on the autonomy of women and it's impact on their reproductive behaviour.

The design of the study with setting of objectives, collection of data, univariate and multi-variate analysis of data has been praise worthy. Unwinding the concept of women's autonomy into eight (8) variables to pierce into reality has laudably been done. The sample size has been very scientifically decided upon indicating the rural-urban divide of three districts of Tamilnadu viz., Kancheepuram, Thiruchirapalli and Villupuram selected on the basis of Gender Development Index (GDI). With the help of interview method combined with 'Focus Group Discussions' organized in rural and urban areas in each of the selected districts, the results of the study has been placed in high relevance in respect of policy-making.

The study has been conducted with great care and the findings are of immense value. I hope this book will meet the requirement of policy makers, programme planners, researchers, academicians, students and individuals who are interested in the study of women autonomy and reproductive behaviour.

Dr. S. Gunasekaran
Associate Professor
Department of Applied Research
Gandhigram Rural University
Gandhigram-624302
Tamil Nadu

Acknowledgements

I am very much grateful to Indian Council of Social Science Research (ICSSR), New Delhi for funding this study without which this research would not have been possible.

I wish to place on record my deep sense of gratitude to Dr. M.A. Sudhir, Professor and Head of the Department of Applied Research, Gandhigram Rural University, for his contineous support, technical advice and motivation through out the implementation of the project.

I express my gratitude to the research investigators Ms. K. Dhanalakshmi and Ms. K. Indiragandhi, who took a lot of effort facing many difficulties, to travel to various parts of Tamil Nadu to collect data from women. I am also thankful to the women respondents for their cooperation in responding to the questions during the personal interview and the focus group discussion.

The contribution made by various academicians, researchers and programme personnel during the dissemination workshop held at Gandhigram Rural University was equally valuable and I am very much thankful to them.

I am also thankful to Dr. S. Muthukrishnaveni, Dr. P. Devi, and Dr. T. Latha, research scholars in the Department of

Applied Research, Gandhigram Rural University for their valuable help at various stages of the preparation of this book.

I take this opportunity to also acknowledge the computer assistance rendered by Shri. S. Arul Gnanaprakasam, working in the ICMR Project in the Department of Applied Research.

Finally I thank Kalpaz Publications, Delhi, for their professional help and support in publishing this book.

Dr. S. Gunasekaran
Associate Professor
Department of Applied Research
Gandhigram Rural University
Gandhigram-624302

1

Introduction

Women are often considered the key to the development challenge. Though they have much to contribute to the development process, a disproportionate percentage of women in the developing world are poor and often lack opportunities for development. Hence a number of development strategies have been adopted in the past throughout the developing world to promote gender equity and participation of women in the development process.

The achieving of equality and equity between men and women in different spheres of life is essential for the attainment of sustainable development. In this context, the need for enhancement of women's participation in national development programmes and their full integration into the development process has been widely recognised in various global and regional forums such as the International Conference on Human Rights (Vienna, 1993), the Declaration on the Elimination of Violence against Women (UN, 1993), the International Conference on Population and Development (Cairo, 1994), the Fourth International Conference on Women (Beijing, 1995) and the

World Health Assembly (Geneva, 1996). The inclusion of gender equality and empowerment of women as one of the Millennium Development Goals showed the international commitment to women's empowerment (UN, 2005).

The Programme of Action adopted by the International Conference on Population and Development at Cairo in 1994 reaffirmed and elaborated the role of women in national development and endorsed a new strategy that emphasises "gender equality, equity and empowerment of women". In this context, the Programme of Action recommends that countries should act to empower women and should take steps to eliminate inequalities between men and women by providing them with more choices through expanded access to education and health services, skill development and employment and eliminating all practices that discriminate against women (United Nations, 1995b).

Despite many international agreements affirming women's human rights, women are much more likely than men to be poor, malnourished and illiterate and to have less access than men to medical care, property ownership, credit, training and employment (United Nations, 1998). Women's equal participation with men in power and decision-making is part of their fundamental right to participate in political life and at the core of gender equality and women's empowerment.

Empowerment implies expansion of assets and capabilities of people to influence, control and hold accountable institutions that affect their lives. Empowerment is a process whereby women become able to organise themselves to increase self reliance, to assert their independent right to make choices and to control resources which will assist in challenging and eliminating their own subordination. Empowerment has multiple dimensions that are interrelated viz. social, economic, political and capability development. The empowerment process encompasses several mutually reinforcing components but begins with and is supported by economic independence, which implies access to and control over production resources; a second component of empowerment is knowledge and awareness; the third is self image; and, the final is autonomy. Empowering women puts the spotlight on their health, education and employment. It is an essential element of sustainable development (Meenakshi Joshi, 2004).

Social empowerment connotes formation of social capacities such as health, education, freedom and opportunities for realizing one's potentialities. Economic empowerment implies entitlement to employment, income, property, productive resources and benefits, regardless of gender differences. Psychological empowerment signifies confidence building, acquisition of a sense of efficacy and ability to overcome the feeling of helplessness. Political empowerment implies equal say in the decision making process in the power structure at all levels from local to global. All these dimensions of empowerment are so intertwined with one another that over reliance on one to the neglect of the others is not likely to work (Sharma, 2000).

Women are now being treated as critical inputs for development. It is felt that women have to be empowered if they have to play a critical role in development. Empowerment of women is a necessary condition for improving the status of women. Any society which has achieved a high degree of social development has its women enjoying better status in terms of education, health, employment, participation in decision making in the family, community, state and civil society (Smita Mishra Panda, 2000). Thus empowerment is a process of awareness and capacity building leading to greater participation, greater decision-making power and control over the transformative action. The empowerment of women covers both individual and collective transformation. It strengthens their innate ability through acquiring knowledge, power and experience (Senthil Vadivoo and Sekar, 2004).

There has been a radical change in the movement for empowerment of women. Recognition is dawning that women are indeed becoming a political force, both nationally and internationally. Since women rights have been accepted as human rights at the international level, the movement for empowerment is bound to gather strength. Once the rights are proclaimed, the process of empowerment can not stop the rights move to the top of the political agenda. However, doubts have been expressed at several forums, including in the Report of the Independent Commission on Population and Quality of Life, about the danger of empowerment being sloganised without coming to realization. There is even danger that empowerment may become devoid of meaning if effective steps are not taken to implement various administrative and constitutional measures. In a country like India, with a strong tradition of democratic functioning, a vibrant public opinion and influential sections of society interested in progress and welfare of women, the movement for women's empowerment is bound to gather strength. Such a powerful onward thrust towards strengthening this movement is bound to make a major contribution towards nation-building (Gupta and Sen, 2002).

According to the draft policy on women, the Government of India plans to set up a National Council for the Empowerment of Women, headed by the Prime Minister, to review the implementation of the recommendations of the National Commission for Women and Child Welfare (Ministry of Human Resource Development). It states that women's equality in power sharing and active participation in decision making, including political decision making at all levels and in all processes, would be ensured for the achievement of the goal of empowerment (Manisha Gangwar and Nita Kandekar, 2004). The National Policy for the Empowerment of Women envisages the creating of an environment through positive economic and social policies for full development of women to enable them to realise their full potential (Bhagyalakshmi, 2004).

Women's empowerment and full, equal participation in all spheres of society, including decision-making and the exercise of power, "are fundamental for the achievement of equality, development and peace"; women's rights are human rights; and these rights include equality of opportunity and access to resources and "the right of all women to control all aspects of their health, in particular their own fertility" (United Nations, 1995b).

Autonomy indicates the ability to obtain information and to use it as the basis for making decisions about one's private concerns and those of one's intimates (Dyson and Moore, 1983). Women's autonomy has been defined as the extent to which women are free of men's control, which may influence childbearing patterns. Autonomy includes freedom in decision-making, freedom to interact with the outside world and freedom of movement (Basu, 1992). After marriage, a woman in India is under the authority of her husband and mother-in-law; a woman generally has little autonomy or voice in decision-making even regarding her own fertility. Sociological and anthropological research on the status of women has suggested that, generally speaking, Indian women enjoy very little autonomy within their household because family decisions relating to finances, kinship relationships, selection of life partners etc. are made by men, and women are rarely consulted. Studies have shown that improvement in the status of women influences them to limit their family size through adoption of family planning methods (Jejeebhoy, 1991). Women having greater income enjoy freedom and develop faith in their own ability to perform various tasks and deal with the outside world with confidence. They are also likely to exercise greater control over their reproduction (Visaria, 1993).

It is thought that constraints on women's autonomy are contributing to the high prevalence of teenage pregnancies and births which occur before an interval of 24 months after the last birth and adoption of family planning methods. However, detailed empirical evidence is yet to become available. Scanty information is available on the relationship between women's autonomy and their reproductive behaviour (child bearing patterns), including the adoption of family planning methods. In this context, an attempt has been made in this study to assess the relationship between women's autonomy and childbearing patterns, focusing in particular on age at first birth, birth interval, parity, gender composition and family planning adoption. Given that women's autonomy has been shown to differ between urban and rural areas, both the rural and the urban areas are included in the study so as to permit comparison. The study is based on married women aged 15-29 years, given the fact that a high proportion of current child bearing occurs within this age group.

2

Review

This chapter presents the results of the review of earlier studies conducted at the international and national level on various aspects of women's autonomy and its relationship with fertility and family planning practices.

2.1 Women's Autonomy

The concept of women's empowerment is very important for the success of family planning and reproductive health programs, but there is no consensus on the meaning of the term. Women's empowerment is such a complex phenomenon that its measurement remains a problem for academicians and policy makers. The review of recent literature on the attempts to measure and examine the validity of indicators of women's empowerment by demographers and other social researchers suggests that the information collected to construct these indicators is sensitive, subjective and varies in dimension. There is certainly a need to develop a standard and valid tool to measure the empowerment of women. There are various indicators and approaches that are collected by various large-scale surveys like the National Family Health Survey (Shastri, 2002).

A growing body of literature strongly suggests that gender inequality has a significant impact on the demographic transition and on the socio-economic development of countries. Data collected through three surveys conducted in Botswana, South Africa and Rajasthan among women aged 15-49 were analyzed using regression models and causal log-linear models to describe the role of different aspects of women's autonomy on fertility. The results of the analysis carried out show some similarities and also very large differences. In particular, the women of Rajasthan have less autonomy (in terms of women's status) than do the women of Botswana and South Africa (Drovandi and Salvini, 2004).

The results of the analysis of data obtained from a qualitative study in Karachi comprising 15 focus group discussions with 114 female participants and 294 semi-structured, in-depth interviews with ever-married women aged 30 years and older on women's autonomy in decision making on physical, emotional and economic showed a continuing strong preference for close cousin unions across all ethnic and religious groups. The key underlying rationale was the socio-cultural advantage such marriages offered in terms of the convenience of finding a suitable bride or a groom. However, there also appeared to be considerable ambivalence surrounding the benefits of kinship marriages. It is noted that women in close cousin unions consistently reported having less autonomy across three of the four domains—decision-making, emotional and economic-in many of the issues affecting their lives. This sense of disempowerment was independent of the type of living arrangement but was perpetuated by the fact that women in close cousin unions often had a lower level of education and a younger age at marriage. With regard to the wider implications of the effect of marriage preferences on women's health and to delineate the impact of kinship structures on female autonomy, a need for more detailed qualitative research is indicated (Hussain, 2001).

The research conducted in northern and southern India and Pakistan on the influence of religion and region on the autonomy of women in these countries put forth two arguments about women's autonomy. Firstly, Pakistani women's position denies them freedom and educational opportunity, as it does in other Islamic settings. Secondly, regional social systems dictate the behavior and norms of Indian women, which characterize more freedom from those in the south. These assertions are explored empirically using data drawn from India and Pakistan. A comparison is presented between the lives of women in three settings—one in Punjab, Pakistan, the other two (Uttar Pradesh and Tamil Nadu) in North and South India, respectively—similarities and differences in women's autonomy are assessed. This is followed by an examination of the extent to which levels of autonomy are in fact explained by such commonly available measures of autonomy as education and economic activity and such traditional providers of status as age and residence patterns. Furthermore, the contextual factors underlying observed differences are explored. It is ascertained whether differences in women's autonomy are attributable to religion, to nationality or to the north-south cultural difference that has been acknowledged within India and that can be investigated with the inclusion of data from Pakistan (Jejeebhoy and Sathar, 2001).

The comparison of changes in gender roles and women's empowerment in China, the Republic of Korea and India revealed that, around 1950, when all these countries had new governments following a revolution or the end of colonial rule, they were largely poor and agrarian, with many cultural commonalities which placed similar severe constraints on women's autonomy. They adopted very different paths of development, which are known to have profoundly affected development outcomes in these countries. However, these choices have also had tremendous impact on gender outcomes and today these countries show striking differences in the extent of gender equity achieved: China has achieved the most and the Republic of Korea the least. It is concluded that States can exert enormous influence over gender equity. They can mitigate cultural influences on women's autonomy (as in China and India) or slow down the pace of change in gender equity despite rapid integration of women in education, formal employment and urbanization (as in the Republic of Korea). The impact of policies to provide opportunities for women's empowerment can be greatly enhanced if accompanied by communication efforts to alter cultural values which place heavy constraints on women's accessing these opportunities (Das Gupta et al., 2000).

An examination of the elements that constitute women's autonomy in rural Pakistan revealed that northern Punjabi women have lower economic autonomy but greater mobility and decision-making authority than women in southern Punjab. Gender systems at the village level are also important predictors of women's autonomy. Economic class has a weak and ambivalent influence on women's autonomy in rural Punjab. Class influences both education and employment of women. These remain the routes to empowerment in rural settings. While most women in rural areas contribute economically, the majority work on the household farm or within the household economic unit. These women do not derive any additional autonomy as a result of this contribution. Paid employment, though offset by other restrictions on poor women, offers greater potential for women's autonomy. Education, on the other hand, has a lesser influence on female autonomy in the rural Punjabi context (Sathar and Kazi, 2000).

A study conducted to examine how aspects of married women's family position influence their domestic power and autonomy in five Southern and Southeastern Asian countries: namely, Pakistan, India, Malaysia, Thailand and the Philippines found that women's power tended to be higher in Southeast Asian countries, especially Thailand and the Philippines. Women's economic power was lowest and coercive interpersonal controls were highest in Pakistan. Freedom of movement was greater in Malaysia and the Philippines. Gender conditions varied between countries. Trust and experience and being the wife of the household head led to greater power in financial decisions. In less traditional settings, the extent of power was determined by personal characteristics, such as age and education. Marrying a related man did not enhance women's economic decision-making. Women with more children had lower autonomy and power. Socioeconomic status was positively related or unrelated to personal power and autonomy. Higher status protected against family coercion. Findings confirm that social context is a strong explanatory factor of variation in women's autonomy and power (Mason, 1997).

Data from the 1988 Egyptian Demographic and Health Survey (EDHS) were analyzed to explore factors which influence women's level and type of autonomy and how different dimensions of autonomy relate to each other. The answers of 7717 women to EDHS queries about women's perceptions of who should have and who does have decision-making powers within the family and about women's freedom of movement were grouped into three indices of autonomy: customary (concerning the procreation and rearing of children), non customary (general areas and household finance) and realized (a combination of who is perceived to have decision-making power and respondent's freedom of movement) autonomy. It was found that modernization had the greatest effect on perceptions of non customary autonomy and that socioeconomic status affected all aspects of autonomy directly and positively (but urban living, while leading to higher levels of noncustomary autonomy, led to lower levels of realized autonomy). Control over earnings, rather than being employed per se, was positively associated with autonomy, but realized autonomy was higher for all women who worked (realized autonomy includes freedom of movement). Being remarried was associated with a lower score on the noncustomary autonomy index. Also, co residence with in-laws and number of sons may not be causally related to women's autonomy. Indeed, higher fertility in general was associated with lower autonomy, even with lower customary autonomy. All aspects of autonomy were positively and significantly related to each other and changes in noncustomary autonomy affected the other indices the most. Thus, manipulating modernization variables (those most amenable to policy changes) may do the most to increase women's autonomy in Egypt (Kishor, 1995).

An analysis of NFHS-2 data on women's empowerment in different states of India shows that socioeconomic development, freedom of decision-making and interactions outside the home are the main dimensions of women's empowerment (Dey, 2002).

A survey conducted in the states of Uttar Pradesh and Tamil Nadu among eligible women aged 15-49 years revealed that a regional divide exists in the level of women's empowerment. It is noted that women in Tamil Nadu showed a greater autonomy in decision making about their own health care, freedom of movement and access to money. On the other hand, women in Uttar Pradesh are found to have a greater self worth, in the sense that they are more critical about wife beating. Of the three direct indicators of autonomy, these women were noted to have the least autonomy in terms of freedom of movement, which is an important indicator of the empowerment (Roy and Niranjan, 2002).

An analysis of data drawn from a 1993-94 community-based study of women's autonomy in Uttar Pradesh and Tamil Nadu states that are, respectively, more and less patriarchal indicate no more than a loose agreement between women and their husbands concerning the dimensions of women's autonomy within the home. Where disagreement is expressed, husbands are more likely to project a comparatively liberal picture of their wives' autonomy than do their wives and the inference can be made that in surveys men tended to provide more "acceptable" responses than when they were questioned in greater depth. Findings also suggest that the cultural context affects the influences that wives' and their husbands' perceptions of women's autonomy have on reproductive outcomes. A clear regional divide is seen, not of individual and household characteristics, in the influence of almost every aspect of women's autonomy (Jejeebhoy, 1991)

Another study conducted in four southern states of India, namely Andhra Pradesh, Karnataka, Tamil Nadu and Kerala revealed that Kerala has better social development and women's empowerment. However, in Tamil Nadu, females are more empowered compared to the state's social development. Karnataka is comparatively well off in social development but not in women's autonomy. In Andhra Pradesh, both are less remarkable. In conclusion, greater attention is to be directed in the states of Karnataka and Andhra Pradesh to improve the conditions of females than the socioeconomic development of the state in general (Sulaja, 2002).

A study conducted to explore the different levels of women's autonomy and the different dimensions of women's autonomy among Rajasthani migrants revealed that, as education increases, women's autonomy increases; and employment is likely to enhance women's autonomy. Almost all respondents were found to have strong decision-making power regarding work and that all respondents have strong decision-making power at the household level. All 14 respondents use appropriate contraceptive; however, only 12 of the respondents jointly take decisions regarding family size. Daughters of respondents were educated as much as possible, indicating a change in women's attitude (Bhatt, 2000).

Delhi migrants from low socioeconomic classes were compared based on their home origins in north or south India. The two groups differed in cultural beliefs, attitudes and practices, but they lived in the same resettlement colony and had the same physical access to services and opportunities. It is found that households from Tamil Nadu in the south were more modern, had greater female autonomy and were open to new ideas. Uttar Pradesh women from the north were more traditional, secluded and restricted in economic activities. The results showed lower fertility, higher levels of contraceptive use and earlier end to childbearing among Tamil Nadu women, who had had more exposure to ideas about smaller family size, healthful childrearing practices and positive attitudes about contraceptive use. The conclusion was that the status of women and their exposure to and interaction with the outside world and control over decision making at home explained the differences between the two groups. Policy implications are to make programs culturally sensitive, for example, providing at-home care for women traditionally sheltered from contact with strangers (Greenspan, 1994).

2.2 Women's Autonomy, Fertility and Family Planning

The persistence of moderate to high fertility in many countries in the South Asian region can be traced to socio-cultural factors that prevent women from translating their family size preferences into practice through conscious use of family planning. Female autonomy — the ability to obtain information and to use it as the basis for decision making — is strongly influenced by factors such as kinship and marriage relationships, age, religion, the political system and the division of labor between the sexes. The complete dependence of younger women on men and older women, deference to age and lack of access to the outside world combine to make it difficult for South Asian women to practice fertility control. Early marriage increases their exposure to the risk of pregnancy even further. Since women in this region are taught that their own interests are subordinate to those of the family group, they are likely to sacrifice their own desire to regulate fertility. Confronted with social isolation and an insecure future, women turn to children as a potential source of security, especially sons. The forces of modernization have the potential to give South Asian women the autonomy they need to resist pronatalist pressures. Such forces include overall development of the locality, opportunities for education and employment, legal reforms, the presence of change agents, the availability of family planning clinics and the adoption of innovations in the immediate environment (United Nations, 1987).

A national study conducted in Oman found that education was a key indicator of women's status. Unmet contraceptive need for women exposed to pregnancy was nearly 25 per cent, but decreased significantly with educational level and paid employment. While empowered women were more likely to use contraception, women's education was a better predictor of "met need" than autonomy, as traditional factors and community influence remain strong. For nearly half the 1,830 women in the study, the husband decided whether contraception was used. Fewer than one per cent were using contraception before their first child as women are expected to have a child within the first year of marriage (Al Riyami et al., 2004).

Another cross-sectional survey of the health status of Omani community found that about 31 per cent of the study population (ever married women) was highly empowered in decision-making and the mean number of decisions taken in the household was 4.46 for the overall sample. As for freedom of movement, 29 per cent of the sample was highly empowered with a mean number of 3.88 for the overall sample. The mean values of both indices varied significantly according to age, residence, level of education and work status. Higher freedom of movement score women were more likely to have less number of children in the first 20 years of marriage. Women of higher score of decision making index were more likely to have a longer closed birth interval. Those who scored low in the decision making index were more likely to get a child at an earlier age. In developing countries where fertility limitation depends on "modern" methods, women's education and autonomy are considered strong tools to make changes in demographic transition (Al Riyami and Afifi, 2003).

A summary of the central findings about gender inequalities in Egypt, India, Ghana and Kenya published by the Population Council in 1994 showed that these countries exhibited gender inequalities in different ways: the legal, economic and educational systems; family planning and reproductive health services; and the health care system. All the countries had in common a high incidence of widowhood. Widowhood was linked with high levels of insecurity, which were linked with high fertility. Children thus became insurance in old age. In Ghana, women's insecurity was threatened through high levels of marital instability and polygyny. In Egypt, insecurity was translated into economic vulnerability because of legal discrimination against women when family systems were disrupted. In all the four countries, insecurity was reflective of limited access to education, an impediment to economic autonomy. In all the four countries, women's status was inferior due to limited control over reproductive decision making about childbearing limits and contraception. In India, the cultural devaluation of girls contributed to higher fertility to satisfy the desire for sons. In India and Egypt, family planning programs were dominated by male-run organizations that were more concerned about demographic objectives than reproductive health. The universal inequality was the burden women carry for contraception. Family planning programs have ignored the local realities of reproductive behavior, family structures and gender relations. The assumption that husbands and wives have similar fertility goals or that fathers fully share the costs of children is mistaken in countries such as Ghana. Consequently, fertility has declined less than 13 per cent in Ghana, but fertility has declined by over 30 per cent in Kenya. Family planning programmes must be aware of gender issues (Population Briefs, 1995).

An analysis of demographic and health survey sample of 3701 married black African women from Zimbabwe revealed that when men dominated all household decisions, women were less likely to approve of contraceptive use, discuss their desired number of children with their spouse, report ever use of a modern method of contraception and intend to use contraception in the future. However, women's decision-making autonomy was not associated with current modern contraceptive use. Women who had no decision-making autonomy had 0.26 more children than women who had some autonomy. These autonomy measures provide additional independent explanatory power of fertility-related behavior not of traditional measures of women's status such as education and labor force participation (Hindin, 2000).

Data for currently married, fecund women aged 15-49 from demographic surveys conducted in the Southern Nations, Nationalities and People's Region of Ethiopia (SNNPR) in 1990 and 1997 are used to investigate contraceptive knowledge and communication and the use of and future need for family planning services in this population. This study focuses on how these processes are affected by household organization and women's status and on their implications for population policies and programs. Considerations of the implications of these results for understanding the fertility transition of a highly diverse African population under severe stress are presented. Although household extension and polygamy characterize one-third of the women sampled, they do not affect the women's contraceptive behavior. Women's literacy and autonomy are, by far, the most significant forces in the movement toward lower fertility in the region (Hogan et al., 1999).

Fertility is declining in all regions of the world, even where women's lives remain severely constrained, as illustrated in the experiences of Bangladesh and Egypt. Population Council researchers analyzed economic, societal and governmental factors in both countries to determine their influence on fertility decline. A comparison between Bangladesh and Egypt suggests that women in both settings have little autonomy. However, a comparison of general socioeconomic conditions suggests that Egypt is relatively better with regard to demographic transition than Bangladesh. Differing development styles may account for some of the factors that lower fertility in Bangladesh. Egypt follows a traditional approach of infrastructure development, whereas Bangladesh follows an approach focused on poverty alleviation that targets resources and services to the poor and to women. The difference in approach is probably most pronounced in the areas of family planning services and the availability of rural credit services (Population Briefs, 1999).

The analysis of data pertaining to women in the demographic registration system for the year 1986 covering 87 villages in Manikganj District of Bangladesh and the matching group of 707 women from the 1994 follow-up survey of 1535 married women 15-49 years old who were nonusers of contraception, found significant differences between 1986 and 1994 in years of schooling, literacy rate, land ownership and husband's education. The increase in literacy reflected the general increase of female education in the country. Both women's autonomy and the involvement with credit-based income generating program had positive and statistically significant effects on contraceptive use regardless of the demographic and socioeconomic differences between women in the villages. Accessibility to credit sources increased the women's autonomy to 28 per cent ($p<0.05$) when the years of schooling was controlled. When the age and socioeconomic variables were added the effects of the involvement in credit programs on women's autonomy diminished. Contraceptive acceptance had statistically significant relationship with the socio-demographic characteristics of women regardless of their involvement with credit-based income generating activities. Model I indicated that the probability of using contraceptives rose to 89 per cent if the women had more autonomy than others, when age and the number of children were controlled. Model II showed that nonusers of contraception involved in the credit program after 1986 were 62 per cent more likely to accept any contraceptive than women who did not receive any credit, controlling for autonomy, age and the number of living children. The effects of autonomy on contraceptive use consistently remained strong in all three models, indicating that socio-demographic variability by women's autonomy in the study population was minimal (Hadi et.al., 1997).

Presenting primary evidence from India, Pakistan, Sri Lanka and Bangladesh and utilising existing census and survey data, an attempt has been made to explore the interrelated issues of women's autonomy, girls schooling and fertility reduction in South Asia. It is concluded that schooling is indeed important for women and should definitely be supported and encouraged, but not because of the possible impact it may have on fertility decline. Further, while resources should continue to be devoted to the spread of education, this should not be at the expense of providing women-friendly contraceptive and maternal/child health services, which give couples the ability to successfully plan the size of the family they want. (Jeffery and Basu, 1996).

An analysis of the 1989 Bangladesh fertility survey aimed at assessing whether or not women's exposure to formal schooling enhances their autonomy in domestic decision making as measured by freedom of movement outside the household and participation in domestic and reproductive decisions showed that there was an increase in self-reported mobility and decision making scores for every increase in educational level from none to primary educated to secondary or higher educated. Maternal education was a strong predictor in the multinomial logistic regression of both autonomy measures, after controlling for urban-rural residence, region, age and socioeconomic status. Schooling had a large and statistically significant effect on traditional and modern reversible contraceptive use. Schooling was not statistically significantly related to sterilization. More educated women were less likely to be sterilized. Under 50 per cent of the influence of schooling on the use of modern reversible contraception was related to factors associated with schooling. After controls for schooling, residence and other factors, there was a highly statistically significant difference between highly mobile women and less autonomous women. The link between domestic decision making and modern contraception was almost as strong as for mobility. The impact of autonomy on sterilization was "less decisive" (Cleland et al., 1996).

A study on the role of women's autonomy in facilitating fertility change in Pakistan suggests that women's autonomy at the community level had a greater influence on fertility than individual autonomy measures. Fertility change was also influenced strongly by gender systems. Women's autonomy at the individual level acted in conflicting ways. Multicollinearity may be an explanatory factor. The shift from joint living to nuclear families did not lead to greater autonomy for women. But, in-laws did inhibit women's autonomy. Greater mobility and decision-making had significant effects on fertility change. Son preference still had a strong impact (Sathar et al., 1996).

A study aimed at assessing women's autonomy in Egypt highlighted some links between women's autonomy and selected aspects of family planning and reproductive health. The study revealed a low autonomy level among Egyptian women. On a scale from 0 to 5, mean autonomy levels were found to be only 1.2. This situation impacted women's ability to control their fertility, to achieve their reproductive intentions, to acquire high quality services, to minimize the gap of unmet need and to seek care when faced with health problems (Nawar, 1995).

Studies from different parts of the country show that there is a broad correlation between women's position and fertility. However, innumerable studies also show that other factors like declining maternal and child mortality, access to reliable health care facilities, confidence over the survival of children, access to contraception and 5-8 years of schooling leading to delay in the age of marriage exert a strong influence on family size, even in situations where women are not empowered or enjoy a good status in society (Ramachandran, 2002).

An attempt made to measure women's empowerment and its relevance to fertility and child mortality by using data from the National Family Health Survey-2, Gujarat State, revealed that older women with long marital duration, those residing in urban areas, belonging to high living standard groups, socially better off castes, engaged in higher non-farm type occupations and Christians are found to have high index value on all indices of women empowerment. The study also found that autonomy indices revealed weak influence on child survival and contraceptive use. However, it is important to note that education of women, a variable highly correlated with female autonomy, has emerged more powerful in the analysis. It is noted that educated women are more likely to have decision making power, freedom of mobility and access to resources in that order, thus enabling them to act upon the aspects that may affect their own health as well as that of their children, thereby leading to increased contraceptive use and reduced child mortality (Dey and Bhavsar, 2002).

The dimensions of women's autonomy and their relationship to maternal health care utilization were investigated in a probability sample of 300 women in Varanasi, India. The study examined the determinants of women's autonomy in three areas: control over finances, decision-making power and freedom of movement. After the control for age, education, household structure and other factors, women with closer ties to natal kin were more likely to have greater autonomy in each of these three areas. Further analyses demonstrated that women with greater freedom of movement obtained higher levels of antenatal care and were more likely to use safe delivery care. The influence of women's autonomy on the use of health care appears to be as important as other known determinants such as education (Bloom et al., 2001)

A field study intended to study and identify women's autonomy in regulating their fertility and adopting family planning methods found that, at the surface level, women seemed to be enjoying choice in fertility regulation behavior. At the deeper level, women actually do not have autonomy in this aspect of life. Their attempts to regulate their own fertility have been controlled and influenced by the tradition of values and importance given to male children and insecurity feelings for not having sons. Decisions on number of children, use of contraceptives and pregnancy termination were determined by having or not having living son(s). Other socioeconomic factors were found to have negligible influence (Sthapit, 1999).

A survey conducted to assess the autonomy or empowerment women have in relation to their reproductive behavior found that the Tamilian woman enjoyed far greater autonomy than their north Indian counterparts. At the regional level, education was far more closely related to autonomy indicators in Tamil Nadu than in Uttar Pradesh and conversely coresidence with a mother-in-law was a stronger inhibitor of autonomy in Uttar Pradesh than in Tamil Nadu. The indicators of female empowerment did indeed affect reproductive choice, contraceptive practice and fertility (Jejeebhoy, 1997).

Findings from 54 developing countries indicate that fertility was most strongly related to the infant mortality rate, female secondary school education, female age at marriage and spousal age difference. Infant mortality rates were highly correlated with total fertility, female education, national income and female marriage age. A reduced form of the model that excludes the infant mortality rate and family planning effort reveals that female education remained highly significant, as did marriage age. Spousal age differences remained insignificant. Urbanization declined in significance. It is concluded that female autonomy had a direct and indirect impact on fertility (Abadian, 1996).

The results of the analysis of data from a survey of 1099 currently married women aged 15-49 years in five villages in Bolangir District of Orissa show that women's autonomy had a strong impact on family size desired, with and without controls for household economic status and had a strong impact on duration of contraceptive use. Smaller family size was associated with better educated women, women with high decision making authority, or women with greater community participation. Women's autonomy in poor households had little impact on desired family size and contraceptive duration. Women's autonomy was insignificant, when income was controlled for in the family size models. Work force participation was the only significant variable. Findings suggest that women's education and autonomy had an independent role in affecting contraceptive duration. Women's autonomy had a strong effect on children ever born, but the effect considerably weakened in poor households (Panda, 1994).

It is inferred from the above review that most of the studies conducted in many parts of the world including India had used very limited variables to measure the various dimensions of women's autonomy. Further studies on rural-urban differentials of women's autonomy are also found to be very rare. Studies on the linkage between women's autonomy and reproductive behaviour are also very limited, particularly in India. Hence, there is a need for a comparative study of women's autonomy in rural and in urban areas and its link to fertility and family planning use. The present study is an attempt in this direction.

3

Methodology

The objectives of the study, hypotheses formulated and the methodology adopted to select the sample, collect the data and analyze the data are presented in detail in this chapter.

3.1 Objectives

(i) To assess the level of various dimensions of women's autonomy in both rural and urban areas;

(ii) To study the socio-economic and demographic determinants of women's autonomy;

(iii) To study the influence of women's autonomy on their reproductive behaviour; and

(iv) To suggest suitable strategies for improving women's autonomy and healthy reproductive behaviour among women in both rural and urban areas.

3.2 Hypotheses

1. The higher the level of education, higher the level of autonomy of women.
2. The higher the level of standard of living, the higher the level of autonomy of women.

3. The higher the level of exposure to mass media, the higher the level of autonomy of women.
4. The higher the level of individual income, the higher the level of autonomy of women.
5. Members of self help group have more autonomy than non-members.
6. The higher the level of autonomy of women, the lower the level of fertility.
7. The higher the level of autonomy of women, the lower the preference for son(s).
8. The higher the level of autonomy of women, the higher the knowledge of family planning methods.
9. The higher the level of autonomy of women, the higher the husband-wife communication about family planning.
10. The higher the level of autonomy of women, the higher the adoption of family planning methods.

3.3 Sample Design

A multi stage random sampling procedure was adopted for the selection of the sample for the study. In the first stage, all the districts in Tamil Nadu were classified into three groups as high, medium and low level of gender development based on the gender development index as per the Tamil Nadu Human Development Report 2001. (The details of gender development indices and classification of districts into three groups are given in Annexure-I). In the next stage one district was selected at random from each of the three (low, medium and high) groups of districts. The districts selected from the three groups are Kancheepuram, representing high, Thiruchirapalli, representing medium and Villupuram, representing low level of gender development.

In the next stage, 10 Primary Sampling Units (PSUs) were selected separately from both the rural and the urban areas of the selected districts based on their distance from the District

Head quarters. The PSUs are revenue villages in rural areas and wards in urban areas. All currently married women aged 15-29 years and having at least one living child at the time of the survey were listed from the records and registers maintained by the Anganwadi Workers for each of the selected PSUs. From the list, 40 eligible women were selected using systematic random sampling procedure from each of the PSUs. Thus a total of 400 eligible women were selected separately for rural and urban areas in each of the selected districts. Overall, the total sample consisted of 1200 women from each of the rural and urban areas. As the Self Help Group (SHG) programme is very vigorously implemented in TamilNadu, the rural sample consisted of an equal number of members and non-members of Self Help Groups in each of the selected districts. Thus the rural sample consisted of 200 members and 200 non-members of women Self Help Group in each of the selected districts.

3.4 Respondents

The respondents for the study were currently married women aged 15-29 years who had at least one living child at the time of the interview. Since most women complete their fertility by the age of 29, the selection of respondents for the study was restricted only to those aged 15-29 years.

3.5 Development of Tools for Data Collection

In order to collect data from the respondents, an interview schedule was developed using simple and short questions and was translated into the local language (Tamil) so as enable the respondents to understand the concept and answer the questions without any difficulty. The interview schedule was pre-tested and finalized. The finalized interview schedule covered a range of subjects which include the socio-economic and demographic characteristics of the respondents, their fertility behaviour, family planning knowledge and adoption and eight different dimensions of women's autonomy.

3.6 Data Collection

The research assistants, who were trained for two weeks on various aspects of the subjects covered in the interview schedule, met the respondents in their home and collected the data through personal interview. The data collection work was carried out during the period from May to October 2005. The data collection work was carried out under the supervision of the Research Associate. The Research Associate spot checked the schedules to verify the genuineness of the data collected by the Research Assistants. At the end of every day, the schedules were checked in the field itself in order to assess the correctness, consistency and completeness of the data collected by the Research Assistants. The Project Director often visited the data collection area and met the project team and the respondents and interacted with them on various aspects of the data collected by the Research Assistants. The data collected in the field was again edited in the office before entering it into the computer. Thus the quality of the data was ensured at each stage of the data collection and analysis work.

3.7 Focus Group Discussions (FGDs)

Besides the data collected through personal interview, focus group discussions were also organized separately for rural and urban areas in each of the selected districts. A total of four FGDs were conducted in each of the selected districts. The respondents for the FGDs were classified into two categories as women aged 15-24 years and those aged 25-29 years. This classification by age was chosen because of the fact that younger women are more likely to discuss freely with other younger women than in a group including older women. The FGDs were organized in the evening hours in a common place free from disturbance and distractions. Each FGD took place for nearly two hours and 10-14 participants participated in each of the FGDs.

3.8 Data Analysis

The computer analysis of data was carried out using the Statistical Package for Social Sciences (SPSS). Both univariate and multivariate analysis were carried out to assess the level of women's autonomy and its socio-economic and demographic determinants in both rural and urban areas. In the second stage, the fertility behaviour of women was assessed based on the number of children ever born, age at first birth, age at last birth, birth interval and sex composition of children. The influence of women's autonomy on the reproductive behaviour of women was assessed using both bivariate and multivariate analysis of the data. The influence of women's autonomy on family planning knowledge and use of contraception was also assessed in this study. The statistical tools used in the analysis of data were mean, standard deviation, analysis of variance, chi-square and regression.

3.9 Variables

Dependent Variables

1. Women's autonomy
2. Fertility behaviour (Age at first birth, birth interval, number of children ever born and sex composition of children).
3. Family Planning (knowledge and adoption)

Each of the dependent variable was considered individually while doing the analysis.

Independent Variables

1. Socio-economic characteristics.
2. Demographic characteristics.
3. Marital characteristics.
4. Reproductive characteristics.
5. Family Planning characteristics.
6. Exposure to mass media.
7. Membership in Self Help Group.

8. Women's autonomy (used only for the dependent variables 2 and 3).

3.10 Measurement of Women's Autonomy

The eight dimensions of women's autonomy used in this study and their measurement procedure are described in the following sections.

3.10.1 Sex-segregated Interaction

The first measure of autonomy is an eight point scale concerned with women's sex- segregated interaction. The questions included to estimate the level of women's autonomy on sex-segregated interaction are: whether women had been denied / deprived of certain basic rights such as taking meals along with the males, present in the same room with other males, accompanying husband to functions, getting adequate nutritious food as the males, getting help from husband in household work, getting equal quality and quantity of food and engaging relatives / friends at home in the absence of husband. The responses were scored as follows: two points for woman who had freedom always, one point for woman who had freedom sometimes and 0 for woman who never had such freedom.

3.10.2 Freedom of movement

The second autonomy measure is a 13 point scale measuring women's freedom of movement. The questions considered to estimate the level of women's autonomy on freedom of movement include whether women can go shopping alone, go shopping with friends / neighbours, go to a movie alone, go to parties / attend village function and community functions alone, visit friends home alone, visit parents' / relatives' home alone, go to hospital, temple, hotel and go out of village / town alone and return home late in the evening. The responses were scored as follows: 2 points for freedom to move alone always, one point for sometimes and 0 for never allowed to move alone anywhere.

3.10.3 Freedom to Participate in Social and Political Activities

The third measure of autonomy is a seven point scale concerned with women's autonomy on freedom to participate in social and political activities. The questions included to estimate the level of women's autonomy on freedom to participate in social and political activities are: taking part in women's group activities, election activities, panchayat activities and community welfare, interact with men and boys and membership in local, social and political institutions. The responses were scored as follows: two points for freedom to participate in social and political activities always, one for sometimes and 0 for never allowed to participate in social and political activities.

3.10.4 Financial management

The fourth measure of autonomy is a three point scale concerned with women's ability to maintain family income, control over jewels and maintaining family property. The responses were scored as follows: two points for financial management by woman alone, one for both husband and wife and 0 for financial management by others.

3.10.5 Household Decisions

The fifth measure of autonomy is a 11 point scale concerned with women's autonomy in household decisions. Women's autonomy in household decisions was estimated based on the questions on the following aspects: purchase of household items, purchase of dress, purchase of property / jewels, lending / borrowing, preparation of household budget, children's education, performing/ attending functions/ ceremonies, inviting friends and weightage given for her views / suggestions. The responses were scored as follows: two points for decision taken by women alone, one for decision taken by both husband and wife and 0 for decisions taken by others.

3.10.6 Freedom of Choice

The sixth measure of autonomy is an eight point scale concerned with women's freedom of choice on dressing, hair style, voting, timing of sex with husband, cooking, talking with neighbours, using household items and worshiping God. The responses were scored as follows: two points for having freedom always, one for having freedom only for sometimes and 0 for never have the freedom of choice.

3.10.7 Violence Against Women

The seventh measure of autonomy is a 10 point scale concerned with the ability of women to oppose violence against women. The autonomy of women to oppose/prevent violence against women was estimated by asking women whether they experienced verbal abuse from husband and in laws, physical abuse by husband and in laws, ill treatment by husband and in laws, drinking habit of husband, harassment from husband/in laws, intimidation by family members and experience of eve teasing. The responses were scored as follows: two points for never experienced violence, one for sometimes and 0 for always.

3.10.8 Decision about Contraception and Child Birth

The eighth measure of autonomy is a four point scale concerned with women's ability to take independent decisions on timing of child birth, number and sex composition of children and adoption of family planning methods. The responses were scored as follows: two points for decision taken by woman herself, one for decision taken by both husband and wife and 0 for decision taken by others.

3.10.9 Total autonomy

The overall autonomy of women was estimated based on the total score attained by each woman for all the above said eight dimensions of autonomy. The maximum score for all the eight measures of autonomy was 128. The women are arranged in the ascending order of the score attained by them. The cumulative total of the score attained by the women was divided into three equal intervals viz., 33.3 percentiles, 33.4 to 66.6 percentiles and 66.7 percentile and above. Those women who came under the 33.3 percentiles were considered as **Low** autonomy women, women who fell between 33.4 to 66.6 percentiles were considered as **Medium** autonomy women and those who fell above 66.6 percentile were considered as **High** autonomy women. As per the above said procedure, the low autonomy women were those who attained a score of 73 or less, the medium autonomy women were those who attained a score between 74 and 86 and the high autonomy women were those who had attained the score of 87 and above.

The details of autonomy variables, scoring pattern and grouping of women into low, medium and high level of autonomy based on the total score attained by women for all the above said eight autonomy measures individually as well as totally are given in annexure-II.

4

Background Characteristics Of The Respondents

The background characteristics of the respondents are important factors in determining the variation in the level of autonomy and reproductive behaviour. Hence a detailed analysis of the background characteristics of the respondents interviewed in the survey was made and the results are presented in the following sections.

4.1 SOCIO-ECONOMIC CHARACTERISTICS

The socio-economic characteristics of the women interviewed in the survey are presented in Table 4.1. Among the 2400 women interviewed in the survey, half were from rural and the remaining half from urban areas. Overall, only 10.7 per cent were illiterate. The proportion of illiterates did not vary much among women in rural and urban areas. It was 11.1 per cent in rural and 10.3 per cent in urban areas. The proportion of women who had illiterate husbands was 9.8 per cent in rural and 7 per cent in urban areas.

Among the total sample, Hindus were predominant at 88.2 per cent. Muslims and Christians constituted only 7.6 per cent and 4.2 per cent respectively. The same phenomenon was observed in both rural and urban areas with 90.2 per cent of Hindus in rural and 86.2 per cent in urban areas. Scheduled caste and schedule tribe respondents together constituted nearly one-fourth (24 per cent) of the total sample. The proportion of SC/ST women was substantially higher in rural (28.3 per cent) than in urban areas (19.6 per cent).

Nearly half of the respondents' (49.7 per cent) family had property worth more than Rs.1,00,000/-. It was 47.7 per cent in rural and 51.6 per cent in urban areas. Overall, only 19.5 per cent of women reported to have engaged in some sort of income earning activities. The proportion of women engaged in income

Table 4.1 Percent distribution of women aged 15-29 years by socio-economic characteristics

Socio-economic Characteristics	*Rural N=1200*	*Urban N=1200*	*Total N=2400*
Education of woman			
Illiterate	11.1	10.3	10.7
Literate & Primary	20.6	15.8	18.2
Middle (6-8)	29.3	26.4	27.9
High School (9-10)	25.8	28.0	26.9
Higher Secondary & above	13.2	19.4	16.3
Education of husband			
Illiterate	9.8	7.0	8.4
Literate & Primary	20.2	14.4	17.3
Middle (6-8)	22.2	22.9	22.5
High School (9-10)	34.0	34.5	34.3
Higher Secondary & above	13.9	21.2	17.5
Religion			
Hindu	90.2	86.2	88.2
Muslim	6.4	8.8	7.6
Christian	3.4	5.0	4.2

(Contd.)

(Contd. Table 4.1)

Socio-economic Characteristics	*Rural N=1200*	*Urban N=1200*	*N=2400*
Community			
Scheduled Caste and Schedule Tribe (SC/ST)	28.3	19.6	24.0
Most Backward Caste (MBC)	32.2	25.3	28.8
Backward caste (BC) and Others	39.5	55.1	47.2
Property ownership of family (Rupees)			
Nil	3.5	5.4	4.5
≤ 50,000	10.8	11.5	11.2
50001 – 1,00,000	38.0	31.4	34.7
100001 – 1,50,000	14.5	12.3	13.4
Above 1,50,000	33.2	39.3	36.3
Involvement in income earning economic activities			
Yes	26.3	12.7	19.5
No	73.8	87.3	80.5
Percent contribution to total family income			
Nil	73.5	87.1	80.3
≤ 25 per cent	12.0	8.3	10.2
Above 25 per cent	14.5	4.6	9.5
Standard of Living Index (SLI)			
Low	41.0	28.1	34.5
Medium	31.6	31.4	31.5
High	27.4	40.5	34.0
Type of family			
Nuclear	60.0	54.9	57.5
Joint	40.0	45.1	42.5

earning economic activities was substantially higher in rural than in urban areas (26.3 per cent in rural and 13 per cent in urban areas). The contribution to total family income was 25 per cent or less for 12 per cent of women in rural and 8.3 per cent of women in urban areas. It was more than 25 per cent for 14.5 per cent of women in rural and 4.6 per cent in urban areas.

The proportion of women contributing to total family income was substantially higher in rural than in urban areas (26.5 per cent in rural and just 12.9 per cent in urban areas). About 73.5 per cent of women in rural and 87.1 per cent in urban areas did not contribute anything to the family income.

The standard of living of each woman was assessed based on the household amenities and possession of selected household items. The details of household items and scoring procedure used for developing a Standard of Living Index* (SLI) are given in Annexure-III. It is observed that overall 34.5 per cent of women had a low standard of living, 31.5 per cent had a medium and 34 per cent had a high standard of living. The proportion of women who had a high standard of living was substantially more in urban (40.5 per cent) than in rural areas (27.4 per cent).

The distribution of the respondents by type of family revealed that 57.5 per cent belonged to nuclear family and the rest belonged to joint family. The proportion of respondents belonged to nuclear family was higher (60 per cent) in rural than in urban areas (54.9 per cent).

The overall socio economic characteristics of the respondents indicate that younger women were more literate and the literacy gap between husband and wife narrowed down in both rural and urban areas. Rural women were contributing more to family income than urban women. The proportion of women with a high standard of living was more in urban than in rural areas. A substantially high proportion of women belonged to nuclear family in both rural and urban areas.

---

* Standard of Living Index (SLI)

In order to assess the standard of living of the family, a standard of living index (SLI) was developed based on the possession of certain household items in the selected households. Each of the household items was given a score depending on the comparative value. The maximum score for each household was 65. Household having a score of 21 or less was classified as low SLI, a household having a score between 22 and 42 was classified as medium SLI and household having a score of 43 and above was classified as high SLI.

4.2 DEMOGRAPHIC CHARACTERISTICS

The demographic characteristics of women presented in Table 4.2 reveal that the majority of the women interviewed (52.6 per cent) were in the age group of 25-29 years, 42.9 per cent were in the age group of 20-24 years and the rest (4.5 per cent) were aged 19 years or less. The overall mean age of the women was 25.48 years. It was 25.69 years for women in rural and 25.26 years for women in urban areas.

It is surprising to see that still a substantial proportion of women (10.5 per cent) got married at the very young age of 16 years or less in TamilNadu. The proportion of women married at ages 16 years or less was substantially higher in rural (12.7 per cent) than in urban areas (8.3 per cent). Overall, the mean age at marriage was 19.23 years for the total sample. The mean age at marriage was higher in urban than in rural areas. It was 18.97 years in rural and 19.50 years in urban areas. The husband–wife age difference was observed to be less than four years for 35.6 per cent of women, 5–8 years for 40.8 per cent and more than 9 years for 23.6 per cent of women. The husband-wife age difference did not vary much between the rural and the urban areas. The mean age difference was 6.31 years for rural and 6.04 years for urban women. The results indicate that the overall mean age difference was about 6 years and there was not much variation in the husband-wife age difference among women in rural and urban areas.

The overall mean number of male children born alive was 0.99 and there was not much variation in the mean number of male children between the rural and urban areas. It was 1.01 in rural and 0.97 in urban areas. The mean number of female children born alive was 0.96 and it was slightly higher at 0.99 in rural and 0.91 in urban areas. The mean number of children ever born to a woman was 1.95. The mean number of children ever born to a woman was high at 2.01 in rural and 1.89 in urban areas.

Overall, it is observed that even among the younger generation, still a substantial proportion of women (40.3 per cent) got married at a very young age (≤ 18 years). However, the mean number of children ever born was just around two in

Table 4.2 Percent distribution of women aged 15-29 years by demographic characteristics

Demographic Characteristics	*Rural N=120 0*	*Urban N=120 0*	*Total N=240 0*
Age (years)			
≤ 19	4.2	4.9	4.5
20 – 24	39.8	45.9	42.9
25 – 29	56.0	49.2	52.6
Mean	**25.69**	**25.26**	**25.48**
Age at marriage (years)			
≤ 16	12.7	8.3	10.5
17 – 18	33.2	26.3	29.8
19 – 20	29.3	34.8	32.1
21 – 22	16.9	19.5	18.2
23 +	7.9	11.0	9.4
Mean	**18.97**	**19.50**	**19.23**
Husband-wife age difference (years)			
≤ 4	34.8	36.5	35.6
5 – 8	41.6	39.9	40.8
9 +	23.7	23.6	23.6
Mean	**6.31**	**6.04**	**6.18**
Number of male children			
0	26.9	29.3	28.1
1	48.9	47.5	48.2
2	20.5	20.3	20.4
3 +	3.7	2.9	4.3
Mean	**1.01**	**0.97**	**0.99**
Number of female children			
0	29.3	32.9	31.1
1	46.4	46.1	46.3

(Contd.)

(Contd. Table 4.2)

Demographic Characteristics	*Rural N=120 0*	*Urban N=120 0*	*Total N=240 0*
2	19.9	17.9	18.9
3 +	4.4	3.1	3.7
Mean	**0.99**	**0.91**	**0.96**
Total number of children			
1	27.0	31.8	29.4
2	49.4	50.2	49.8
3 +	23.6	18.2	20.8
Mean	**2.01**	**1.89**	**1.95**

both rural and urban areas, indicating a positive demographic change.

4.3 Marital Characteristics

The marital characteristics of women presented in Table 4.3 reveal that 34.3 per cent of women had consanguineous marriage and there was not much variation in the type of marriage among women in rural and urban areas. It is observed that 33.3 per cent of women in rural and 35.4 per cent in urban areas had consanguineous marriage. Among those who had consanguineous marriage, 53.2 per cent had married persons from the maternal side and 46.8 per cent had married persons from the paternal side. About 89.5 per cent of women had arranged marriage and the remaining 10.5 per cent had love marriage. The prevalence of arranged marriage did not vary much between rural and urban areas (89.8 per cent in rural and 89.3 per cent in urban areas).

Overall 92.7 per cent had got married to persons belonging to their own caste and only 7.3 per cent had inter-caste / inter religious marriage. The proportion of inter-caste/inter religious marriage was only six per cent in rural and 8.7 per cent in urban areas.

The results indicate that about one third of marriages were consanguineous in both rural and urban areas. More than half of

Table 4.3 Percent distribution of women aged 15-29 years by marital characteristics

Marital characteristics	*Rural N=1200*	*Urban N=1200*	*Total N=2400*
Type of marriage			
Consanguineous	33.3	35.4	34.3
Non – consanguineous	66.8	64.6	65.7
Consanguineous type*			
Maternal	52.4	53.9	53.2
Paternal	47.6	46.1	46.8
Kind of marriage			
Arranged marriage	89.8	89.3	89.5
Love marriage	10.2	10.8	10.5
Inter caste / inter religious marriage			
Inter caste / inter religious marriage	6.0	8.7	7.3
Same caste marriage	94.0	91.3	92.7

*Percent computed only for those who had consanguineous type of marriage.

the consanguineous marriages were from the maternal side. Love marriages constituted about one tenth of the total marriages in both rural and urban areas. Though small in proportion, the prevalence of inter-caste / inter religious marriage was slightly higher in urban than in rural areas.

4.4 Reproductive Characteristics

The reproductive characteristics of women presented in Table 4.4 show that nearly one third (32.1 per cent) of women had their first birth within 19 years of age. The proportion of women who had their first birth at 19 years or less was substantially higher in rural (36.5 per cent) than in urban areas (27.9 per cent). The overall mean age at first birth was 20.71 years. The mean age at first birth did not vary much between rural and urban areas. It was 20.49 years in rural and 20.94 years in urban areas.

About 61.6 per cent of women reported to have completed their fertility on the date of survey. A comparatively higher proportion of women in rural areas (66.2 per cent) had completed their fertility than their urban counterparts (57 per cent). It is also observed that nearly one third of women (32 per cent) had completed their child bearing within 3 years of marriage and most of them (98 per cent) had completed their child bearing within 9 years of their marriage. However, the mean duration of child bearing was only 4.64 years. The mean duration of child bearing period did not vary much between rural and urban areas. It was 4.74 years in rural and 4.51 years in urban areas.

Among those who had completed their fertility, 4.3 per cent had their last birth at ages less than 19 years, 62.3 per cent had their last birth at ages 20-24 years and 33.4 per cent had their last birth at ages 25-29 years. Overall, the mean age at last birth was 23.46 years and there was not much variation in the mean age at last birth among women in rural and urban areas. The mean age at last birth was 23.26 years for women in rural and 23.69 years for women in urban areas.

In order to assess the tendency of women to go in for higher parity, a parity progression ratio was worked out and it was found that all women had gone for first child, 69.9 per cent had gone for second child, 20.5 per cent had gone for third child,

Table 4.4 Percent distribution of women aged 15-29 years by their reproductive characteristics

Reproductive Characteristics	*Rural N=1200*	*Urban N=1200*	*Total N=2400*
Age at first birth			
≤19	36.5	27.9	32.1
20 – 22	44.2	48.6	46.4
23 – 25	15.9	19.1	17.5
26+	3.4	4.5	4.0
Mean	**20.49**	**20.94**	**20.71**
Fertility completion status			
Completed	66.2	57.0	61.6
Not completed	33.8	43.0	38.4
Reproductive span			
≤3	30.5	33.8	32.0
4-6	50.5	52.9	51.6
7-9	16.6	11.8	14.4
10+	2.4	1.5	2.0
Mean	**4.74**	**4.51**	**4.64**
Age at last birth			
≤19	5.9	2.3	4.3
20 – 24	63.9	60.5	62.3
25 – 29	30.2	37.1	33.4
Mean	**23.26**	**23.69**	**23.46**
Parity progression			
1	100.0	100.0	100.0
2	72.0	67.5	69.9
3	23.5	17.5	20.5
4	3.6	1.6	2.6
5	0.5	0.25	0.4

(Contd.)

(Contd. Table 4.4)

Reproductive Characteristics	*Rural N=1200*	*Urban N=1200*	*Total N=2400*
Mean birth interval (months)			
Between 1-2	28.1	28.7	28.4
Between 2-3	28.8	27.5	28.2
Between 3-4	26.9	25.1	26.3
Between 4-5	30.3	31.7	30.7

2.6 per cent had gone for the fourth child and just 0.4 per cent had gone for fifth child. The proportion of women going for higher parity was comparatively higher in rural than in urban areas.

It is observed that the mean birth interval was 28.4 months between first and second birth, 28.2 months between second and third birth, 26.3 months between third and fourth birth and 30.7 months between fourth and fifth birth. The mean birth interval did not vary much between the rural and urban areas.

5

Women's Autonomy

The results of the analysis of data on the level of women's autonomy measured based on the mean score attained by women on each of the eight different dimensions of autonomy by selected socio-economic, demographic, marital and mass media variables are presented in this chapter.

5.1 Sex-segregated Interaction

The autonomy of women on sex-segregated interaction measured by mean autonomy score attained by women on various indicators of sex-segregated interaction by selected background characteristics is presented in Tables 5.1.1 to 5.1.4. The results show that rural women were more autonomous than their urban counterparts. On a scale of 0-16, the mean autonomy score on sex-segregated interaction was highest at 14.06 for women in rural areas compared to 12.63 observed for women in urban areas. The influence of various socio-economic, demographic, marital and mass media variables on the autonomy of women on sex-segregated interaction is discussed in the following sections 5.1.1 to 5.1.4.

5.1.1 Women's autonomy on sex – segregated interaction and Socio-economic characteristics

The distribution of women according to their level of autonomy on sex- segregated interaction by selected socio-economic characteristics is presented in Table 5.1.1. The level of autonomy of women on sex-segregated interaction is measured based on the mean score attained by women for each of the selected socio-economic characteristics. The mean autonomy score on sex-segregated interaction increased significantly with education in both rural and urban areas. In rural areas, the mean score increased significantly from 11.18 for illiterates to 13.22 for higher secondary and above. In urban areas, the mean score increased significantly from 11.06 for illiterates to 13.08 for higher secondary and above educated respondents. It is to be noted that the mean autonomy score was slightly higher among women in rural areas at all levels of education than among women in urban areas. Education of husband also showed significant influence on the autonomy of women on sex segregated interaction in both rural and urban areas. In rural areas, the mean autonomy score increased significantly from 11.65 for women who had illiterate husband to 12.82 for women who had husband with high school and higher level of education. In urban areas, the mean score increased significantly from 10.90 for illiterates to 12.69 for higher secondary and above.

Muslim women had comparatively lower autonomy on sex-segregated interaction than Hindu and Christian women in both rural and urban areas. However, these differences were not statistically significant. The mean autonomy score on sex-segregated interaction did not vary much among women from different caste groups in rural areas. The mean score was 12.04 for SC/ST, 12.36 for MBC and 12.21 for BC and others. However in urban areas, the mean score on sex-segregated interaction varied significantly among women from different caste groups. It is observed that SC/ST women had significantly lower autonomy than

Table 5.1.1 Mean autonomy score attained by women on sex-segregated interaction by socio-economic characteristics

Socio-economic characteristics	*Rural*			*Urban*			*Total*		
	Mean	*N*	*SD*	*Mean*	*N*	*SD*	*Mean*	*N*	*SD*
All	**12.21**	**1200**	**2.76**	**12.19**	**1200**	**2.66**	**12.20**	**2400**	**2.71**
Education of woman									
Illiterate	11.18	133	3.21	11.06	124	3.24	11.12	257	3.22
Literate & Primary	11.65	247	2.77	11.56	190	2.57	11.61	437	2.69
Middle (6-8)	12.25	352	2.72	12.15	317	2.60	12.20	669	2.66
High School (9-10)	12.54	310	2.57	12.37	336	2.55	12.45	646	2.56
Higher Secondary & above	13.22	158	2.27	13.08	233	2.25	13.14	391	2.26
		F-14.186	P<0.000		F-15.956	P<0.000		F-29.784	P<0.000
Education of husband									
Illiterate	11.65	117	3.13	10.90	84	3.17	11.34	201	3.16
Literate & Primary	12.04	242	2.71	11.65	173	2.90	11.88	415	2.80
Middle (6-8)	11.97	266	2.67	12.03	275	2.66	12.00	541	2.66
High School (9-10)	12.38	408	2.77	12.46	414	2.55	12.42	822	2.66
Higher Sec. & above	12.82	167	2.53	12.69	254	2.25	12.74	421	2.36
		F- 4.430	P<0.001		F-10.558	P<0.000		F-13.112	P<0.000

(Contd.)

(Contd. Table 5.1.1)

Socio-economic characteristics	*Rural*			*Urban*			*Total*		
	Mean	*N*	*SD*	*Mean*	*N*	*SD*	*Mean*	*N*	*SD*
Religion									
Hindu	12.25	1082	2.77	12.19	1034	2.68	12.22	2116	2.72
Muslim	11.60	77	2.62	12.05	105	2.13	11.86	182	2.35
Christian	12.34	41	2.69	12.26	61	3.10	12.29	102	2.93
		F-2.055	P<0.129		F-0.176	P<0.838		F-1.600	P<0.202
Community									
SC / ST	12.04	340	2.79	11.54	235	2.99	11.83	575	2.89
MBC	12.36	386	2.72	12.29	304	2.71	12.33	690	2.72
BC & Others	12.21	474	2.76	12.37	661	2.47	12.30	1135	2.59
		F-1.254	P<0.286		F-8.877	P<0.000		F-6.940	P<0.001
Standard of living									
Low	11.60	492	2.95	11.09	337	3.06	11.39	829	3.00
Medium	12.41	379	2.62	12.32	377	2.55	12.36	756	2.58
High	12.90	329	2.11	12.85	486	2.15	12.87	815	2.26
		F-24.093	P<0.000		F-47.347	P<0.000		F-66.201	P<0.000

(Contd.)

(Contd. Table 5.1.1)

Socio-economic characteristics	*Rural*			*Urban*			*Total*		
	Mean	*N*	*SD*	*Mean*	*N*	*SD*	*Mean*	*N*	*SD*
Economic activities									
Yes	12.28	315	2.87	11.82	152	2.99	12.13	467	2.91
No	12.18	885	2.71	12.24	1048	2.60	12.21	1933	2.66
		F-0.295	P<0.587		F-3.408	P<0.065		F-0.367	P<0.545
Percent Contribution to total income									
Nil	12.18	882	2.72	12.24	1045	2.60	12.21	1927	2.66
25 %	12.50	144	2.72	11.61	100	2.91	12.13	244	2.83
≤ 25 %	12.11	174	2.97	12.25	55	3.05	12.15	229	2.98
		F-0.946	P<0.388		F-2.581	P<0.076		F-0.132	P<0.876
Type of family									
Nuclear	12.23	720	2.73	12.15	659	2.70	12.19	1379	2.72
Joint	12.17	480	2.80	12.23	541	2.60	12.20	1021	2.69
		F-0.129	P<0.720		F-0.201	P<0.654		F-0.002	P<0.963

most backward caste and backward and other caste women. The mean autonomy score was lowest at 11.54 for SC/ST compared to 12.29 for MBC and 12.37 for BC and others.

The standard of living had significantly positive effect on the autonomy of women on sex-segregated interaction in both rural and urban areas. The mean autonomy score increased significantly with standard of living in both rural and urban areas. In rural areas, the mean autonomy score increased significantly from 11.60 for low standard of living to 12.41 for medium and to 12.90 for high standard of living. In urban areas, the mean score increased from 11.09 for low standard of living to 12.32 for medium and to 12.85 for high standard of living.

Involvement of women in income earning economic activities did not make much difference to the autonomy of women on sex-segregated interaction in rural areas. It is observed that the mean autonomy score was 12.18 for women not involved in any income earning economic activities and it was nearly the same at 12.28 for women involved in economic activities. In urban areas, involvement of women in economic activities showed significantly negative effect on the autonomy of women on sex-segregated interaction. It is observed that the mean score was lowest at 11.82 for women involved in economic activities compared to 12.24 for women not involved in economic activities.

The contribution of women to total family income did not make any significant difference in the autonomy of women on sex-segregated interaction in rural areas. It is observed that the mean score was 12.18 for women who did not contribute anything to the family income, 12.50 for women who contributed up to 25 per cent of the total family income and 12.11 for women who contributed more than 25 per cent to the total family income. However in urban areas, women's contribution to total family income significantly increased the autonomy of women on sex-segregated interaction. It is observed that the mean autonomy score was 12.24 for women who made no contribution to the total family income, 11.61 for women who contributed up to 25 per cent and 12.25 for women who contributed more than 25 per cent to the total family income.

The type of family did not make any significant difference in the autonomy of women on sex-segregated interaction in both rural and urban areas. In rural areas, the mean autonomy score was 12.23 for women in nuclear family and 12.17 for women in joint family. In urban areas, the mean score was 12.15 for women in nuclear family and 12.23 for women in joint family.

The results indicate that the education of women and their husband and the standard of living significantly improved the autonomy of women on sex-segregated interaction in both rural and urban areas. Involvement in income earning economic activities and contribution to the total family income had significantly positive influence on women's autonomy on sex-segregated interaction only in urban areas. Higher caste women (BC and others) had significantly more autonomy than others in urban areas.

5.1.2 Women's Autonomy on Sex-segregated Interaction and Demographic Characteristics

The distribution of women according to the mean autonomy score on sex-segregated interaction by selected demographic characteristics is presented in Table 5.1.2. The autonomy of women on sex-segregated interaction increased significantly with the age of women in both rural and urban areas. In rural areas, the mean score increased from 11.52 for women aged 19 years or less to 12.00 for women aged 20–24 years and to 12.41 for women aged 25-29 years. In urban areas, the mean score increased from 10.83 for women aged 19 years or less to 12.57 for women aged 25–29 years.

Age at marriage of women did not make much difference in the autonomy of women on sex-segregated interaction among women in rural areas. However in urban areas, age at marriage significantly influenced the autonomy of women on sex-segregated interaction. The mean autonomy score significantly increased from

Table 5.1.2 Mean autonomy score attained by women on sex-segregated interaction by demographic characteristics

Demographic characteristics	*Rural*			*Urban*			*Total*		
	Mean	*N*	*SD*	*Mean*	*N*	*SD*	*Mean*	*N*	*SD*
All	**12.21**	**1200**	**2.76**	**12.19**	**1200**	**2.66**	**12.20**	**2400**	**2.71**
Age (years)									
≤ 19	11.52	50	3.06	10.83	59	3.27	11.15	109	3.18
20 – 24	12.00	478	2.68	11.92	551	2.73	11.96	1029	2.70
25 – 29	12.41	672	2.77	12.57	590	2.45	12.49	1262	2.63
		F-4.758	P<0.009		F17.017	P<0.000		F19.663	P<0.000
Age at marriage (years)									
≤ 16	11.76	152	3.00	11.29	100	2.99	11.58	252	2.99
17 – 18	12.22	398	2.60	11.79	316	2.84	12.03	714	2.71
19 – 20	12.23	352	2.77	12.47	418	2.57	12.36	770	2.67
21 – 22	12.36	203	2.96	12.32	234	2.44	12.34	437	2.69
23 +	12.49	95	2.46	12.67	132	2.35	12.60	227	2.39
		F-1.407	P<0.229		F-7.137	P<0.000		F-6.283	P<0.000

(Contd.)

(Contd. Table 5.1.2)

Demographic characteristics	*Rural*			*Urban*			*Total*		
	Mean	*N*	*SD*	*Mean*	*N*	*SD*	*Mean*	*N*	*SD*
Husband-wife age difference (years)									
≤ 4	12.17	417	2.71	12.16	438	2.67	12.16	855	2.69
5 – 8	12.27	499	2.74	12.40	479	2.53	12.33	978	2.64
9 +	12.17	284	2.87	11.88	283	2.83	12.02	567	2.85
		F-0.206	P<0.814		F-3.452	P<0.032		F- 2.467	P<0.085
Marital duration (years)									
≤ 3	12.05	223	2.78	12.06	300	2.71	12.06	523	2.74
4 – 6	12.05	376	2.77	12.08	437	2.55	12.07	813	2.65
7 – 9	12.35	347	2.72	12.34	318	2.71	12.35	665	2.71
10+	12.39	254	2.76	12.43	145	2.77	12.40	399	2.76
		F-1.320	P<0.267		F- 1.163	P<0.323		F- 2.485	P<0.059

(Contd.)

(Contd. Table 5.1.2)

Demographic characteristics	*Rural*			*Urban*			*Total*		
	Mean	*N*	*SD*	*Mean*	*N*	*SD*	*Mean*	*N*	*SD*
Number of male children									
0	11.80	335	2.97	12.24	363	2.78	12.03	698	2.88
1	12.39	596	2.61	12.15	574	2.62	12.27	1170	2.62
2+	12.30	269	2.77	12.20	263	2.58	12.25	532	2.68
		F-5.118	P<0.006		F-0.150	P<0.861		F- 1.854	P<0.157
Number of female children									
0	12.42	357	2.64	12.26	400	2.49	12.34	757	2.56
1	12.24	568	2.76	12.32	558	2.68	12.28	1126	2.72
2 +	11.86	275	2.88	11.77	242	2.84	11.82	517	2.86
		F-3.312	P<0.037		F-3.384	P<0.022		F- 6.633	P<0.001
Total number of children									
1	12.12	345	2.87	12.27	402	2.58	12.20	747	2.72
2	12.42	604	2.62	12.36	605	2.65	12.39	1209	2.63
3 +	11.83	251	2.89	11.49	193	2.74	11.68	444	2.83
		F-4.213	P<0.015		F-8.224	P<0.000		F-11.082	P<0.000

11.29 for women married at ages 16 years or less to 12.67 for women married at ages 23 years or more. The husband-wife age difference did not make any significant difference in the autonomy of women on sex-segregated interaction in rural areas. However in urban areas, it had significant influence on the autonomy of women on sex-segregated interaction. In urban areas, the mean autonomy score was 12.16 for an age difference of four years or less, 12.40 for five to eight years and 11.88 for 9 years and above.

Women who had male child(ren) had significantly more autonomy on sex-segregated interaction than those who had no male child in rural areas. However in urban areas, the number of male children did not make any significant difference in the autonomy of women on sex-segregated interaction.

The autonomy of women on sex-segregated interaction decreased significantly with the number of female children in both rural and urban areas. In rural areas, the mean autonomy score on sex-segregated interaction decreased from 12.42 for women who had no female child to 11.86 for those who had two or more female children. In urban areas, the mean autonomy score was more among women who had one female child compared to those who had no female child and those who had two or more female children.

Women who had a total of two living children had significantly more autonomy on sex-segregated interaction than those who had one child or three or more children in both rural and urban areas. In rural areas, the mean score was highest at 12.42 for women who had two children compared to 12.12 for women who had one living child and 11.83 for women who had three or more children. In urban areas, the mean score was highest at 12.36 for women who had two living children compared to 12.27 for women who had one living child and 11.49 for women who had three or more children.

The results indicate that age and age at marriage of women had significantly positive effect on women's autonomy on sex-segregated interaction in both rural and urban areas. Women

Table 5.1.3 Mean autonomy score attained by women on sex-segregated interaction by marital characteristics

Marital characteristics	*Rural*			*Urban*			*Total*		
	Mean	*N*	*SD*	*Mean*	*N*	*SD*	*Mean*	*N*	*SD*
All	**12.21**	**1200**	**2.76**	**12.19**	**1200**	**2.66**	**12.20**	**2400**	**2.71**
Type of marriage									
Consanguineous	12.21	399	2.70	12.22	425	2.63	12.21	824	2.66
Non-consanguineous	12.21	801	2.79	12.17	775	2.67	12.19	1576	2.73
		F-0.000	P<0.996		F-0.091	P<0.763		F-0.044	P<0.834
Consanguineous type									
Maternal	12.07	209	2.79	12.09	229	2.58	12.08	438	2.68
Paternal	12.36	190	2.60	12.36	196	2.69	12.36	386	2.64
		F-1.158	P<0.282		F -1.081	P<0.299		F-2.242	P<0.135

(Contd.)

(Contd. Table 5.1.3)

Marital characteristics	*Rural*			*Urban*			*Total*		
	Mean	*N*	*SD*	*Mean*	*N*	*SD*	*Mean*	*N*	*SD*
Kind of marriage									
Arranged marriage	12.19	1078	2.75	12.21	1071	2.61	12.20	2149	2.68
Love marriage	12.34	122	2.86	12.03	129	3.07	12.18	251	2.96
		F-0.3228	P<0.571		F-0.500	P<0.479		F-0.009	P<0.924
Inter caste / inter religious marriage									
Same caste marriage	12.21	1128	2.75	12.17	1096	2.63	12.19	2224	2.69
Inter caste / inter religious marriage	12.14	72	2.94	12.39	104	2.97	12.29	176	2.96
		F-0.051	P<0.822		F-0.688	P<0.407		F-0.214	P<0.643

who had two or more number of female children had significantly lower autonomy than others in both rural and urban areas. Women who had a total of two children had significantly more autonomy than others in both rural and urban areas.

5.1.3 Women's Autonomy on Sex-segregated Interaction and Marital Characteristics

In order to assess the influence of the type of marriage on women's autonomy on sex-segregated interaction, the data were analysed according to the type of marriage and autonomy of women on sex-segregated interaction. The results presented in Table 5.1.3 show that the type of marriage did not make any significant difference in the autonomy of women on sex-segregated interaction in both rural and urban areas. Among those who had consanguineous marriage, women who had married a person from the paternal side had more autonomy than those who had married a person from the maternal side in both rural and urban areas. However, the differences were not statistically significant in both rural and urban areas. The kind of marriage, such as arranged marriage and love marriage did not make any significant difference in the autonomy on sex-segregated interaction in both rural and urban areas. Similarly, inter-caste / inter-religious marriage did not make any significant difference in the autonomy of women in both rural and urban areas.

The results indicate that none of the marital characteristics of women had any significant association with women's autonomy on sex-segregated interaction in both rural and urban areas.

5.1.4 Women's Autonomy on Sex-segregated Interaction and Exposure to Mass Media

The results of the analysis of data on the influence of mass media on women's autonomy on sex-segregated interaction are presented in Table 5.1.4. Women who were listening to radio at least once a week had significantly more autonomy on

Table 5.1.4 Mean autonomy score attained by women on sex-segregated interaction by exposure to mass media

Exposure to mass media	*Rural*			*Urban*			*Total*		
	Mean	*N*	*SD*	*Mean*	*N*	*SD*	*Mean*	*N*	*SD*
All	**12.21**	**1200**	**2.76**	**12.19**	**1200**	**2.66**	**12.20**	**2400**	**2.71**
Listening to radio									
Yes	12.48	683	2.72	12.52	630	2.40	12.50	1313	2.57
No	11.85	517	2.77	11.82	570	2.87	11.83	1087	2.82
		F-15.738	P<0.000		F-20.965	P<0.000		F-36.483	P<0.000
Watching television									
Yes	12.34	1050	2.71	12.30	1088	2.59	12.33	2138	2.65
No	11.29	150	2.90	11.01	112	3.04	11.17	262	2.96
		F – 19.504	P<0.000		F - 24.751	P<0.000		F - 43.349	P<0.000
Going to movies									
Yes	12.84	172	2.47	13.01	242	2.36	12.94	414	2.40
No	12.10	1028	2.79	11.98	958	2.69	12.04	1986	2.74
		F -10.462	P<0.001		F - 30.186	P<0.000		F - 38.260	P<0.000

(Contd.)

(Contd. Table 5.1.4)

Exposure to mass media	*Rural*			*Urban*			*Total*		
	Mean	*N*	*SD*	*Mean*	*N*	*SD*	*Mean*	*N*	*SD*
Reading newspapers / magazines									
Yes	12.97	458	2.47	12.74	456	2.36	12.86	914	2.42
No	11.74	742	2.82	11.85	744	2.77	11.79	1486	2.80
		F - 58.852	P<0.000		F -33.009	P<0.000		F -90.340	P<0.000
Mass media index									
No exposure	10.83	76	3.20	10.06	53	3.29	10.51	129	3.25
Low exposure	11.93	752	2.71	12.00	759	2.69	11.97	1511	2.70
High exposure	13.06	372	2.52	12.84	388	2.28	12.95	760	2.40
		F -32.514	P<0.000		F -32.262	P<0.000		F -62.685	P<0.000
Membership in SHG									
Yes	12.66	600	2.63	12.66	304	2.40	12.66	904	2.56
No	11.77	600	2.81	12.03	896	2.72	11.92	1496	2.76
		F -32.039	P<0.000		F -13.051	P<0.000		F -12.210	P<0.000

sex-segregated interaction than those who were not listening to radio in both rural and urban areas. In rural areas, the mean score on sex-segregated interaction was 12.48 for women who were listening to radio compared to 11.85 for those who were not listening to radio. In urban areas, the mean score for women who were listening to radio was more at 12.52 compared to 11.82 for those who were not listening to radio. Watching television significantly influenced women's autonomy on sex-segregated interaction in both rural and urban areas. In rural areas, the mean score was highest at 12.34 for women who were watching television once a week compared to 11.29 observed for women who were not having the habit of watching television. In urban areas, the mean score was highest at 12.30 for women who were watching television compared to 11.01 observed for those who were not having the habit of watching television once a week.

Going to movies at least once a month showed significant difference in the autonomy of women on sex-segregated interaction in both rural and urban areas. In rural areas, the mean autonomy score was more at 12.84 for women going to movies compared to only 12.10 for women who were not going to movies. In urban areas also, the mean autonomy score was comparatively highest at 13.01 for women who were going to movies compared to only 11.98 for women who were not going to movies. Reading newspapers / magazines also showed significant influence on the autonomy of women on sex-segregated interaction in both rural and urban areas. In rural areas, the mean score was significantly highest at 12.97 for women who were reading newspapers / magazines compared to 11.74 for women who were not having the habit of reading newspapers / magazines. In urban areas also, the mean autonomy score on sex-segregated interaction was highest at 12.74 for women who were reading newspapers / magazines compared to 11.85 for women who were not having the habit of reading newspapers / magazines.

Figure 5.1.1 Autonomy of women on sex-segregated interaction by exposure to mass media

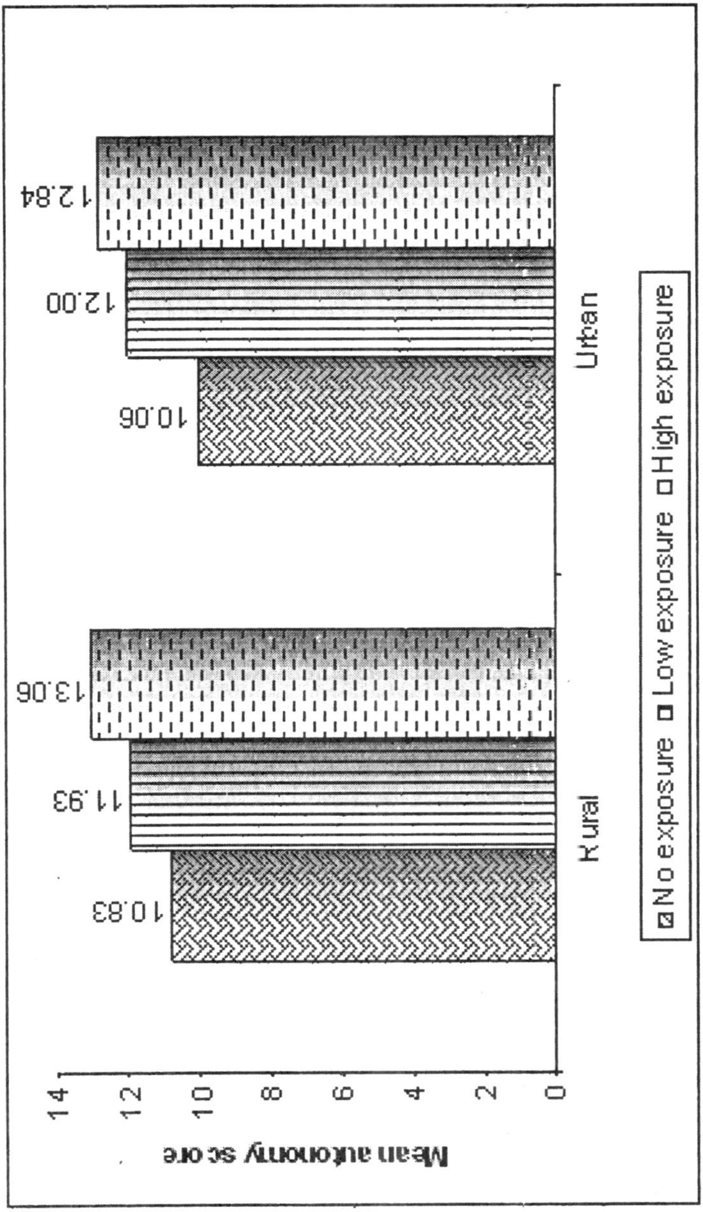

A mass media index was developed based on the exposure of women to all the four mass media. As per the mass media index, women were grouped into three categories as no exposure, low level of exposure and high level of exposure based on the total score attained by each woman for all the four mass media variables (The details of scoring for the mass media index is given in Annexure – IV). The analysis of data on the influence of mass media on women's autonomy on sex-segregated interaction reveal that increase in the level of exposure to mass media increases the level of women's autonomy on sex-segregated interaction in both rural and urban areas (Figure 5.1.1). In rural areas, the mean score significantly increased from 10.83 for women who had no exposure to mass media to 11.93 for women who had a low level of exposure and to 13.06 for women who had a high level of exposure. In urban areas, the mean score significantly increased from 10.06 for women who had no exposure to 12 for women who had a low level of exposure and to 12.84 for women who had a high level of exposure to mass media.

Membership in Self Help Group (SHG) significantly influenced the autonomy of women in both rural and urban areas. In both rural and urban areas, members of SHGs had significantly higher autonomy on sex-segregated interaction than non-members. In rural areas, the members had a mean autonomy score of 12.66 and non-members had a mean score of 11.77. In urban areas, the members had a mean autonomy score of 12.66 and non-members had a mean autonomy score of 12.03.

Overall, the results indicate that all mass media variables included in the analysis and the membership of women in self help group had significantly positive effect on women's autonomy on sex-segregated interaction in both rural and urban areas. Thus the exposure of women to mass media and membership in self help groups played a vital role in improving the autonomy of women on sex-segregated interaction in both rural and urban areas.

5.2 Freedom of Movement

The autonomy of women on freedom of movement measured by mean autonomy score attained by women on various indicators of freedom of movement by selected background characteristics is presented in Tables 5.2.1 to 5.2.4. Overall, the results show that rural women had substantially more autonomy on freedom of movement than their urban counterparts. On the scale of 0 to 26, the mean autonomy score attained by women was 14.06 in rural and 12.63 in urban areas. The influence of various background characteristics of women on their autonomy on freedom of movement are discussed in the following sections 5.2.1 to 5.2.4.

5.2.1 Women's Autonomy on Freedom of Movement and Socio-economic Characteristics

The distribution of women by mean autonomy score on freedom of movement and selected socio-economic characteristics is presented in Table 5.2.1. The level of autonomy of women on freedom of movement was measured based on the mean score attained by women on each of the selected socio-economic characteristics. The autonomy of women on freedom of movement increased with education in both rural and urban areas. In rural areas, the mean score on freedom of movement increased from 13.19 for illiterates to 15.03 for higher secondary and above educated respondents except for a declining trend observed for women with high school education. In urban areas, the mean score on freedom of movement increased from 11.69 for illiterates to 13.43 for higher secondary and above educated respondents. Education of husband did not make significant difference in the autonomy of women on freedom of movement in both rural and urban areas.

Muslim women had a significantly lower autonomy on freedom of movement than others in both rural and urban areas. The level of autonomy on freedom of movement varied significantly among women belonging to different communities in both rural and urban areas. It is observed that scheduled caste/scheduled tribe women and most backward caste women

Table 5.2.1 Mean autonomy score attained by women on freedom of movement by socio-economic characteristics

Socio-economic characteristics	*Rural*			*Urban*			*Total*		
	Mean	*N*	*SD*	*Mean*	*N*	*SD*	*Mean*	*N*	*SD*
All	14.06	1200	6.08	12.63	1200	6.19	13.35	2400	6.18
Education of woman									
Illiterate	13.19	133	5.89	11.69	124	5.40	12.47	257	5.70
Literate & Primary	13.91	247	5.93	12.17	190	5.69	13.16	437	5.88
Middle (6-8)	14.33	352	5.91	12.27	317	6.28	13.35	669	6.17
High School (9-10)	13.78	310	6.35	12.97	336	6.33	13.36	646	6.35
Higher Sec. & above	15.03	158	6.26	13.48	233	6.59	14.10	391	6.49
		F-2.059	P<0.084		F-2.559	P<0.037		F-2.867	P<0.022
Education of husband									
Illiterate	14.77	117	6.15	13.04	84	5.25	14.04	201	5.84
Literate & Primary	14.54	242	5.87	12.68	173	5.85	13.76	415	5.93
Middle (6-8)	13.77	266	5.81	12.05	275	6.24	12.90	541	6.09
High School (9-10)	13.89	408	6.18	13.13	414	6.21	13.51	822	6.20
Higher Sec. & above	13.77	167	6.51	12.27	254	6.60	12.86	421	6.60
		F-1.099	P<0.355		F-1.593	P<0.174		F-2.618	P<0.034

(Contd.)

(Contd. Table 5.2.1)

Socio-economic characteristics	Rural			Urban			Total		
	Mean	*N*	*SD*	*Mean*	*N*	*SD*	*Mean*	*N*	*SD*
Religion									
Hindu	14.32	1082	6.01	12.92	1034	6.09	13.63	2116	6.09
Muslim	10.09	77	6.38	9.62	105	6.58	9.82	182	6.48
Christian	14.78	41	4.78	12.92	61	6.11	13.67	102	5.66
		F-18.157	P<0.000		F-13.858	P<0.000		F-32.915	P<0.000
Community									
SC / ST	14.26	340	5.84	12.34	235	5.73	13.47	575	5.87
MBC	14.60	386	6.09	13.92	304	5.72	14.30	690	5.94
BC & Others	13.48	474	6.21	12.14	661	6.49	12.70	1135	6.40
		F-3.894	P<0.021		F-9.097	P<0.000		F-14.830	P<0.000
Standard of living									
Low	14.23	492	5.78	11.59	337	5.71	13.15	829	5.89
Medium	14.34	379	5.98	13.37	377	5.98	13.85	756	5.99
High	13.50	329	6.62	12.78	486	6.59	13.07	815	6.61
		F-1.977	P<0.139		F-7.649	P<0.001		F-3.709	P<0.023

(Contd.)

(Contd. Table 5.2.1)

Socio-economic characteristics	*Rural*			*Urban*			*Total*		
	Mean	*N*	*SD*	*Mean*	*N*	*SD*	*Mean*	*N*	*SD*
Economic activities									
Yes	16.16	315	5.52	13.91	152	6.02	15.43	467	5.78
No	13.32	885	6.10	12.44	1048	6.20	12.84	1933	6.17
		F-52.955	P<0.000		F-7.523	P<0.006		F-67.689	P<0.000
Contribution to total income									
Nil	13.33	882	6.09	12.42	1045	6.20	12.84	1927	6.17
25 %	15.63	144	5.40	13.69	100	6.07	14.83	244	5.75
≤ 25 %	16.51	174	5.69	14.67	55	5.96	16.07	229	5.80
		F-26.264	P<0.000		F-5.082	P<0.006		F-36.836	P<0.000
Type of family									
Nuclear	14.84	720	5.66	13.51	659	5.92	14.20	1379	5.82
Joint	12.90	480	6.51	11.55	541	6.36	12.19	1021	6.46
		F-29.658	P<0.000		F-30.439	P<0.000		F-63.927	P<0.000

Figure 5.2.1 Autonomy of women on freedom of movement by age (years)

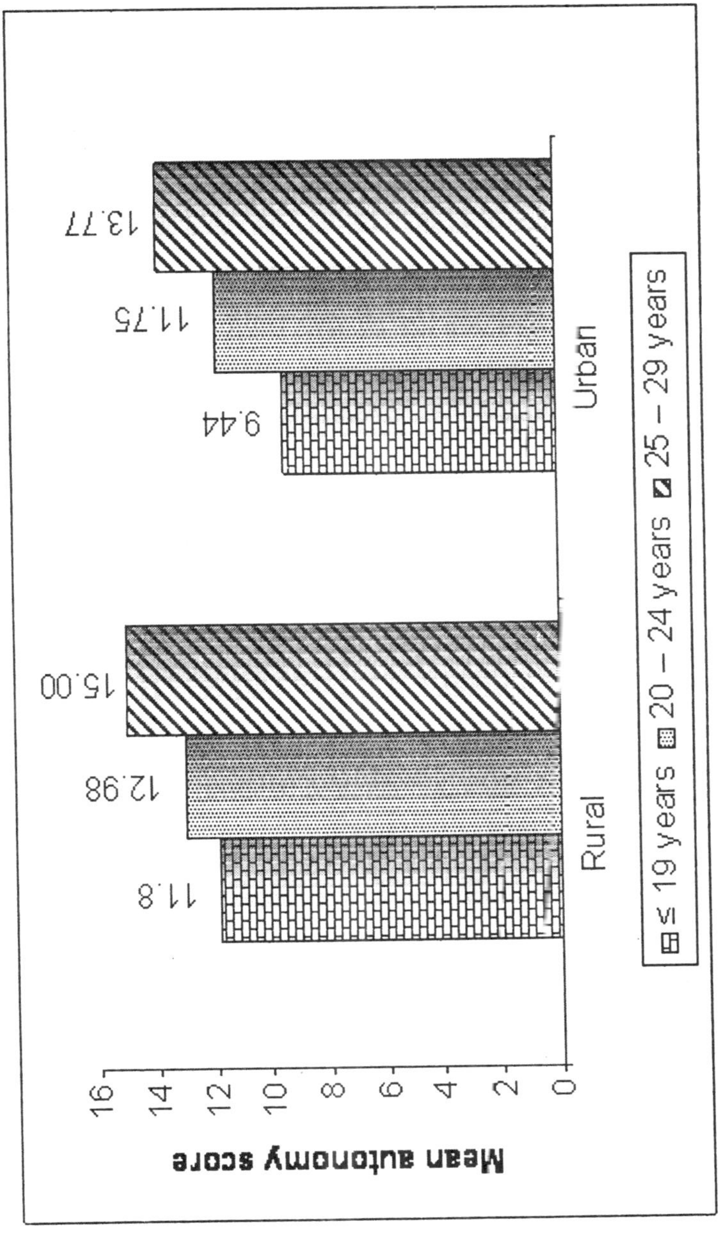

had more autonomy on freedom of movement than backward and other caste women in rural areas. However, in urban areas, the most backward caste women had more autonomy than SC/ ST and BC and others. In rural areas, the mean autonomy score on freedom of movement was highest at 14.26 for SC/ST followed by MBC (14.60) and BC and others (13.48). In urban areas, the mean autonomy score was highest at 13.92 for MBC, followed by SC/ST (12.34) and BC and others (12.14).

The standard of living did not make significant difference in the autonomy of women on freedom of movement in rural areas. It is observed that the mean autonomy score on freedom of movement was 14.23 for a low standard of living, 14.34 for a medium and 13.50 for a high standard of living. However in urban areas, the standard of living showed significant differences in the level of autonomy on freedom of movement. It is observed that the mean autonomy score on freedom of movement was significantly lowest at 11.59 for low standard of living compared to the mean score of 13.37 for medium and 12.78 for high standard of living women.

Involvement in income earning economic activities showed significantly positive effect on the autonomy of women on freedom of movement in both rural and urban areas. It is observed that the mean autonomy score on freedom of movement was significantly more among women involved in economic activities (16.16) compared to women not involved in economic activities (13.32). In urban areas also, the mean score was significantly more among women involved in economic activities (13.91) compared to women not involved in economic activities (12.44).

The contribution of women to total family income significantly influenced the autonomy of women on freedom of movement in both rural and urban areas. The mean score was significantly lowest at 13.33 for women who did not contribute anything to the family income compared to the mean score of 15.63 for women who contributed up to 25 per cent and 16.51 for women who contributed more than 25 per cent to the total family income. In urban areas, the mean autonomy score was

12.42 for women who did not contribute anything to family income compared to the mean score of 13.69 for women who contributed up to 25 per cent and 14.67 for women who contributed more than 25 per cent to the total family income.

The type of family significantly influenced the autonomy of women on freedom of movement in both rural and urban areas. Women in nuclear family had significantly more autonomy on freedom of movement than women in joint family in both rural and urban areas. In rural areas, the mean autonomy score on freedom of movement was significantly higher at 14.84 for women in nuclear family compared to 12.90 for women in joint family. In urban areas, the mean autonomy score on freedom of movement was significantly higher at 13.51 for women in nuclear family compared to 11.55 observed for women in joint family

The results indicate that education of women, involvement in income earning economic activities and contribution to the total family income significantly improved the autonomy of women on freedom of movement in both rural and urban areas. Muslim women and backward caste women had a significantly lower autonomy than others in both rural and urban areas. Women in nuclear family had significantly more autonomy than others in both rural and urban areas. The standard of living seemed to have significant association only in urban areas.

5.2.2 Women's Autonomy on Freedom of Movement and Demographic Characteristics

The mean autonomy score on freedom of movement by selected demographic characteristics of the women are presented in Table 5.2.2. The mean autonomy score on freedom of movement increased with the age of women in both rural and urban areas. In rural areas, the mean score increased from 11.80 for women aged 19 years or less to 12.98 for women aged 20 – 24 years and to 15.00 for women aged 25-29 years. In urban areas also, the mean score increased with the age of women. It increased from 9.44 for women aged 19 years or less to 13.77 for women aged 25–29 years. (Figure 5.2.1)

Women married at younger ages (d" 20 years) had more autonomy on freedom of movement compared to women married at later ages (21+). It is observed that in rural areas, the mean autonomy score on freedom of movement decreased from 14.22 for women married at ages 16 years or less to 11.70 for women married at ages 23 years and above. In urban areas, the mean autonomy score was 12.45 for women married at ages 16 years or less and 11.69 for women married at ages 23 years and above.

The husband-wife age difference did not make any significant difference in the level of autonomy on freedom of movement in both rural and urban areas. Marital duration significantly influenced women's autonomy on freedom of movement in both rural and urban areas. In rural areas, the mean autonomy score on freedom of movement increased significantly from 11.26 for marital duration of three years or less to 15.98 for women who had marital duration of 10 years or more. In urban areas, the mean autonomy score increased with the marital duration of up to 9 years and then showed a declining trend for a marital duration of 10 years or more.

The autonomy of women on freedom of movement increased with the number of male children in both rural and urban areas. In rural areas, the mean autonomy score on freedom of movement increased from 13.68 for women who had no male child to 14.63 for women who had two or more male children. In urban areas, the mean score increased with increase in the number of male children. It increased from 12.39 for no male child to 12.86 for two or more number of male children. Though differences are observed in the mean score, the differences are not statistically significant.

The autonomy of women on freedom of movement increased significantly with number of female children in both rural and urban areas. In rural areas, the mean autonomy score on freedom of movement increased significantly from 13.46 for women who had no female child to 14.60 for women who had two or more female children. In urban areas also, the mean

Table 5.2.2 Mean autonomy score attained by women on freedom of movement by demographic characteristics

Demographic characteristics	Rural			Urban			Total		
	Mean	*N*	*SD*	*Mean*	*N*	*SD*	*Mean*	*N*	*SD*
All	**14.06**	**1200**	**6.08**	**12.63**	**1200**	**6.20**	**13.35**	**2400**	**6.18**
Age (years)									
≤ 19	11.80	50	5.75	9.44	59	5.84	10.52	109	5.89
20 – 24	12.98	478	6.20	11.75	551	6.04	12.32	1029	6.15
25 – 29	15.00	672	5.85	13.77	590	6.14	14.43	1262	6.02
		F-19.677	P<0.000		F-24.354	P<0.000		F-46.622	P<0.000
Age at marriage (years)									
≤ 16	14.22	152	6.10	12.45	100	5.98	13.52	252	6.10
17 – 18	14.24	398	6.28	12.64	316	5.63	13.53	714	6.05
19 – 20	14.74	352	5.67	13.31	418	6.37	13.96	770	6.09
21 – 22	13.54	203	6.12	12.01	234	6.38	12.72	437	6.30
23 +	11.70	95	6.09	11.69	132	6.61	11.69	227	6.39
		F-5.254	P<0.000		F-2.636	P<0.033		F-7.392	P<0.000

(Contd.)

(Contd. Table 5.2.2)

Demographic characteristics	Rural			Urban			Total		
	Mean	*N*	*SD*	*Mean*	*N*	*SD*	*Mean*	*N*	*SD*
Husband-wife age difference (years)									
≤ 4	14.02	417	5.95	12.59	438	6.09	13.29	855	6.06
5 – 8	13.75	499	6.12	12.79	479	6.36	13.28	978	6.26
9 +	14.68	284	6.18	12.42	283	6.10	13.55	567	6.24
		F-2.119	P<0.121		F-0.324	P<0.724		F-0.410	P<0.664
Marital duration (years)									
≤ 3	11.26	223	6.14	10.40	300	6.12	10.77	523	6.14
4 – 6	13.59	376	5.90	12.39	437	6.11	12.95	813	6.04
7 – 9	14.97	347	5.64	14.38	318	5.84	14.69	665	5.74
10+	15.98	254	5.94	14.11	145	5.89	15.30	399	5.98
		F-29.321	P<0.000		F-25.880	P<0.000		F-59.086	P<0.000

(Contd.)

(Contd. Table 5.2.2)

Demographic characteristics	*Rural*			*Urban*			*Total*		
	Mean	*N*	*SD*	*Mean*	*N*	*SD*	*Mean*	*N*	*SD*
Number of male children									
0	13.68	335	6.12	12.39	363	6.14	13.01	698	6.16
1	14.02	596	6.14	12.68	574	6.43	13.36	1170	6.32
2 +	14.63	269	5.89	12.86	263	5.76	13.75	532	5.89
		F-1.852	P<0.157		F-0.459	P<0.632		F -2.194	P<0.112
Number of female children									
0	13.46	357	6.29	12.04	400	6.26	12.71	757	6.31
1	14.19	568	6.06	12.78	558	6.34	13.49	1126	6.24
2 +	14.60	275	5.80	13.26	242	5.68	13.97	517	5.78
		F -2.959	P<0.052		F-3.221	P<0.040		F- 6996	P<0.001
Total Number of children									
1	12.58	345	6.49	11.28	402	6.47	11.88	747	6.51
2	14.75	604	5.80	13.56	605	5.95	14.15	1209	5.91
3 +	14.47	251	5.82	12.51	193	5.88	13.62	444	5.92
		F-15.040	P<0.000		F-16.886	P<0.000		F-32.692	P<0.000

autonomy score increased significantly from 12.04 for women who had no female child to 13.26 for women who had two or more female children. Overall, women who had a total of two living children had significantly more autonomy on freedom of movement than women who had one child or three or more children in both rural and urban areas. In rural areas, the mean autonomy score on freedom of movement was highest at 14.75 for women who had two children compared to 12.58 for women who had one living child and 14.47 for women who had three or more children. In urban areas, the mean autonomy score was highest at 13.56 for women who had two living children compared to 11.28 for women who had one living child and 12.51 for women who had three or more children.

The results indicate that the autonomy of women on freedom of movement increased with the age of women in both rural and urban areas. Women married at younger ages had more autonomy than women married at older ages (21+) in both rural and urban areas. Marital duration and number of female children had significantly positive effect on women's autonomy in both rural and urban areas. Women who had a total of two children had significantly more autonomy on freedom of movement in both rural and urban areas.

5.2.3 Women's Autonomy on Freedom of Movement and Marital Characteristics

The distribution of women according to mean autonomy score on freedom of movement by marital characteristics of the women is presented in Table 5.2.3. It is observed that there was not much variation in the mean autonomy score on freedom of movement among women who had consanguineous and non-consanguineous type of marriage in both rural and urban areas.

In rural areas, women who had married a person from the paternal side had more autonomy on freedom of movement than women who had married a person from the maternal side. However, in urban areas, it was vice versa. Though differences are observed

Table 5.2.3 Mean autonomy score attained by women on freedom of movement by marital characteristics

Marital characteristics	*Rural*			*Urban*			*Total*		
	Mean	*N*	*SD*	*Mean*	*N*	*SD*	*Mean*	*N*	*SD*
All	**14.06**	**1200**	**6.08**	**12.63**	**1200**	**6.19**	**13.35**	**2400**	**6.18**
Type of marriage									
Consanguineous	14.05	399	6.24	12.79	425	6.13	13.40	824	6.21
Non-consanguineous	14.07	801	6.01	12.54	775	6.24	13.32	1576	6.17
		F-0.002	P<0.963		F- 0.420	P<0.517		F-0.091	P<0.763
Consanguineous type									
Maternal	13.70	209	6.44	13.00	229	6.20	13.34	438	6.32
Paternal	14.44	190	6.01	12.54	196	6.05	13.47	386	6.09
		F-1.376	P<0.241		F-0.605	P<0.437		F-0.098	P<0.754

(Contd.)

(Contd. Table 5.2.3)

Marital characteristics	*Rural*			*Urban*			*Total*		
	Mean	*N*	*SD*	*Mean*	*N*	*SD*	*Mean*	*N*	*SD*
Kind of marriage									
Arranged	13.99	1078	6.14	12.46	1071	6.28	13.24	2149	6.26
Love marriage	14.70	122	5.52	14.05	129	5.28	14.37	251	5.40
		F-1.506	P<0.220		F-7.598	P<0.006		F-7.648	P<0.006
Inter caste / inter religious marriage									
Same caste	14.06	1128	6.10	12.50	1096	6.26	13.29	2224	6.23
Inter caste / inter religious	14.07	72	5.82	13.98	104	5.30	14.02	176	5.50
		F-0.000	P<0.994		F-5.434	P<0.020		F-2.234	P<0.135

in the mean score among women married to persons from paternal and maternal side, the differences are not significant for both rural and urban areas. Women who had love marriage had more autonomy on freedom of movement than those who had arranged marriage in both rural and urban areas. Though differences are observed in the mean score between women who had love marriage and arranged marriage, the differences are statistically significant only for women in urban areas. Inter-caste / inter-religious marriage did not make any significant difference in the level of autonomy of women on freedom of movement in rural areas. However in urban areas, women who had inter-caste / inter-religious marriage had significantly more autonomy on freedom of movement than those who had same caste marriage.

Overall, the results indicate that the autonomy of women on freedom of movement was significantly higher among women who had love marriage and inter-caste / inter religious marriage than among others in urban areas. None of the marital characteristics variables showed any significant relationship with the autonomy of women in rural areas.

5.2.4 Women's Autonomy on Freedom of Movement and Exposure to Mass Media

The results of the analysis of data on the influence of mass media on women's autonomy on freedom of movement are presented in Table 5.2.4. Listening to radio did not make any significant difference in the autonomy of women on freedom of movement in both rural and urban areas. In rural areas, the mean autonomy score on freedom of movement was 14.25 for women who had the habit of listening to radio and 13.81 for women who were not having the habit of listening to radio. In urban areas, the mean autonomy score on freedom of movement was 12.90 for women who had the habit of listening to radio and 12.34 for those who were not having the habit of listening to radio. Though women who had the habit of listening to radio were having a comparatively higher autonomy, the differences are not statistically significant.

Watching television at least once a week seemed to have a significant influence on women's autonomy on freedom of movement in both rural and urban areas. In rural areas, the mean autonomy score on freedom of movement was significantly highest at 14.21 for women who were watching television at least once a week compared to 13.01 for women who were not watching television. In urban areas also, the mean autonomy score was significantly higher (12.84) for women who were watching television once a week than for women who were not watching television (10.62).

Going to movies did not make any significant difference in the level of women's autonomy on freedom of movement in rural areas. However in urban areas, going to movies showed significant difference in the autonomy of women on freedom of movement. It is observed that the mean autonomy score was highest at 13.97 for women going to movies compared to 12.29 observed for those who were not going to movies. Reading newspapers / magazines showed significant difference in the level of women's autonomy on freedom of movement in both rural and urban areas. In rural areas, the mean score was significantly higher (14.94) for those who were reading newspapers / magazines than for those who were not having the habit of reading newspapers / magazines (13.53). In urban areas also, the mean autonomy score on freedom of movement was significantly highest at 13.38 for women who had the habit of reading newspapers / magazines compared to 12.17 for women who were not having the habit of reading newspapers / magazines.

The results of the analysis of data on the overall level of women's exposure to various mass media reveals that the increase in the level of exposure to mass media increased the level of women's autonomy on freedom of movement in both rural and urban areas (Figure 5.2.2). In rural areas, the mean autonomy score on freedom of movement significantly increased from 11.95 for women who had no exposure to mass media to 13.84 for women who had a low level of exposure and to 14.95

Table 5.2.4 Mean autonomy score attained by women on freedom of movement by exposure to mass media

Exposure to mass media	*Rural*			*Urban*			*Total*		
	Mean	*N*	*SD*	*Mean*	*N*	*SD*	*Mean*	*N*	*SD*
All	**14.06**	**1200**	**6.08**	**12.63**	**1200**	**6.19**	**13.35**	**2400**	**6.18**
Listening to radio									
Yes	14.25	683	6.16	12.90	630	6.31	13.60	1313	6.27
No	13.81	517	5.97	12.34	570	6.06	13.04	1087	6.06
		F-1.532	P<0.216		F-2.447	P<0.118		F- 4.940	P<0.026
Watching television									
Yes	14.21	1050	6.06	12.84	1088	6.21	13.51	2138	6.17
No	13.01	150	6.16	10.62	112	5.74	11.99	262	6.09
		F-5.130	P<0.024		F-13.160	P<0.000		F-14.269	P<0.000
Going to movies									
Yes	14.61	172	6.23	13.97	242	6.08	14.24	414	6.14
No	13.97	1028	6.06	12.29	958	6.19	13.16	1986	6.17
		F-1.654	P<0.199		F-14.275	P<0.000		F-10.408	P<0.001

(Contd.)

(Contd. Table 5.2.4)

Exposure to mass media	*Rural*			*Urban*			*Total*		
	Mean	*N*	*SD*	*Mean*	*N*	*SD*	*Mean*	*N*	*SD*
Reading newspapers / magazines									
Yes	14.94	458	6.08	13.38	456	6.50	14.16	914	6.34
No	13.53	742	6.03	12.17	744	5.96	12.85	1486	6.03
		F-15.410	P<0.000		F -10.926	P<0.001		F-25.862	P<0.000
Mass media index									
No exposure	11.95	76	6.29	10.09	53	5.46	11.19	129	6.01
Low exposure	13.84	752	5.95	12.29	759	6.12	13.06	1511	6.08
High exposure	14.95	372	6.17	13.63	388	6.29	14.28	760	6.26
		F-9.161	P<0.000		F-10.823	P<0.000		F-18.345	P<0.000
Membership in SHG									
Yes	15.90	600	5.47	14.62	304	5.63	15.47	904	5.55
No	12.23	600	6.12	11.95	896	6.24	12.06	1496	6.19
		F-119.821	P<0.000		F -43.561	P<0.000		F-183.918	P<0.000

Figure 5.2.2 Autonomy of women on freedom of movement by exposure to mass media

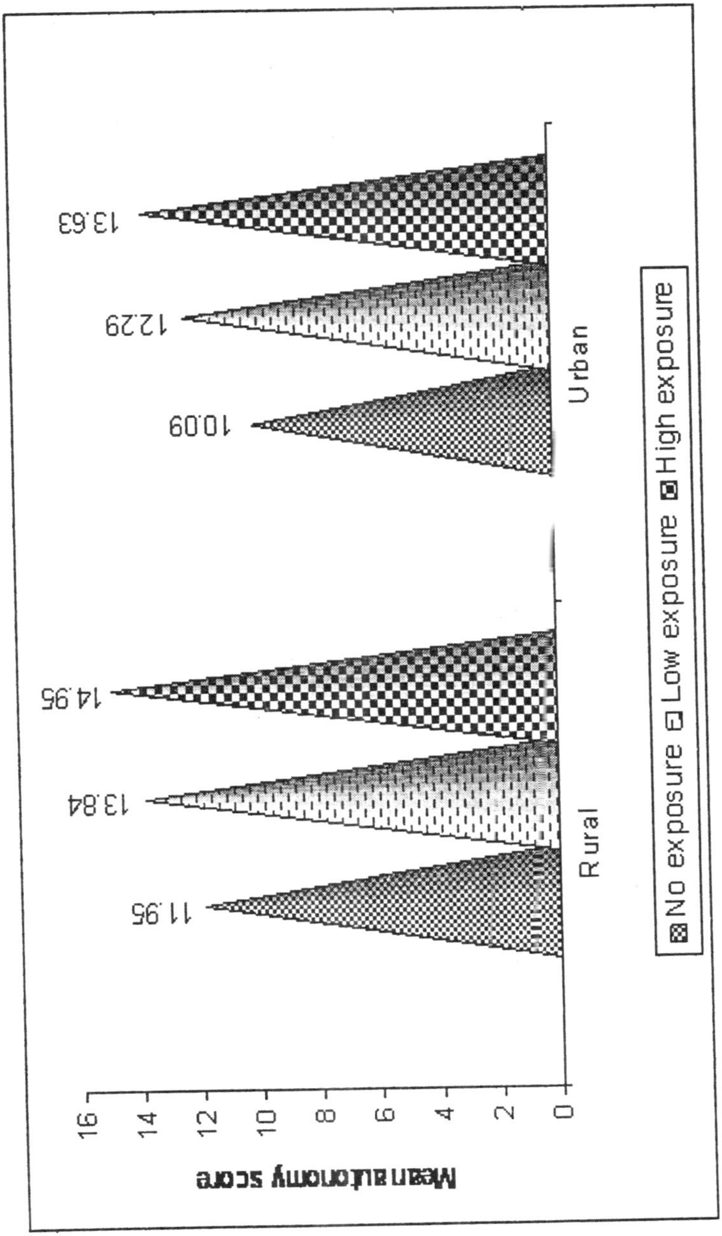

Figure 5.2.3 Autonomy of women on freedom of movement by membership in SHG

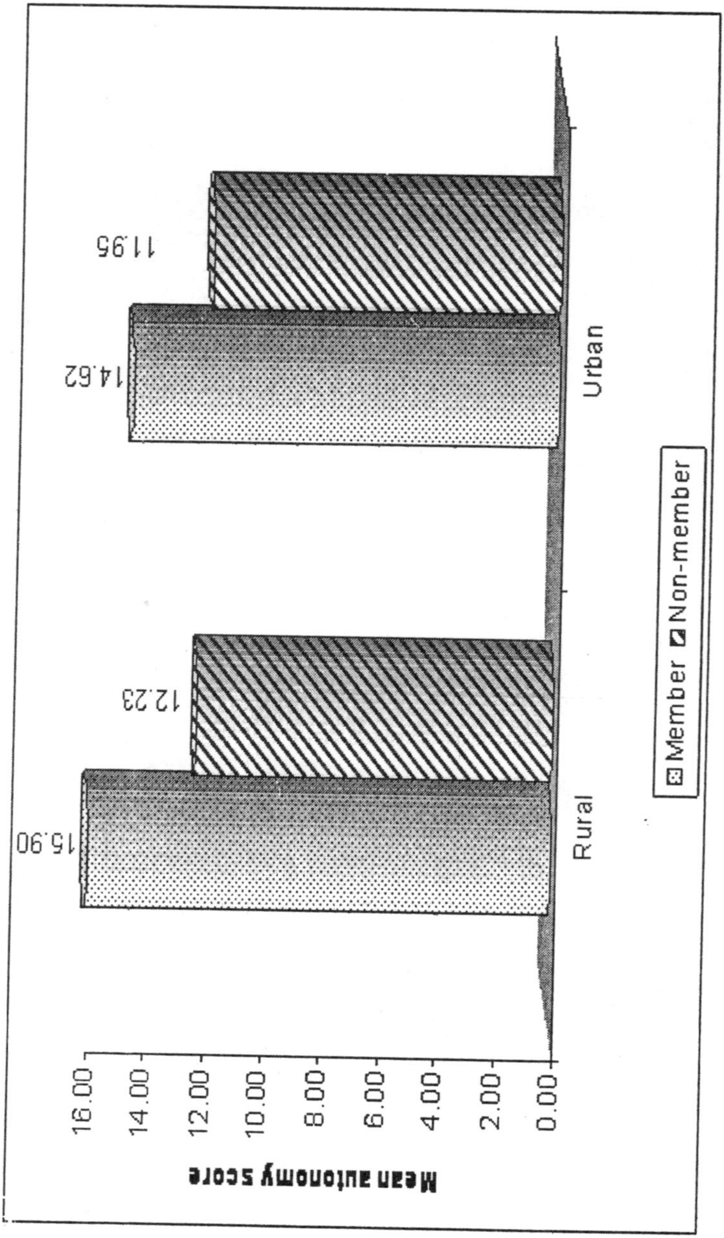

for those who had a high level of exposure. In urban areas, the mean autonomy score on freedom of movement significantly increased from 10.09 for women who had no exposure to mass media to 12.29 for women who had a low level of exposure and to 13.63 for women who had a high level of exposure to mass media.

It is observed that in both rural and urban areas, members of SHG had significantly more autonomy on freedom of movement than non-members (Figure 5.2.3). In rural areas, members had a mean autonomy score of 15.90 compared to only 12.23 observed for non-members. In urban areas also, members of SHG had a mean score of 14.62 compared to only 11.95 observed for non-members.

The results indicate that watching television, reading newspapers / magazines, overall level of exposure to mass media and membership in self help group had significantly positive effect on the autonomy of women on freedom of movement in both rural and urban areas. Going to movies had significantly positive influence on women's autonomy only in urban areas. In general, women's exposure to mass media and membership in SHG are the important factors in improving the autonomy of women on freedom of movement.

5.3 Freedom to Participate in Social and Political Activities

The distribution of women by their level of autonomy on freedom to participate in social and political activities and selected background characteristics is presented in Tables 5.3.1 to 5.3.4. Overall, the results indicate that the level of autonomy of women on freedom to participate in social and political activities was more among women in rural than among women in urban areas. On a scale of 0-14, the mean autonomy score was higher for women in rural (4.24) than for women in urban areas (2.56). The influence of various socio-economic, demographic, marital and mass media variables on the autonomy of women on freedom to participate in social and political activities is discussed in the following sections 5.3.1 to 5.3.4.

5.3.1 Women's Autonomy on Freedom to Participate in Social and Political Activities and Socio-economic Characteristics

The distribution of women according to the mean autonomy score on freedom to participate in social and political activities by selected socio-economic characteristics is presented in Table 5.3.1. The autonomy of women on freedom to participate in social and political activities increased significantly with education in both rural and urban areas. In rural areas, the mean score increased from 3.33 for illiterates to 4.92 for higher secondary and above educated respondents. In urban areas, the mean score increased from 1.91 for illiterates to 2.88 for higher secondary and above educated respondents. It is to be noted that the mean score among women in rural areas was higher at all levels of education than among women in urban areas. Education of husband did not make any significant difference in the level of autonomy of women on freedom to participate in social and political activities in both rural and urban areas.

Muslim women had a significantly lower autonomy on freedom to participate in social and political activities than others in both rural and urban areas.

The autonomy of women on freedom to participate in social and political activities varied significantly among women of different caste groups in both rural and urban areas. Scheduled Caste / Scheduled Tribe (SC/ST) women in rural areas and Most Backward Caste (MBC) women in urban areas had more autonomy on freedom to participate in social and political activities than others. In rural areas, the mean autonomy score was highest at 4.60 for SC/ST women compared to 4.48 for MBC and 3.79 for BC and others. In urban areas, the mean score was 2.76 for SC/ST women, 2.81 for MBC and 2.36 for BC and others.

The standard of living did not make significant difference in the autonomy of women on freedom to participate in social

Table 5.3.1 Mean autonomy score attained by women on freedom to participate in social and political activities by socio-economic characteristics

Socio-economic characteristics	*Rural*			*Urban*			*Total*		
	Mean	*N*	*SD*	*Mean*	*N*	*SD*	*Mean*	*N*	*SD*
All	**4.24**	**1200**	**3.65**	**2.56**	**1200**	**2.66**	**3.40**	**2400**	**3.30**
Education of woman									
Illiterate	3.33	133	3.25	1.91	124	1.92	2.65	257	2.77
Literate & Primary	3.92	247	3.44	2.33	190	2.18	3.23	437	3.05
Middle (6-8)	4.07	352	3.63	2.49	317	2.54	3.32	669	3.25
High School (9-10)	4.74	310	3.84	2.76	336	2.81	3.71	646	3.48
Higher Sec. & above	4.92	158	3.73	2.88	233	3.18	3.70	391	3.55
		F- 5.631	P<0.000		F -3.594	P<0.006		F -6.033	P<0.000
Education of husband									
Illiterate	4.45	117	3.61	2.54	84	2.19	3.65	201	3.23
Literate & Primary	4.55	242	3.78	2.31	173	2.19	3.62	415	3.39
Middle (6-8)	4.04	266	3.55	2.47	275	2.63	3.24	541	3.21
High School (9-10)	4.24	408	3.69	2.83	414	2.92	3.53	822	3.39
Higher Sec. & above	3.96	167	3.53	2.37	254	2.64	3.00	421	3.12
		F-0.975	P<0.420		F-1.888	P<0.110		F-2.944	P<0.019

(Contd.)

(Contd. Table 5.3.1)

Socio-economic characteristics	*Rural*			*Urban*			*Total*		
	Mean	*N*	*SD*	*Mean*	*N*	*SD*	*Mean*	*N*	*SD*
Religion									
Hindu	4.33	1082	3.68	2.61	1034	2.71	3.49	2116	3.35
Muslim	3.18	77	3.39	1.68	105	1.77	2.31	182	2.68
Christian	4.05	41	3.02	3.13	61	2.67	3.50	102	2.84
		F- 3.607	P<0.027		F-7.474	P<0.001		F-10.739	P<0.000
Community									
SC / ST	4.60	340	3.51	2.76	235	2.91	3.84	575	3.40
MBC	4.48	386	3.94	2.81	304	2.63	3.74	690	3.52
BC & Others	3.79	474	3.44	2.36	661	2.56	2.96	1135	3.04
		F- 6.040	P<0.002		F-3.821	P<0.022		F -19.286	P<0.000
Standard of living									
Low	4.16	492	3.58	2.06	337	2.28	3.30	829	3.28
Medium	4.40	379	3.71	2.93	377	2.99	3.67	756	3.45
High	4.17	329	3.68	2.60	486	2.57	3.23	815	3.16
		F-0.579	P<0.561		F-9.788	P<0.000		F-3.875	P<0.021

(Contd.)

(Contd. Table 5.3.1)

Socio-economic characteristics	*Rural*			*Urban*			*Total*		
	Mean	*N*	*SD*	*Mean*	*N*	*SD*	*Mean*	*N*	*SD*
Economic activities									
Yes	5.65	315	3.81	3.25	152	3.16	4.87	467	3.78
No	3.74	885	3.45	2.45	1048	2.56	3.04	1933	3.07
		F-67.495	P<0.000		F-12.006	P<0.001		F-121.229	P<0.000
Percent contribution to total income									
Nil	3.74	882	3.45	2.45	1045	2.55	3.04	1927	3.06
≤25 %	5.58	144	3.77	3.00	100	3.04	4.52	244	3.70
Above 25 %	5.68	174	3.87	3.78	55	3.45	5.23	229	3.85
		F-33.421	P<0.000		F-8.205	P<0.000		F-63.969	P<0.000
Type of family									
Nuclear	4.51	720	3.68	2.67	659	2.67	3.63	1379	3.36
Joint	3.04	480	3.57	2.41	541	2.64	3.08	1021	3.19
		F-9.832	P<0.002		F-2.922	P<0.088		F-16.442	P<0.000

and political activities in rural areas. However, in urban areas, the standard of living showed significant difference in the level of autonomy. It is observed that in urban areas, low standard of living women had significantly low level of autonomy compared to those who had medium and high standard of living.

Involvement of women in income earning economic activities showed significantly positive influence on the autonomy of women on freedom to participate in social and political activities in both rural and urban areas. In rural areas, the mean autonomy score was significantly higher at 5.65 for women who were involved in economic activities compared to only 3.74 observed for women who were not involved in economic activities. In urban areas also, the mean autonomy score was significantly higher at 3.25 for women who were involved in economic activities compared to only 2.45 observed for women were had not involved in economic activities.

Contribution to the total family income significantly increased the autonomy of women on freedom to participate in social and political activities in both rural and urban areas. In rural areas, the mean score was significantly lowest at 3.74 for women who did not contribute anything to the family income compared to a significantly high mean score of 5.58 observed for women who contributed up to 25 per cent of the total family income and 5.68 observed for women who contributed more than 25 per cent to the total family income. In urban areas, it is observed that the mean score was 2.45 for women who did not contribute anything to the family income compared to a mean score of 3.00 for women who contributed up to 25 per cent and 3.78 for women who contributed more than 25 per cent to the total family income.

The type of family showed significant influence on the autonomy of women on freedom to participate in social and political activities in both rural and urban areas. Women in nuclear family had significantly higher autonomy than women in joint family. In rural areas, the mean score was significantly highest at 4.51 for women in nuclear family compared to only 3.84 observed for women in joint family. In urban areas, the mean score was significantly highest at 2.67 for women in nuclear family compared to 2.41 observed for women in joint family.

Overall, the results showed that the education of women, involvement of women in income earning economic activities and contribution of women to the total family income significantly improved the autonomy of women on their participation in social and political activities in both rural and urban areas. Muslim women had significantly lower autonomy than others in both rural and urban areas. Higher caste women (BC and others) in both rural and urban areas had significantly lower autonomy than others. Women in nuclear family had significantly more autonomy than women in joint family in both rural and urban areas.

5.3.2 Women's Autonomy on Freedom to Participate in Social and Political Activities and Demographic Characteristics

The distribution of women according to mean autonomy score on freedom to participate in social and political activities by selected demographic characteristics of women is presented in Table 5.3.2. The autonomy of women on freedom to participate in social and political activities increased with the age of women in both rural and urban areas (Figure 5.3.1). In rural areas, the mean autonomy score increased significantly from 2.24 for women aged 19 years or less to 3.69 for women aged 20 – 24 years and to 4.78 for women aged 25-29 years. In urban areas also, the mean score increased significantly with the age of women. It has increased from 1.54 for women aged 19 years or less to 2.28 for women aged 20-24 years and to 2.91 for women aged 25-29 years.

While the age at marriage of women showed significant difference in the level of autonomy on freedom to participate in social and political activities in rural areas, no significant differences were observed in urban areas. In rural areas, the mean score significantly decreased from 4.43 for women married at ages 16

Table 5.3.2 Mean autonomy score attained by women on freedom to participate in social and political activities by demographic characteristics

Demographic characteristics	*Rural*			*Urban*			*Total*		
	Mean	*N*	*SD*	*Mean*	*N*	*SD*	*Mean*	*N*	*SD*
All	**4.24**	**1200**	**3.65**	**2.56**	**1200**	**2.66**	**3.40**	**2400**	**3.30**
Age (years)									
≤ 19	2.24	50	2.81	1.54	59	2.04	1.86	109	2.44
20 – 24	3.69	478	3.36	2.28	551	2.42	2.94	1029	2.98
25 – 29	4.78	672	3.79	2.91	590	2.86	3.90	1262	3.51
		F-20.929	P<0.000		F-12.857	P<0.000		F-38.051	P<0.000
Age at marriage (years)									
≤ 16	4.43	152	3.85	2.32	100	2.42	3.59	252	3.50
17 – 18	4.35	398	3.89	2.69	316	2.95	3.61	714	3.59
19 – 20	4.49	352	3.47	2.62	418	2.71	3.47	770	3.21
21 – 22	3.96	203	3.42	2.59	234	2.47	3.23	437	3.02
23 +	3.20	95	3.20	2.14	132	2.21	2.58	227	2.71
		F-2.858	P<0.023		F-1.298	P<0.269		F-4.893	P<0.001

(Contd.)

(Contd. Table 5.3.2)

Demographic characteristics	Rural			Urban			Total		
	Mean	N	SD	Mean	N	SD	Mean	N	SD
Husband-wife age difference (years)									
≤ 4	4.29	417	3.56	2.57	438	2.59	3.40	855	3.21
5 – 8	4.18	499	3.66	2.70	479	2.82	3.45	978	3.36
9+	4.29	284	3.76	2.29	283	2.47	3.30	567	3.33
		F-0.141	P<0.869		F-2.067	P<0.127		F-0.402	P<0.669
Marital duration (years)									
≤ 3	2.73	223	2.95	1.91	300	2.04	2.26	523	2.50
4 – 6	3.96	376	3.40	2.40	437	2.45	3.13	813	3.03
7 – 9	4.42	347	3.50	3.03	318	2.95	3.76	665	3.33
10 +	5.73	254	4.13	3.28	145	3.29	4.84	399	4.02
		F-29.739	P<0.000		F–13.867	P<0.000		F-53.817	P<0.000

(Contd.)

(Contd. Table 5.3.2)

Demographic characteristics	*Rural*			*Urban*			*Total*		
	Mean	*N*	*SD*	*Mean*	*N*	*SD*	*Mean*	*N*	*SD*
Number of male children									
0	3.79	335	3.61	2.41	363	2.32	3.07	698	3.08
1	4.19	596	3.59	2.64	574	2.80	3.43	1170	3.32
2+	4.91	275	3.73	2.65	242	2.50	3.59	517	3.37
		F-0.400	P<0.670		F-0.244	P<0.784		F-1.197	P<0.302
Number of female children									
0	4.20	357	3.52	2.49	400	2.68	3.30	757	3.22
1	4.18	568	3.66	2.56	558	2.71	3.38	1126	3.32
2 +	4.41	275	3.79	2.65	242	2.50	3.59	517	3.37
		F-0.400	P<0.670		F-0.244	P<0.784		F-1.495	P<0.214
Total No. of children									
1	3.35	345	3.28	2.22	402	2.37	2.74	747	2.88
2	4.58	604	3.69	2.80	605	2.79	3.69	1209	3.39
3 +	4.65	251	3.81	2.48	193	2.75	3.70	444	3.56
		F-14.737	P<0.000		F-5.819	P<0.003		F-21.600	P<0.000

Figure 5.3.1 Autonomy of women to participate in social and political activities by age (years)

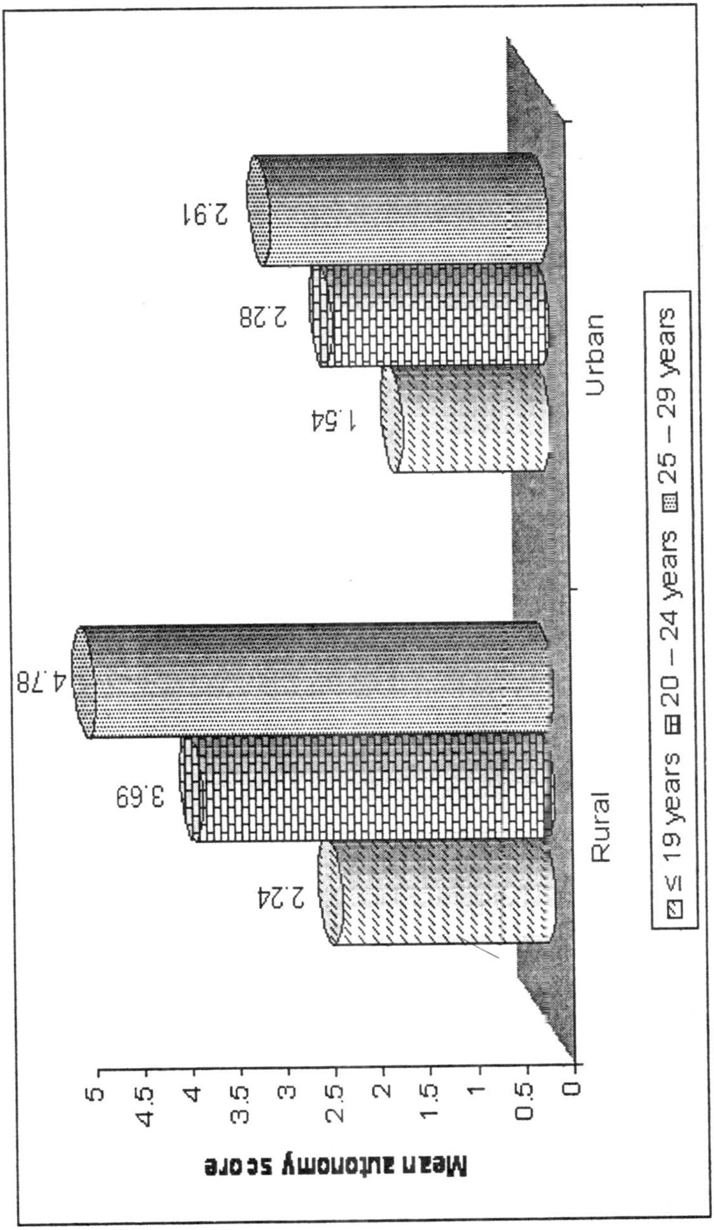

Figure 5.3.2 Autonomy of women to participate in social and political activities by marital duration (years)

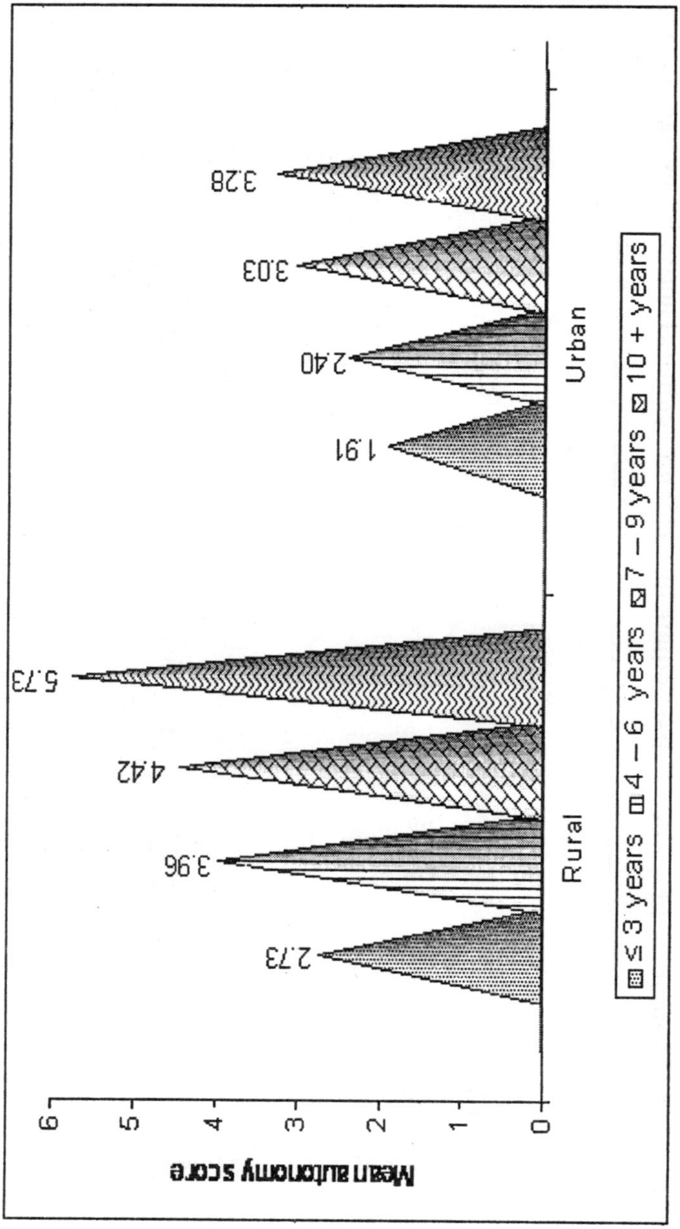

years or less to 3.20 for women married at ages 23 years and above. The husband-wife age difference did not make any significant difference in the level of women's autonomy on freedom to participate in social and political activities in both rural and urban areas.

The autonomy of women on freedom to participate in social and political activities increased significantly with marital duration in both rural and urban areas (Figure 5.3.2). In rural areas, the mean score significantly increased from 2.73 for women who had a marital duration of three years or less to 5.73 for women who had a marital duration of ten years or more. In urban areas also, the mean score significantly increased from 1.91 for women who had a marital duration of three years or less to 3.28 for women who had a marital duration of ten years or more.

Autonomy of women on freedom to participate in social and political activities increased with the number of male children in both rural and urban areas. In rural areas, the mean autonomy score on freedom to participate in social and political activities increased from 3.79 for women who had no male child to 4.91 for women who had two or more number of male children. In urban areas, the mean score increased from 2.41 for women who had no male child to 2.64 for women who had one male child and to 2.65 for women who had two or more number of male children. However, the differences are not statistically significant in both rural and urban areas. The number of female children did not make any significant difference in the autonomy of women in both rural and urban areas. Overall, it is observed that the mean score increased significantly with increase in the total number of children in rural areas. It increased from 3.35 for one living child to 4.65 for three or more number of living children. In urban areas, women who had two children had higher autonomy (2.80) than those who had one child (2.22) and three or more number of children (2.48).

Overall, the results showed that the age of women and marital duration had significantly positive influence on the autonomy of women on freedom to participate in social and political activities in both rural and urban areas. Age at marriage showed significantly negative effect and total number of children showed significantly positive effect among women in rural areas. Women who had a total of two children had significantly more autonomy than women who had only one child and three or more number of children in urban areas.

5.3.3 Women's Autonomy on Freedom to Participate in Social and Political Activities and Marital Characteristics

In order to assess the influence of the type of marriage on women's autonomy on freedom to participate in social and political activities, the data were analysed according to the type of marriage and autonomy score. The results presented in Table 5.3.3 show that the type of marriage and consanguineous type did not make any significant difference in the autonomy of women on freedom to participate in social and political activities in both rural and urban areas. However, love marriage significantly improved the autonomy of women in both rural and urban areas. In rural areas, women who had love marriage had a significantly high mean score of 4.77 compared to only 4.18 for arranged marriage. In urban areas also, the mean score was significantly highest at 3.21 for women who had love marriage compared to only 2.48 for arranged marriage. Inter-caste / inter-religious marriage did not make any significant difference in the autonomy of women on freedom to participate in social and political activities in both rural and urban areas.

The results indicate that except for love marriage, none of the other marital characteristics variables had any significant influence on the autonomy of women on freedom to participate in social and political activities in both rural and urban areas. Women who had love marriage had significantly higher autonomy than women who had arranged marriage in both rural and urban areas.

Table 5.3.3 Mean autonomy score attained by women on freedom to participate in social and political activities by marital characteristics

Marital characteristics	*Rural*			*Urban*			*Total*		
	Mean	*N*	*SD*	*Mean*	*N*	*SD*	*Mean*	*N*	*SD*
All	**4.24**	**1200**	**3.65**	**2.56**	**1200**	**2.66**	**3.40**	**2400**	**3.30**
Type of marriage									
Consanguineous	4.37	399	3.81	2.56	425	2.63	3.43	824	3.38
Non-consanguineous	4.18	801	3.57	2.55	775	2.67	3.38	1576	3.26
		F-0.684	P<0.408		F-0.000	P<0.998		F-0.128	P<0.721
Consanguineous type									
Maternal	4.17	209	3.89	2.42	229	2.62	3.26	438	3.40
Paternal	4.58	190	3.71	2.71	196	2.64	3.63	386	3.34
		F-1.136	P<0.287		F–1.328	P<0.250		F-2.555	P<0.110
Kind of marriage									
Arranged	4.18	1078	3.62	2.48	1071	2.59	3.33	2149	3.26
Love	4.77	122	3.82	3.21	129	3.11	3.97	251	3.56
		F-2.850	**P<0.092**		F–8.814	**P<0.003**		F-8.367	**P<0.004**
Inter caste / inter roligious marriage									
Same caste	4.25	1128	3.67	2.53	1096	2.67	3.40	2224	3.33
Inter caste / inter religious	4.08	72	3.27	2.77	104	2.58	3.30	176	2.95
		F-0.146	P<0.703		F- 0.739	P<0.390		F-0.147	P<0.701

5.3.4 Women's Autonomy on Freedom to Participate in Social and Political Activities and Exposure to Mass Media

The results of the analysis of data on the influence of mass media on women's autonomy on freedom to participate in social and political activities are presented in Table 5.3.4. Listening to radio and going to movies did not make any significant difference in the autonomy of women on freedom to participate in social and political activities in both rural and urban areas. However, watching television and reading newspapers had a significant influence on women's autonomy on freedom to participate in social and political activities in both rural and urban areas. In rural areas, the mean score was highest at 4.35 for women who were watching television at least once a week compared to the mean score of 3.48 observed for women who were not watching television. In urban areas, the mean score was highest at 2.62 for women who were watching television compared to 1.89 for women who were not having the habit of watching television. Women who had the habit of reading newspapers / magazines had significantly more autonomy than women who were not having the habit of reading newspapers / magazines in both rural and urban areas. In rural areas, the mean score was significantly highest at 5.00 for women who had the habit of reading newspapers / magazines compared to 3.77 observed for women who were not having the habit of reading newspapers / magazines. In urban areas, the mean score was highest at 2.97 for women reading newspapers/ magazines compared to 2.30 observed for women who were not having the habit of reading newspapers / magazines.

Exposure to mass media significantly increased the level of women's autonomy on participation in social and political activities in both rural and urban areas (Figure 5.3.3). In rural areas, the mean score significantly increased from 3.43 for women who had no exposure to mass media to 3.97 for women

Table 5.3.4 Mean autonomy score attained by women on freedom to participate in social and political activities by exposure to mass media

Exposure to mass media	*Rural*			*Urban*			*Total*		
	Mean	*N*	*SD*	*Mean*	*N*	*SD*	*Mean*	*N*	*SD*
All	**4.24**	**1200**	**3.65**	**2.56**	**1200**	**2.66**	**3.40**	**2400**	**3.30**
Listening to radio									
Yes	4.33	683	3.70	2.65	630	2.60	3.52	1313	3.33
No	4.13	517	3.57	2.45	570	2.71	3.25	1087	3.26
		F-0.931	P<0.335		F-1.611	P<0.205		F-4.129	P<0.042
Watching television									
Yes	4.35	1050	3.68	2.62	1088	2.70	3.47	2138	3.33
No	3.48	150	3.33	1.89	112	2.10	2.80	262	2.97
		F-7.531	P<0.006		F-7.707	P<0.006		F-9.664	P<0.002
Going to movies									
Yes	4.30	172	3.47	2.74	242	2.82	3.39	414	3.20
No	4.23	1028	3.68	2.50	958	2.61	3.40	1986	3.32
		F-0.054	P<0.816		F-1.530	P<0.216		F-0.003	P<0.960

(Contd.)

(Contd. Table 5.3.4)

Exposure to mass media	*Rural*			*Urban*			*Total*		
	Mean	*N*	*SD*	*Mean*	*N*	*SD*	*Mean*	*N*	*SD*
Reading newspapers /magazines									
Yes	5.00	458	3.85	2.97	456	3.04	3.99	914	3.62
No	3.77	742	3.44	2.30	744	2.36	3.04	1486	3.04
		F-32.982	P<0.000		F-17.733	P<0.000		F-47.600	P<0.000
Mass media index									
No exposure	3.43	76	3.21	1.64	53	1.99	2.70	129	2.90
Low exposure	3.97	752	3.54	2.45	759	2.55	3.21	1511	3.18
High exposure	4.95	372	3.84	2.89	388	2.89	3.90	760	3.54
		F-11.126	P<0.000		F-6.878	P<0.001		F-14.331	P<0.000
Membership in SHG									
Yes	6.43	600	3.37	4.95	304	3.10	5.93	904	3.35
No	2.06	600	2.39	1.74	896	1.89	1.87	1496	2.11
		F-668.824	P<0.000		F-456.235	P<0.000		F-1321.656	P<0.000

Figure 5.3.3 Autonomy of women to participate in social and political activities by level of exposure to mass media

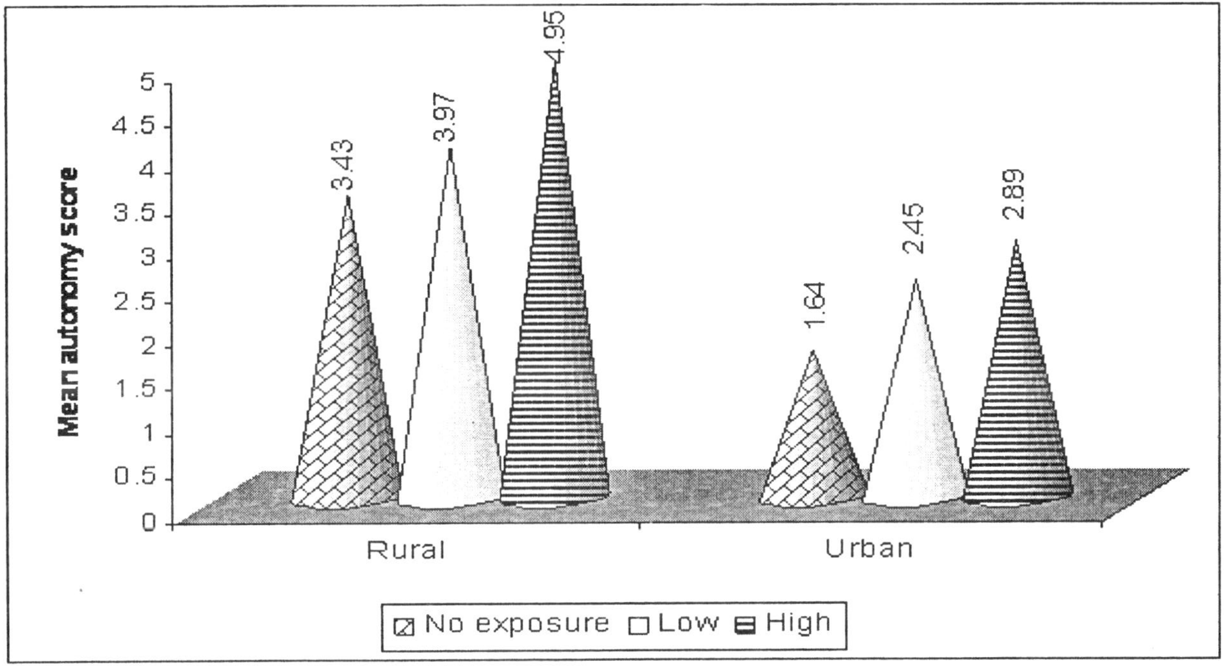

Figure 5.3.4 Autonomy of women to participate in social and political activities by membership in SHG

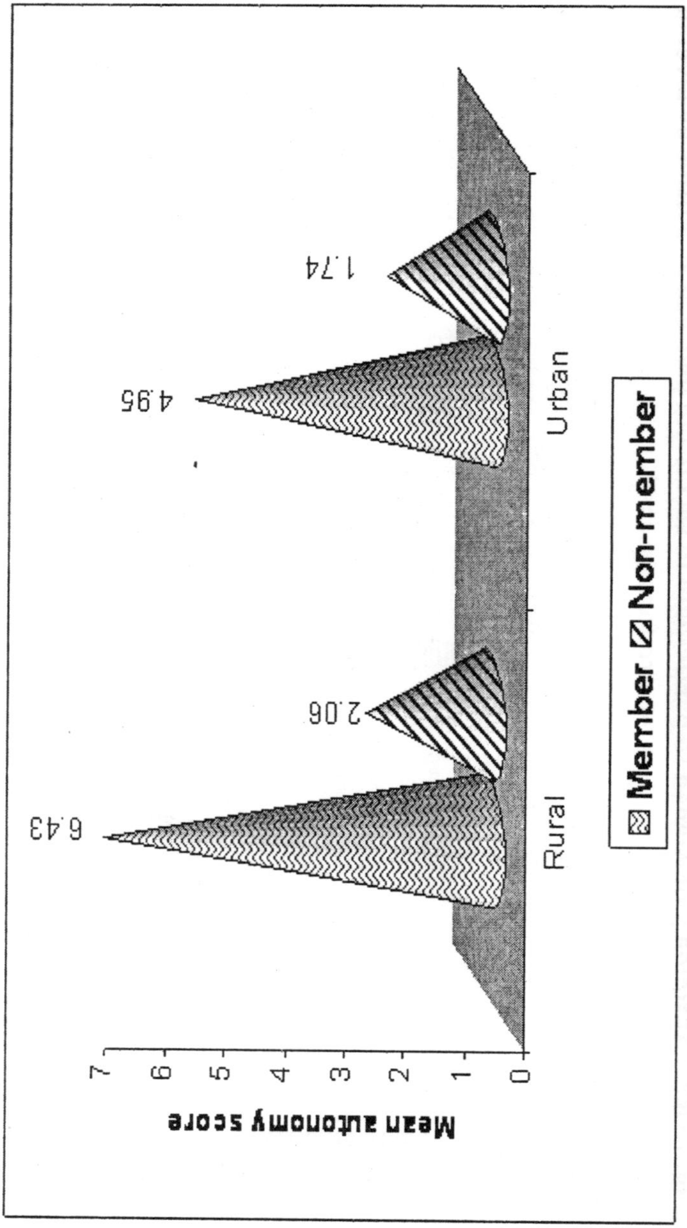

who had a low level of exposure and to 4.95 for women who had a high level of exposure. In urban areas, the mean score significantly increased from 1.64 for women who had no exposure to 2.45 for women who had a low level of exposure and to 2.89 for women who had a high level of exposure to mass media.

Membership in Self Help Group (SHG) helped women to gain more autonomy to participate in social and political activities in both rural and urban areas (Figure 5.3.4). In both rural and urban areas, members of SHG had significantly more autonomy than non-members. In rural areas, the members had a mean score of 6.43 and non-members had a mean score of only 2.06. In urban areas, the members had a mean score of 4.95 and non-members had a mean score of only 1.74.

Overall, the results indicate that the exposure of women to mass media had significant influence on the autonomy of women to participate in social and political activities in both rural and urban areas. Among the various mass media variables examined in this study, watching television and reading newspapers/magazines showed significantly positive effect on the autonomy of women. Participation of women in self help group activities also showed significantly positive effect on the autonomy of women on freedom to participate in social and political activities in both rural and urban areas.

5.4 Financial Management

The distribution of women by their level of autonomy on financial management and selected background characteristics is presented in Tables 5.4.1 to 5.4.4. Overall, it is observed that rural women had more autonomy on financial management than urban women. On a scale of 0 to 6, the mean autonomy score on financial management was higher at 3.07 for rural women compared to only 2.76 for urban women. The influence of socio-economic, demographic, marital and mass media variables on the autonomy of women on financial management is discussed in the following sections 5.4.1 to 5.4.4.

5.4.1 Women's Autonomy on Financial Management and Socio-economic Characteristics

The mean autonomy score of women on financial management according to selected socio-economic characteristics is presented in Table 5.4.1. Education of women did not make any significant difference in the autonomy of women on financial management in both rural and urban areas. However, education of husband had significantly negative effect on the autonomy of women on financial management in both rural and urban areas. Increase in the education of husband significantly decreased the level of women's autonomy on financial management in both rural and urban areas. In rural areas, the mean score decreased from 3.66 for women who had illiterate husband to 2.88 for women who had husband with higher secondary and above. In urban areas, the mean score decreased from 3.01 for women who had illiterate husband to 2.50 for women who had husband with higher secondary and above level of education. The results indicated the dominance of the educated husband in the management of finance at home.

Christian women had higher autonomy on financial management than others in both rural and urban areas. However, the differences are not statistically significant. The level of autonomy on financial management varied significantly among women belonging to different community in rural areas. It is observed that Scheduled Caste / Scheduled Tribe (SC/ST) women had significantly higher autonomy (3.37) compared to MBC (2.95) and BC and others (2.95). However, in urban areas there was no significant variation in the mean score on financial management among women belonging to different communities.

Surprisingly, high standard of living women had low autonomy on financial management in both rural and urban areas. However, the differences are not statistically significant in urban areas. In rural areas, the mean autonomy score was significantly lowest at 2.85 for high standard of living women compared to 3.14 for low standard of living and 3.17 for medium standard of living women.

Table 5.4.1 Mean autonomy score attained by women on financial management by socio-economic characteristics

Socio-Economic characteristics	*Rural*			*Urban*			*Total*		
	Mean	*N*	*SD*	*Mean*	*N*	*SD*	*Mean*	*N*	*SD*
All	**3.07**	**1200**	**1.80**	**2.76**	**1200**	**1.85**	**2.91**	**2400**	**1.83**
Education of woman									
Illiterate	3.02	133	1.97	2.98	124	2.09	3.00	257	2.03
Literate & Primary	3.15	247	1.93	2.78	190	1.93	2.99	437	1.94
Middle (6-8)	3.03	352	1.79	2.60	317	1.78	2.83	669	1.80
High school (9-10)	3.14	310	1.70	2.70	336	1.77	2.91	646	1.75
Higher sec. & above	2.92	158	1.66	2.91	233	1.82	2.91	391	1.76
		F-0.566	P<0.687		F-1.475	P<0.207		F-0.691	P<0.598
Education of husband									
Illiterate	3.66	117	1.90	3.01	84	1.98	3.39	201	1.96
Literate & Primary	3.18	242	1.81	2.91	173	1.95	3.07	415	1.87
Middle (6-8)	2.97	266	1.83	2.64	275	1.87	2.80	541	1.86
High school (9-10)	2.98	408	1.76	2.88	414	1.83	2.93	822	1.79
Higher sec. & above	2.88	167	1.70	2.50	254	1.65	2.65	421	1.69
		F-4.313	P<0.002		F-2.747	P<0.027		F-6.940	P<0.000

(Contd.)

(Contd. Table 5.4.1)

Socio-Economic characteristics	*Rural*			*Urban*			*Total*		
	Mean	*N*	*SD*	*Mean*	*N*	*SD*	*Mean*	*N*	*SD*
Religion									
Hindu	3.09	1082	1.79	2.76	1034	1.84	2.93	2116	1.82
Muslim	2.69	77	1.93	2.56	105	1.87	2.61	182	1.89
Christian	3.29	41	1.89	3.01	61	1.85	3.13	102	1.86
		F-2.096	P<0.123		F-1.194	P<0.303		F-3.186	P<0.042
Community									
SC / ST	3.37	340	1.87	2.86	235	2.03	3.16	575	1.95
MBC	2.95	386	1.77	2.86	304	1.79	2.90	690	1.78
BC & others	2.95	474	1.76	2.68	661	1.79	2.79	1135	1.79
		F-6.830	P<0.001		F-1.400	P<0.247		F-7.948	P<0.000
Standard of living									
Low	3.14	492	1.90	2.76	337	1.96	2.99	829	1.93
Medium	3.17	379	1.78	2.90	377	1.88	3.04	756	1.84
High	2.85	329	1.66	2.64	486	1.73	2.72	815	1.70
		F-3.363	P<0.035		F-2.226	P<0.108		F-6.771	P<0.001

(Contd.)

(Contd. Table 5.4.1)

Socio-Economic characteristics	Rural			Urban			Total		
	Mean	N	SD	Mean	N	SD	Mean	N	SD
Economic activities									
Yes	3.66	315	1.85	3.05	152	2.03	3.46	467	1.93
No	2.86	885	1.74	2.71	1048	1.81	2.78	1933	1.78
		F-47.203	P<0.000		F-4.296	P<0.038		F-52.604	P<0.000
Contribution to total income									
Nil	2.86	882	1.74	2.70	1045	1.81	2.78	1927	1.78
25 %	3.63	144	1.79	3.06	100	2.01	3.39	244	1.90
≤ 25 %	3.67	174	1.92	3.15	55	2.11	3.54	229	1.98
		F-23.140	P<0.000		F-2.960	P<0.052		F-27.819	P<0.000
Type of family									
Nuclear	3.41	720	1.75	3.15	659	1.81	3.28	1379	1.78
Joint	2.56	480	1.76	2.28	541	1.77	2.41	1021	1.77
		F-67.258	P<0.000		F-68.693	P<0.000		F-140.139	P<0.000

Figure 5.4.1 Autonomy of women on financial management by type of family

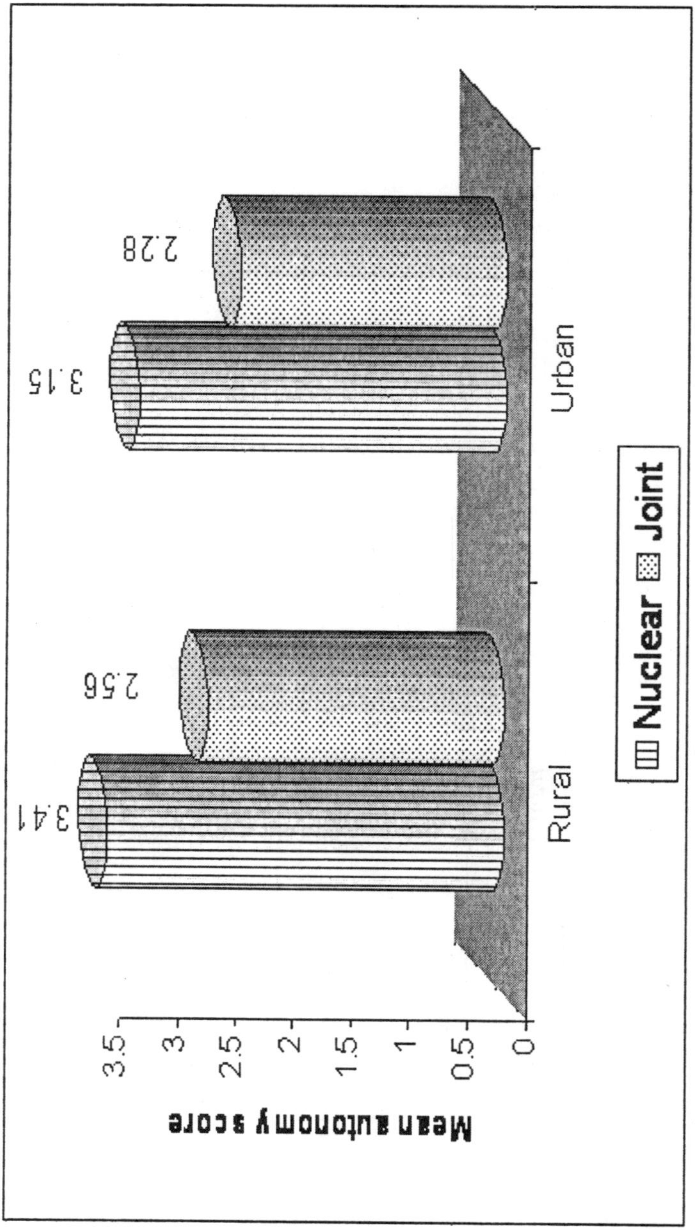

Involvement in income earning economic activities showed significant influence on the autonomy of women on financial management in both rural and urban areas. In rural areas, the mean autonomy score was highest at 3.66 for women involved in income earning economic activities compared to only 2 86 observed for women not involved in income earning activities. In urban areas, it was 3.05 for women involved in income earning economic activities compared 2.71 for women not involved in economic activities. Contribution to the total family income had significant effect on the level of autonomy in both rural and urban areas. In rural areas, the mean autonomy score on financial management significantly increased with the level of contribution to the total family income. The mean autonomy score was 2.86 for women who did not contribute anything to the family income compared to the mean score of 3.63 observed for women who contributed up to 25 per cent and 3.67 observed for women who contributed more than 25 per cent to the total family income. In urban areas also, the mean score increased with the level of contribution to the total family income. It is observed that the mean score increased from 2.70 for women who did not contribute anything to the family income to 3.06 for women who contributed up to 25 per cent of the total family income and to 3.15 for women who contributed more than 25 per cent to the total family income.

The type of family had significant influence on the autonomy of women on financial management in both rural and urban areas (Figure 5.4.1). Women in nuclear family had significantly higher autonomy on financial management than women in joint family in both rural and urban areas. In rural areas, the mean score was 3.41 for women in nuclear family compared to the mean score of 2.56 observed for women in joint family. In urban areas, the mean score was significantly higher at 3.15 for women in nuclear family compared to only 2.28 observed for women in joint family.

Overall, the results indicate that while the education of husband had significantly negative effect on women's autonomy on financial management, involvement in income earning economic activities and contribution to the total family income had significantly positive effect in both rural and urban areas. Women in nuclear family had significantly more autonomy than women in joint family in both rural and urban areas. SC/ST women had significantly more autonomy than others in rural areas. High standard of living women in rural areas had significantly lower autonomy on financial management.

5.4.2 Women's Autonomy on Financial Management and Demographic Characteristics

The mean autonomy score on financial management by selected demographic characteristics of the women is presented in Table 5.4.2. Women's autonomy on financial management increased significantly with the age of women in both rural and urban areas. In rural areas, the mean score increased significantly from 2.18 for women aged 19 years or less to 2.78 for women aged 20–24 years and to 3.34 for women aged 25-29 years. In urban areas also, the mean score increased significantly from 1.69 for women aged 19 years or less to 3.11 for women aged 25-29 years.

Age at marriage of women did not make any significant difference in the autonomy of women on financial management in urban areas. However, in rural areas, age at marriage had significantly negative effect on the autonomy of women on financial management. The mean autonomy score decreased from 3.39 for women married at ages 16 years or less to 2.67 for women married at ages 23 years and above. The husband-wife age difference did not make any significant difference in the autonomy of women on financial management in both rural and urban areas. However, marital duration had significantly positive effect on women's autonomy on financial management in both rural and urban areas. The mean autonomy score on financial management significantly increased with marital duration in both rural and urban areas (Figure 5.4.2). In rural areas, the mean score increased from 2.45 for women who had a marital duration of three years or less to 3.76 for women who had a marital duration of ten years or more. In urban areas, the mean score increased from 2.29 for women who had a marital duration of 3 years or less to 3.35 for women who had a marital duration of ten years or more.

Women's autonomy on financial management increased with the number of male children in both rural and urban areas. However, the differences are significant only in rural areas. It is observed that, in rural areas, the mean score increased from 2.99 for women who had no male child to 3.02 for women who had one male child and to 3.27 for women who had two or more male children. In urban areas, the mean score was 2.69 for women who had no male child, 2.73 for women who had one male child and 2.91 for women who had two or more male children.

Women's autonomy on financial management increased with the number of female children in both rural and urban areas. In rural areas, the mean score was significantly highest at 3.42 for women who had two or more female children compared to 3.05 observed for women who had no female child and 2.91 for women who had one female child. In urban areas, the mean score was highest at 2.84 for women who had two or more female children compared to 2.76 observed for women who had one female child and 2.69 for women who had no female child. Overall, women's autonomy on financial management significantly increased with the total number of children in rural areas. In urban areas, women who had two living children had significantly more autonomy than others. In rural areas, the mean score increased from 2.74 for women who had one child to 3.30 for women who had three or more children. In urban areas, the mean autonomy score was highest at 2.93 for women who had two children compared to the mean score of 2.47 for one child and 2.79 for three or more children.

Overall, the results showed that age, marital duration and total number of children showed significantly positive effect

Table 5.4.2 Mean autonomy score attained by women on financial management by demographic characteristics

Demographic characteristics	*Rural*			*Urban*			*Total*		
	Mean	*N*	*SD*	*Mean*	*N*	*SD*	*Mean*	*N*	*SD*
All	**3.07**	**1200**	**1.80**	**2.76**	**1200**	**1.84**	**2.91**	**2400**	**1.83**
Age (years)									
≤ 19	2.18	50	1.60	1.69	59	1.74	1.91	109	1.69
20 – 24	2.78	478	1.77	2.50	551	1.74	2.63	1029	1.76
25 – 29	3.34	672	1.79	3.11	590	1.87	3.23	1262	1.83
		F-20.496	P<0.000		F-27.057	P<0.000		F-49.670	P<0.000
Age at marriage (years)									
≤ 16	3.39	152	1.89	2.55	100	2.01	3.06	252	1.98
17 – 18	3.10	398	1.87	2.72	316	1.95	2.93	714	1.91
19 – 20	2.97	352	1.80	2.74	418	1.75	2.84	770	1.77
21 – 22	3.12	203	1.67	2.94	234	1.80	3.02	437	1.74
23 +	2.67	95	1.58	2.73	132	1.83	2.70	227	1.73
		F-2.766	P<0.026		F-0.906	P<0.459		F-1.812	P<0.124

(Contd.)

(Contd. Table 5.4.2)

Demographic characteristics	*Rural*			*Urban*			*Total*		
	Mean	*N*	*SD*	*Mean*	*N*	*SD*	*Mean*	*N*	*SD*
Husband-wife age difference (years)									
≤ 4	3.14	417	1.87	2.75	438	1.90	2.94	855	1.89
5 – 8	3.10	499	1.77	2.82	479	1.84	2.96	978	1.81
9 +	2.90	284	1.75	2.66	283	1.77	2.78	567	1.76
		F-1.613	P<0.200		F-0.626	P<0.535		F-1.849	P<0.158
Marital duration(years)									
≤ 3	2.45	223	1.61	2.29	300	1.67	2.36	523	1.65
4 – 6	2.80	376	1.71	2.70	437	1.84	2.75	813	1.78
7 – 9	3.25	347	1.84	3.00	318	1.81	3.13	665	1.83
10 +	3.76	254	1.76	3.35	145	2.02	3.61	399	1.87
		F-26.997	P<0.000		F-14.046	P<0.000		F-43.343	P<0.000
Number of male children									
0	2.99	335	1.85	2.69	363	1.78	2.83	698	1.82
1	3.02	596	1.74	2.73	574	1.84	2.88	1170	1.80
2 +	3.27	269	1.85	2.91	263	1.93	3.10	532	1.90
		F-2.317	P<0.099		F-1.243	P<0.289		F-3.558	P<0.029

(Contd.)

(*Contd. Table 5.4.2*)

Demographic characteristics	*Rural*			*Urban*			*Total*		
	Mean	*N*	*SD*	*Mean*	*N*	*SD*	*Mean*	*N*	*SD*
Number of female children									
0	3.05	357	1.74	2.69	400	1.88	2.86	757	1.82
1	2.91	568	1.80	2.76	558	1.80	2.84	1126	1.80
2 +	3.42	275	1.85	2.84	242	1.90	3.15	517	1.89
		F-7.574	P<0.001		F-0.472	P<0.624		F-5.644	P<0.004
Total Number of children									
1	2.74	345	1.74	2.47	402	1.75	2.59	747	1.75
2	3.16	604	1.79	2.93	605	1.81	3.05	1209	1.80
3 +	3.30	251	1.86	2.79	193	2.04	3.08	444	1.96
		F-9.051	P<0.000		F-7.778	P<0.000		F-16.992	P<0.000

Figure 5.4.2 Autonomy of women on financial management by marital duration (years)

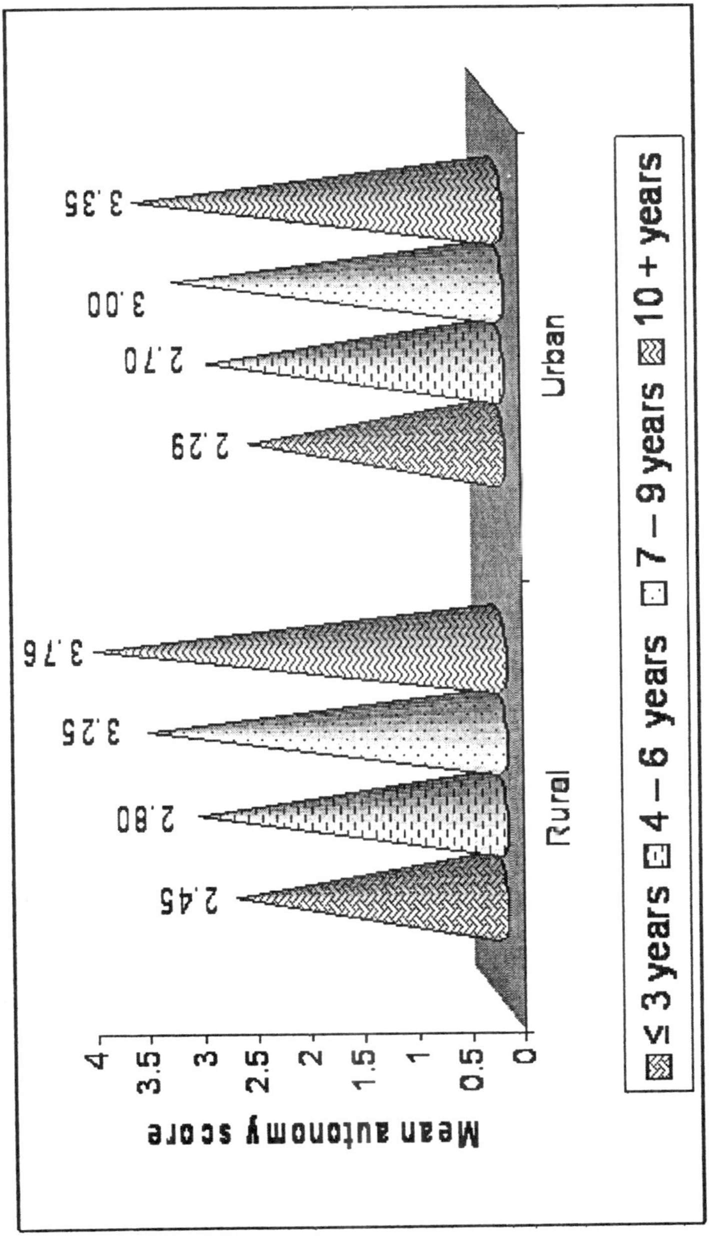

on the autonomy of women on financial management in both rural and urban areas. Age at marriage showed significantly negative effect and the number of male children showed significantly positive effect on the autonomy of women on financial management in rural areas.

5.4.3 Women's Autonomy on Financial Management and Marital Characteristics

In order to assess the influence of the type of marriage on women's autonomy on financial management, the data were analysed according to the type of marriage and mean autonomy score on financial management. The results presented in Table 5.4.3 reveal that the mean autonomy score on financial management was higher among women who had non-consanguineous marriage than those who had consanguineous marriage in both rural and urban areas. However, the differences are significant only for women in urban areas. In urban areas, women who had non-consanguineous marriage had a significantly higher mean score of 2.85 compared to only 2.59 observed for women who had consanguineous marriage. Among the women who had consanguineous marriage, those who had married a person from the paternal side had more autonomy on financial management than those who had married a person from the maternal side in both rural and urban areas. However, the differences are not statistically significant.

Women who had love marriage had significantly more autonomy on financial management than those who had arranged marriage in both rural and urban areas. In rural areas, the mean autonomy score on financial management was 3.39 for women who had love marriage compared to only 3.03 observed for women who had arranged marriage. In urban areas also, the mean autonomy score was 3.41 for women who had love marriage compared to only 2.68 observed for women who had arranged marriage. Women who had inter-caste / inter-religious marriage had more autonomy than those who had same caste

Table 5.4.3 Mean autonomy score attained by women on financial management by marital characteristics

Marital characteristics	*Rural*			*Urban*			*Total*		
	Mean	*N*	*SD*	*Mean*	*N*	*SD*	*Mean*	*N*	*SD*
All	**3.07**	**1200**	**1.80**	**2.76**	**1200**	**1.84**	**2.91**	**2400**	**1.83**
Type of marriage									
Consanguineous	3.06	399	1.80	2.59	425	1.82	2.82	824	1.82
Non-Consanguineous	3.08	801	1.80	2.85	775	1.85	2.96	1576	1.83
		F-0.036	P<0.849		F-5.203	P<0.023		F-3.469	P<0.063
Consanguineous type									
Maternal	2.93	209	1.85	2.58	229	1.81	2.75	438	1.84
Paternal	3.19	190	1.73	2.60	196	1.84	2.89	386	1.81
		F-2.030	P<0.155		F-0.022	P<0.882		F-1.295	P<0.255

(Contd.)

(Contd. Table 5.4.3)

Marital characteristics	*Rural*			*Urban*			*Total*		
	Mean	*N*	*SD*	*Mean*	*N*	*SD*	*Mean*	*N*	*SD*
Kind of marriage									
Arranged marriage	3.03	1078	1.79	2.68	1071	1.82	2.86	2149	1.81
Love marriage	3.39	122	1.91	3.41	129	1.91	3.40	251	1.91
		F-4.187	P<0.041		F-18.447	P<0.000		F-19.887	P<0.000
Inter caste / inter religious marriage									
Same caste	3.05	1128	1.80	2.70	1096	1.82	2.88	2224	1.81
Inter caste / inter religious marriage	3.39	72	1.80	3.33	104	1.96	3.35	176	1.91
		F-2.413	P<0.121		F-10.975	P<0.001		F-10.995	P<0.001

marriage in both rural and urban areas. However, the differences are statistically significant only in urban areas. It is observed that, in urban areas, the mean score was significantly highest at 3.33 for women who had inter-caste/ inter-religious marriage compared to only 2.70 observed for women who had same caste marriage.

Overall, the results indicate that women who had love marriage had significantly high autonomy on financial management than women who had arranged marriage in both rural and urban areas. Inter-caste / inter religious marriage showed significantly positive effect on women's autonomy on financial management only in urban areas. In general, women who had love marriage and those who had inter-caste / inter religious marriage had significantly more autonomy on financial management than others in both rural and urban areas.

5.4.4 Women's Autonomy on Financial Management and Exposure to Mass Media

The results of the analysis of data on the influence of mass media on women's autonomy on financial management are presented in Table 5.4.4. Listening to radio and watching television did not make any significant difference in the autonomy of women on financial management in both rural and urban areas. Going to movies showed significant difference only in rural areas.

While reading newspapers / magazines did not make any significant difference in the autonomy of women on financial management in rural areas, it showed significant difference in urban areas. In rural areas, the mean score was highest at 3.12 for women who were having the habit of reading newspapers / magazines compared to 3.04 observed for women who were not having the habit of reading newspapers/ magazines. In urban areas, the mean score was 2.90 for women who had the habit of reading newspapers / magazines compared to 2.67 for women who were not having the habit of reading newspapers / magazines.

Table 5.4.4 Mean autonomy score attained by women on financial management by exposure to mass media

Exposure to mass media	*Rural*			*Urban*			*Total*		
	Mean	*N*	*SD*	*Mean*	*N*	*SD*	*Mean*	*N*	*SD*
All	**3.07**	**1200**	**1.80**	**2.76**	**1200**	**1.85**	**2.91**	**2400**	**1.83**
Listening to radio									
Yes	3.08	683	1.70	2.69	630	1.68	2.90	1313	1.70
No	3.05	517	1.92	2.83	570	2.00	2.93	1087	1.97
		F-0.100	P<0.752		F-1.628	P<0.202		F-0.258	P<0.612
Watching television									
Yes	3.09	1050	1.79	2.76	1088	1.84	2.92	2138	1.82
No	2.93	150	1.92	2.70	112	1.92	2.83	262	1.92
		F-1.072	P<0.301		F-0.132	P<0.717		F-0.630	P<0.428
Going to movies									
Yes	2.81	172	1.70	2.71	242	1.67	2.76	414	1.68
No	3.11	1028	1.82	2.77	958	1.89	2.95	1986	1.86
		F-4.036	P<0.045		F-0.156	P<0.693		F-3.681	P<0.055

(Contd.)

(Contd. Table 5.4.4)

Exposure to mass media	*Rural*			*Urban*			*Total*		
	Mean	*N*	*SD*	*Mean*	*N*	*SD*	*Mean*	*N*	*SD*
Reading newspapers / magazines									
Yes	3.12	458	1.71	2.90	456	1.79	3.01	914	1.75
No	3.04	742	1.86	2.67	744	1.88	2.85	1486	1.87
		F-0.541	P<0.462		F-4.676	P<0.031		F-4.242	P<0.040
Mass media index									
No exposure	2.93	76	2.15	2.74	53	2.08	2.85	129	2.11
Low exposure	3.05	752	1.83	2.75	759	1.92	2.90	1511	1.88
High exposure	3.14	372	1.68	2.78	388	1.65	2.96	760	1.67
		F-0.523	P<0.593		F-0.050	P<0.951		F-0.332	P<0.717
Membership in SHG									
Yes	3.51	600	1.76	3.21	304	1.93	3.41	904	1.82
No	2.63	600	1.73	2.60	896	1.79	2.61	1496	1.77
		F-75.677	P<0.000		F-25.899	P<0.000		F-112.160	P<0.000

Figure 5.4.3 Autonomy of women on financial management by membership in SHG

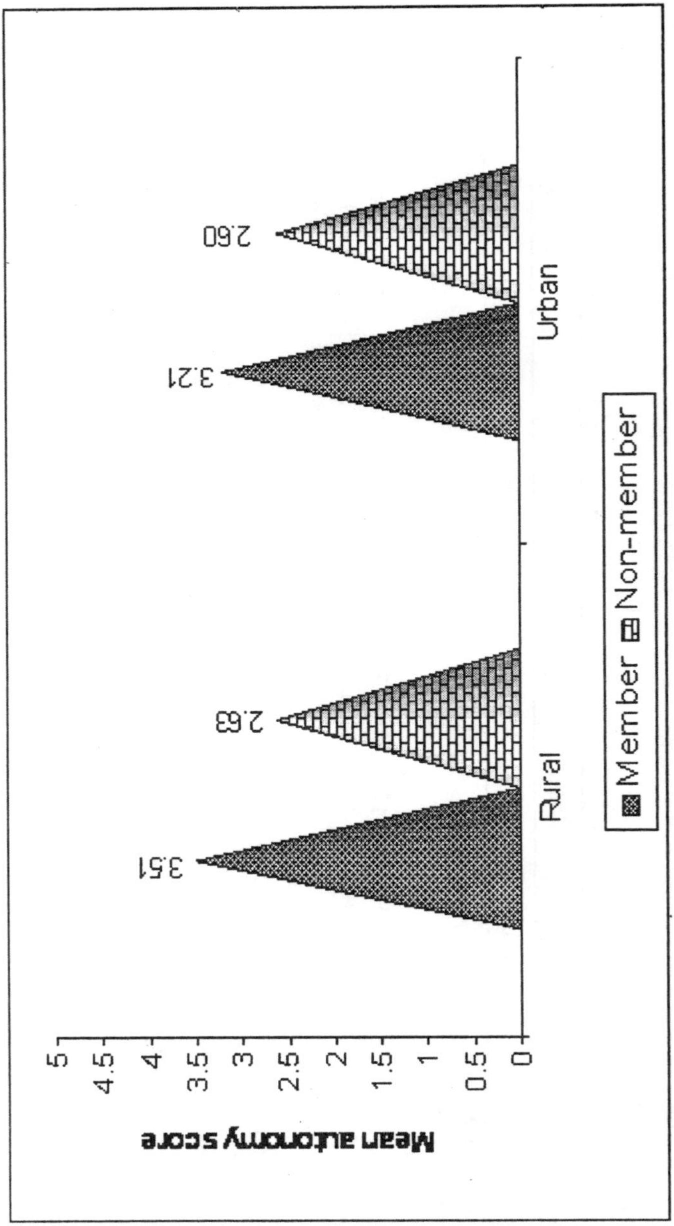

The overall level of exposure of women estimated based on all the four mass media variables did not make any significant difference in the autonomy of women on financial management in both rural and urban areas. So the effect of mass media on women's autonomy on financial management is not significant.

Membership in Self Help Group (SHG) showed significantly positive effect on women's autonomy on financial management in both rural and urban areas (Figure 5.4.3). Members of SHG had significantly more autonomy than non-members in both rural and urban areas. In rural areas, members had a significantly higher autonomy score of 3.51 compared to only 2.63 observed for non-members. In urban areas also, the members had a significantly high autonomy score of 3.21 compared to only 2.60 for non-members.

The results indicate that the overall level of exposure of women to mass media did not make any significant difference in the autonomy of women on financial management in both rural and urban areas. However, members of self help group had significantly more autonomy on financial management than non-members in both rural and urban areas.

5.5 Household Decisions

The distribution of women by their level of autonomy on household decisions and selected background characteristics is presented in Tables 5.5.1 to 5.5.4. In general, the overall autonomy of women on household decisions was more among women in rural than among women in urban areas. On a scale of 0-22, the mean autonomy score was 11.56 for women in rural and 10.81 for women in urban areas. The influence of socio-economic, demographic, marital and mass media variables on women's autonomy on household decisions is discussed in the following sections 5.5.1 to 5.5.4.

5.5.1 Women's Autonomy on Household Decisions and Socio-economic Characteristics

The distribution of women according to their level of autonomy on household decisions and socio-economic characteristics is presented in Table 5.5.1. Education of women did not make any significant difference in the autonomy of women on household decisions in both rural and urban areas. Education of husband showed significantly negative effect on the autonomy of women on household decisions in rural areas. The mean autonomy score on household decisions significantly decreased with increase in the education of husband in rural areas. However, in urban areas, though the education of husband showed negative effect on women's autonomy on household decisions, the differences are not statistically significant.

Muslim women had lower autonomy on household decisions than others in both rural and urban areas. However, the differences are significant only for women in rural areas. The level of autonomy of women on household decisions varied significantly among women of different caste groups in rural areas. Scheduled Caste / Scheduled Tribe (SC/ST) women had more autonomy on household decisions than Most Backward Caste (MBC) and backward caste women in rural areas. The mean score was highest at 12.17 for SC/ST women compared to 11.23 for MBC and 11.38 for BC and other caste women. In urban areas, the mean autonomy score did not show any significant difference among women of various caste groups. Standard of living also did not make any significant difference in the autonomy of women on household decisions in both rural and urban areas.

Women who were involved in income earning economic activities had more autonomy on household decisions in both rural and urban areas. However, the differences are significant only in rural areas. The mean autonomy score was significantly highest at 13.14 for women involved in economic activities compared to 11.00 for women not involved in economic activities in urban areas.

Contribution to total family income showed positive effect on the autonomy of women on household decisions in both rural and urban areas. However, the effect was significant only in rural areas. In rural areas, the mean autonomy score was

Table 5.5.1 Mean autonomy score attained by women on household decisions by socio-economic characteristics

Socio-economic characteristics	*Rural*			*Urban*			*Total*		
	Mean	*N*	*SD*	*Mean*	*N*	*SD*	*Mean*	*N*	*SD*
All	**11.56**	**1200**	**4.29**	**10.81**	**1200**	**4.07**	**11.18**	**2400**	**4.20**
Education of woman									
Illiterate	11.51	133	5.34	10.60	124	4.71	11.07	257	5.06
Literate & primary	11.51	247	4.29	10.73	190	4.02	11.17	437	4.18
Middle (6-8)	11.29	352	4.50	10.43	317	4.19	10.88	669	4.37
High school (9-10)	11.73	310	3.90	11.10	336	3.99	11.41	646	3.96
Higher sec. & above	11.92	158	3.49	11.12	233	3.67	11.44	391	3.62
		F-0.768	P<0.546		F-1.563	P<0.182		F-1.736	P<0.139
Education of husband									
Illiterate	12.80	117	4.20	11.13	84	4.24	12.10	201	4.30
Literate & primary	11.93	242	4.57	10.95	173	4.28	11.52	415	4.47
Middle (6-8)	11.23	266	4.29	10.52	275	4.07	10.87	541	4.19
High school (9-10)	11.38	408	4.21	10.95	414	4.20	11.16	822	4.21
Higher sec. & above	11.10	167	3.94	10.70	254	3.64	10.86	421	3.70
		F-3.998	P<0.003		F-0.705	P<0.588		F-4.504	P<0.001

(Contd.)

(Contd. Table 5.5.1)

Socio-economic characteristics	Rural			Urban			Total		
	Mean	*N*	*SD*	*Mean*	*N*	*SD*	*Mean*	*N*	*SD*
Religion									
Hindu	11.60	1082	4.29	10.85	1034	4.11	11.24	2116	4.22
Muslim	10.50	77	4.36	10.29	105	3.82	10.38	182	4.05
Christian	12.15	41	3.98	11.05	61	3.75	11.49	102	3.86
		F-2.782	P<0.062		F-1.032	P<0.356		F-3.808	P<0.022
Community									
SC / ST	12.17	340	4.50	10.79	235	4.65	11.60	575	4.61
MBC	11.23	386	4.30	10.98	304	4.04	11.12	690	4.18
BC & Others	11.38	474	4.09	10.74	661	3.87	11.00	1135	3.97
		F-4.984	P<0.007		F-0.365	P<0.694		F-3.931	P<0.020
Standard of living									
Low	11.73	492	4.48	10.52	337	4.60	11.24	829	4.56
Medium	11.67	379	4.22	11.10	377	3.84	11.39	756	4.04
High	11.17	329	4.06	10.79	486	3.85	10.94	815	3.94
		F-1.883	P<0.153		F-1.847	P<0.158		F-2.335	P<0.097

(Contd.)

(Contd. Table 5.5.1)

Socio-economic characteristics	Rural			Urban			Total		
	Mean	*N*	*SD*	*Mean*	*N*	*SD*	*Mean*	*N*	*SD*
Economic activities									
Yes	13.14	315	4.48	11.24	152	4.75	12.52	467	4.65
No	11.00	885	4.08	10.75	1048	3.96	10.86	1933	4.01
		F-61.174	P<0.000		F-1.883	P<0.170		F-60.159	P<0.000
Contribution to total income									
Nil	11.00	882	4.07	10.74	1045	3.96	10.86	1927	4.01
≤ 25 %	12.94	144	4.28	11.02	100	4.70	12.15	244	4.55
Above 25 %	13.24	174	4.69	11.84	55	4.85	12.90	229	4.75
		F-29.738	P<0.000		F-2.038	P<0.131		F-32.346	P<0.000
Type of family									
Nuclear	12.30	720	4.05	11.69	659	3.75	12.00	1379	3.92
Joint	10.45	480	4.41	9.75	541	4.19	10.08	1021	4.30
		F-55.828	P<0.000		F-71.273	P<0.000		F-130.284	P<0.000

significantly lowest at 11.00 for women who did not contribute anything to the family income compared to the mean score of 12.94 for women who contributed up to 25 per cent of the total family income and 13.24 for women who contributed more than 25 per cent to the total family income. In urban areas, the mean score increased from 10.74 for women who made no contribution to the total family income to 11.02 for women who contributed up to 25 per cent and to 11.84 for women who contributed more than 25 per cent to the total family income.

The type of family showed significant effect on the autonomy of women on household decisions in both rural and urban areas. Women in nuclear family had significantly more autonomy than women in joint family. In rural areas, the mean autonomy score on household decisions was significantly highest at 12.30 for women in nuclear family compared to only 10.45 for women in joint family. In urban areas also, the mean score was significantly highest at 11.69 for women in nuclear family compared to only 9.75 for women in joint family.

Overall, the results indicate that education of husband, religion, community, standard of living, involvement in income earning activities, percentage contribution to the total family income and type of family had significant association with autonomy of women on household decisions in rural areas. While the education of husband and the standard of living showed negative effect, involvement in income earning economic activities and contribution to the total family income showed positive effect on women's autonomy on household decisions in rural areas. Muslim women and most backward caste women in rural areas had significantly more autonomy than others. Women in nuclear family had significantly more autonomy on household decisions in both rural and urban areas.

5.5.2 Women's Autonomy on Household Decisions and Demographic Characteristics

The mean autonomy score on household decisions by selected demographic characteristics of women is presented in

Table 5.2.2. Autonomy of women on household decisions increased significantly with the age of women in both rural and urban areas (Figure 5.5.1). In rural areas, the mean autonomy score on household decisions increased from 9.10 for women aged 19 years or less to 10.90 for women aged 20–24 years and to 12.21 for women aged 25-29 years. In urban areas, the mean autonomy score increased from 8.53 for women aged 19 years or less to 11.55 for women aged 25 - 29 years.

Age at marriage of women and husband-wife age difference did not make any significant difference in the autonomy of women on household decisions in both rural and urban areas.

Marital duration showed significantly positive effect on women's autonomy on household decisions in both rural and urban areas. In rural areas, the mean score increased from 10.09 for women who had a marital duration of three years or less to 13.04 for women who had a marital duration of 10 years or more. In urban areas, the mean score increased from 9.92 for women who had a marital duration of three years or less to 11.86 for women who had a marital duration of 10 years or more.

Women's autonomy on household decisions increased with the number of male children in both rural and urban areas. In rural areas, the mean score increased from 11.23 for women who had no male child to 11.91 for women who had two or more number of male children. In urban areas, the mean autonomy score on household decisions increased significantly from 10.45 for women who had no male child to 11.26 for women who had two or more number of male children. Though differences are observed in the mean autonomy score in both rural and urban areas, the differences are significant only for women in urban areas. The number of female children showed significant influence on the autonomy of women on household decisions only in rural areas. In urban areas, the number of female children did not make any significant difference in the autonomy of women in household decisions. The total number of children showed significant influence on women's autonomy on household decision in both rural and urban areas. In rural areas, the

Table 5.5.2 Mean autonomy score attained by women on household decisions by demographic characteristics

Demographic characteristics	*Rural*			*Urban*			*Total*		
	Mean	*N*	*SD*	*Mean*	*N*	*SD*	*Mean*	*N*	*SD*
All	**11.56**	**1200**	**4.29**	**10.81**	**1200**	**4.07**	**11.18**	**2400**	**4.20**
Age (years)									
≤ 19	9.10	50	3.97	8.53	59	4.86	8.79	109	4.46
20 – 24	10.90	478	4.03	10.27	551	4.17	10.56	1029	4.11
25 – 29	12.21	672	4.36	11.55	590	3.72	11.90	1262	4.09
		F-22.262	P<0.000		F-24.780	P<0.000		F-49.197	P<0.000
Age at marriage (years)									
≤ 16	12.02	152	5.09	10.75	100	4.39	11.52	252	4.86
17 – 18	11.73	398	4.32	10.62	316	4.39	11.24	714	4.38
19 – 20	11.22	352	4.43	10.87	418	3.97	11.02	770	4.19
21 – 22	11.57	203	3.56	10.97	234	3.85	11.25	437	3.72
23 +	11.27	95	3.60	10.89	132	3.77	11.05	227	3.70
		F-1.255	P<0.286		F-0.293	P<0.883		F-0.774	P<0.542

(Contd.)

(Contd. Table 5.5.2)

Demographic characteristics	Rural			Urban			Total		
	Mean	*N*	*SD*	*Mean*	*N*	*SD*	*Mean*	*N*	*SD*
Husband-wife age difference (years)									
≤ 4	11.60	417	4.47	10.70	438	4.21	11.13	855	4.36
5 – 8	11.66	499	3.94	11.00	479	3.76	11.33	978	3.87
9 +	11.32	284	4.60	10.69	283	4.36	11.00	567	4.49
		F-0.570	P<0.566		F-0.782	P<0.458		F-1.177	P<0.309
Marital duration (years)									
≤ 3	10.09	223	3.86	9.92	300	4.20	9.99	523	4.05
4 - 6	11.03	376	3.99	10.67	437	4.05	10.83	813	4.03
7 – 9	11.97	347	4.30	11.39	318	3.85	11.69	665	4.10
10+	13.04	254	4.52	11.86	145	3.95	12.61	399	4.36
		F-22.987	P<0.000		F-10.537	P<0.000		F-36.083	P<0.000

(Contd.)

(Contd. Table 5.5.2)

Demographic characteristics	*Rural*			*Urban*			*Total*		
	Mean	*N*	*SD*	*Mean*	*N*	*SD*	*Mean*	*N*	*SD*
Number of male children									
0	11.28	335	4.34	10.45	363	4.04	10.85	698	4.20
1	11.55	596	4.22	10.83	574	4.17	11.20	1170	4.21
2 +	11.91	269	4.36	11.26	263	3.87	11.60	532	4.13
		F-1.648	P<0.193		F-3.025	P<0.049		F-4.752	P<0.009
Number of female children									
0	11.30	357	4.13	10.80	400	4.02	11.04	757	4.08
1	11.26	568	4.32	10.89	558	3.96	11.08	1126	4.15
2 +	12.51	275	4.30	10.64	242	4.41	11.63	517	4.44
		F-8.936	P<0.000		F-0.308	P<0.735		F-4.3	P<0.007
Total No. of children									
1	10.50	345	4.10	10.20	402	3.98	10.33	747	4.04
2	11.93	604	4.21	11.29	605	3.96	11.61	1209	4.09
3 +	12.13	251	4.49	10.61	193	4.43	11.47	444	4.52
		F-15.435	P<0.000		F-9.045	P<0.000		F-22.819	P<0.000

Figure 5.5.1 Autonomy of women on household decision by age (years)

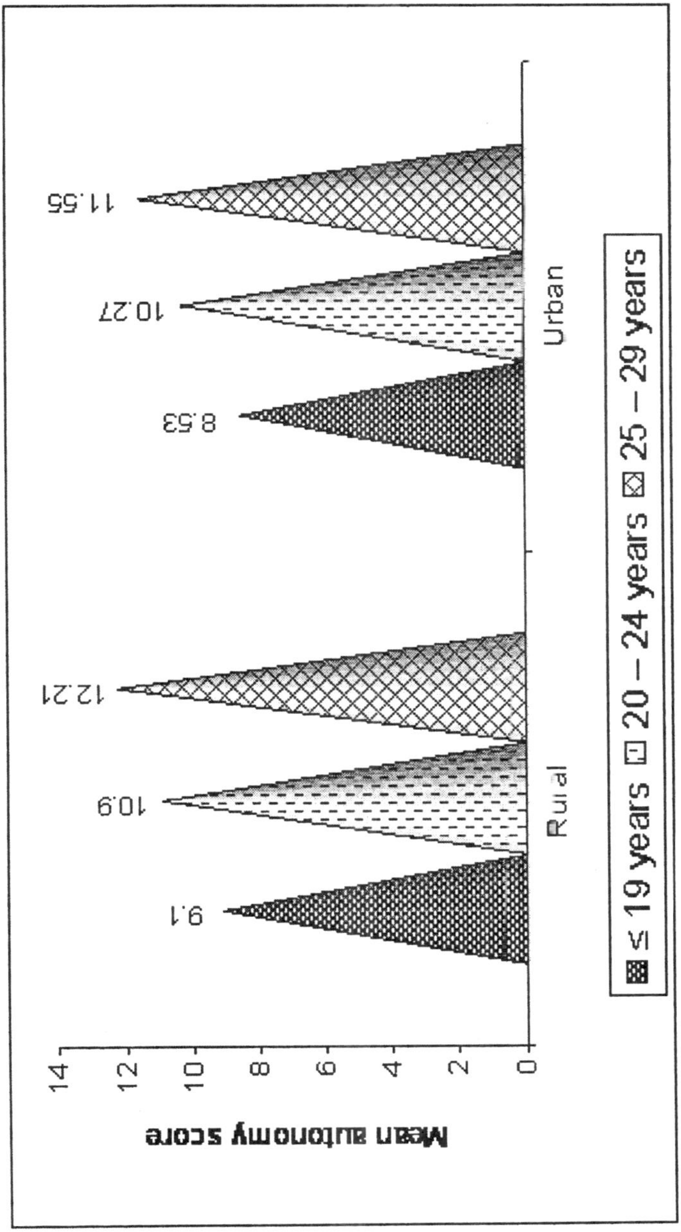

autonomy of women on household decisions increased significantly with increase in the total number of children. In urban areas, women who had two children had significantly more autonomy than those who had one child and three or more number of children.

Overall, the results showed that the age of women, marital duration and total number of children had significantly positive effect on the autonomy of women on household decisions in both rural and urban areas. The number of male children had significantly positive influence on the autonomy of women on household decisions in urban areas and the number of female children had significantly positive influence in rural areas.

5.5.3 Women's Autonomy on Household Decisions and Marital Characteristics

In order to assess the influence of the type of marriage on women's autonomy on household decisions, the data were analysed according to the type of marriage and mean autonomy score on household decisions. The results are presented in Table 5.5.3 reveal that the consanguineous type of marriage did not make any significant difference in the autonomy of women on household decisions in both rural and urban areas. Love marriage showed significantly positive effect on women's autonomy on household decisions in both rural and urban areas (Figure 5.5.2). Inter-caste / inter-religious marriage also showed significantly positive effect on women's autonomy on household decisions in both rural and urban areas.

Overall, the results indicate that women who had love marriage and inter-caste / inter religious marriage had significantly more autonomy on household decisions in both rural and urban areas.

5.5.4 Women's Autonomy on Household Decisions and Exposure to Mass Media

The results of the analysis of data on the influence of mass media on women's autonomy on household decisions are

Table 5.5.3 Mean autonomy score attained by women on household decisions by marital characteristics

Marital characteristics	*Rural*			*Urban*			*Total*		
	Mean	*N*	*SD*	*Mean*	*N*	*SD*	*Mean*	*N*	*SD*
All	**11.56**	**1200**	**4.29**	**10.81**	**1200**	**4.07**	**11.18**	**2400**	**4.19**
Type of marriage									
Consanguineous	11.68	399	4.31	10.65	425	4.05	11.15	824	4.21
Non-consanguineous	11.49	801	4.28	10.90	775	4.09	11.20	1576	4.19
		F-0.515	P<0.473		F-1.036	P<0.309		F-0.083	P<0.774
Consanguineous type									
Maternal	11.80	209	4.53	10.70	229	4.07	11.22	438	4.33
Paternal	11.55	190	4.07	10.60	196	4.03	11.07	386	4.07
		F-0.325	P<0.569		F-0.055	P<0.815		F-0.266	P<0.606

(Contd.)

(Contd. Table 5.5.3)

Marital characteristics	*Rural*			*Urban*			*Total*		
	Mean	*N*	*SD*	*Mean*	*N*	*SD*	*Mean*	*N*	*SD*
Kind of marriage									
Arranged	11.44	1078	4.26	10.67	1071	4.02	11.05	2149	4.16
Love	12.59	122	4.40	12.01	129	4.28	12.30	251	4.34
		F-7.945	P<0.005		F-12.716	P<0.000		F-19.762	P<0.000
Inter caste / inter religious marriage									
Same caste	11.48	1128	4.27	10.70	1096	4.04	11.09	2224	4.18
Inter caste / inter religious	12.67	72	4.45	12.04	104	4.26	12.30	176	4.34
		F-5.156	P<0.023		F-10.384	P<0.001		F-13.369	P<0.000

Figure 5.5.2 Autonomy of women on household decisions by kind of marriage

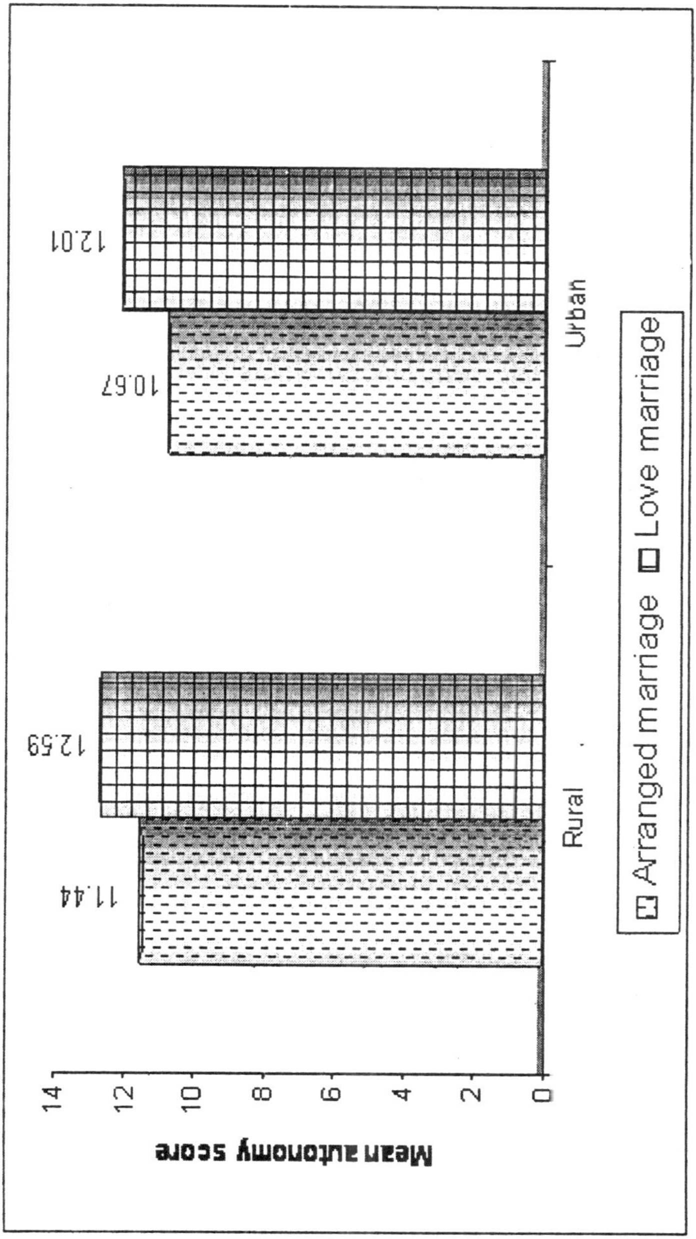

presented in Table 5.5.4. Listening to radio and watching television did not make any significant difference in the autonomy of women on household decisions in both rural and urban areas.

Going to movies did not make any significant difference in the autonomy of women on household decisions in rural areas. However, in urban areas, going to movies showed significantly positive effect on the autonomy of women on household decisions. In urban areas, the mean autonomy score for women who had the habit of going to movies was highest at 11.41 compared to 10.67 observed for those who were not going to movies. Reading newspapers / magazines showed significantly positive effect on the autonomy of women on household decisions in both rural and urban areas. In rural areas, the mean score was highest at 11.94 for women who had the habit of reading newspapers / magazines compared to 11.32 observed for women who were not having the habit of reading newspapers / magazines. In urban areas, the mean score was higher at 11.20 for women who had the habit of reading newspapers / magazines compared to 10.58 observed for women who were not having the habit of reading newspapers / magazines.

The combined mass media index derived from all the four mass media variables showed that the autonomy of women on household decisions increased with increase in the exposure of women to mass media in both rural and urban areas. However the increase was significant only in urban areas. In rural areas, the mean autonomy score increased from 10.89 for women who had no exposure to mass media to 11.48 for women who had a low level of exposure and to 11.84 for women who had a high level of exposure. In urban areas, the mean score significantly increased from 9.66 for those who had no exposure to 10.67 for those who had a low level of exposure and to 11.26 for those who had a high level of exposure to mass media.

Membership in SHG showed significantly positive effect on the autonomy of women on household decisions in both rural

Table 5.5.4 Mean autonomy score attained by women on household decisions by exposure to mass media

Exposure to mass media	*Rural*			*Urban*			*Total*		
	Mean	*N*	*SD*	*Mean*	*N*	*SD*	*Mean*	*N*	*SD*
All	**11.56**	**1200**	**4.29**	**10.81**	**1200**	**4.07**	**11.18**	**2400**	**4.19**
Listening to radio									
Yes	11.61	683	4.21	10.91	630	3.75	11.27	1313	4.00
No	11.49	517	4.39	10.71	570	4.41	11.08	1087	4.42
		F-0.231	P<0.631		F-0.715	P<0.398		F-1.254	P<0.263
Watching television									
Yes	11.56	1050	4.28	10.85	1088	4.05	11.20	2138	4.18
No	11.53	150	4.37	10.48	112	4.33	11.08	262	4.37
		F-0.008	P<0.929		F-0.817	P<0.366		F-0.182	P<0.670
Going to movies									
Yes	11.37	172	3.72	11.41	242	3.61	11.39	414	3.65
No	11.59	1028	4.38	10.07	958	4.17	11.14	1086	4.30
		F-0.368	P<0.544		F-6.426	P<0.011		F-1.213	P<0.271

(Contd.)

(Contd. Table 5.5.4)

Exposure to mass media	*Rural*			*Urban*			*Total*		
	Mean	*N*	*SD*	*Mean*	*N*	*SD*	*Mean*	*N*	*SD*
Reading newspapers / magazines									
Yes	11.94	458	3.84	11.20	456	3.78	11.57	914	3.83
No	11.32	742	4.53	10.58	744	4.23	10.95	1486	4.40
		F-6.000	P<0.014		F-6.722	P<0.010		F-12.648	P<0.000
Mass media index									
No exposure	10.89	76	4.84	9.66	53	5.30	10.39	129	5.05
Low exposure	11.48	752	4.41	10.67	759	4.16	11.07	1511	4.30
High exposure	11.84	372	3.89	11.26	388	3.65	11.54	760	3.77
		F-1.843	P<0.159		F-4.922	P<0.007		F-5.639	P<0.004
Membership in SHG									
Yes	12.80	600	4.02	11.84	304	3.94	12.48	904	4.02
No	10.31	600	4.19	10.47	896	4.06	10.40	1496	4.11
		F-110.183	P<0.000		F-26.358	P<0.000		F-145.714	P<0.000

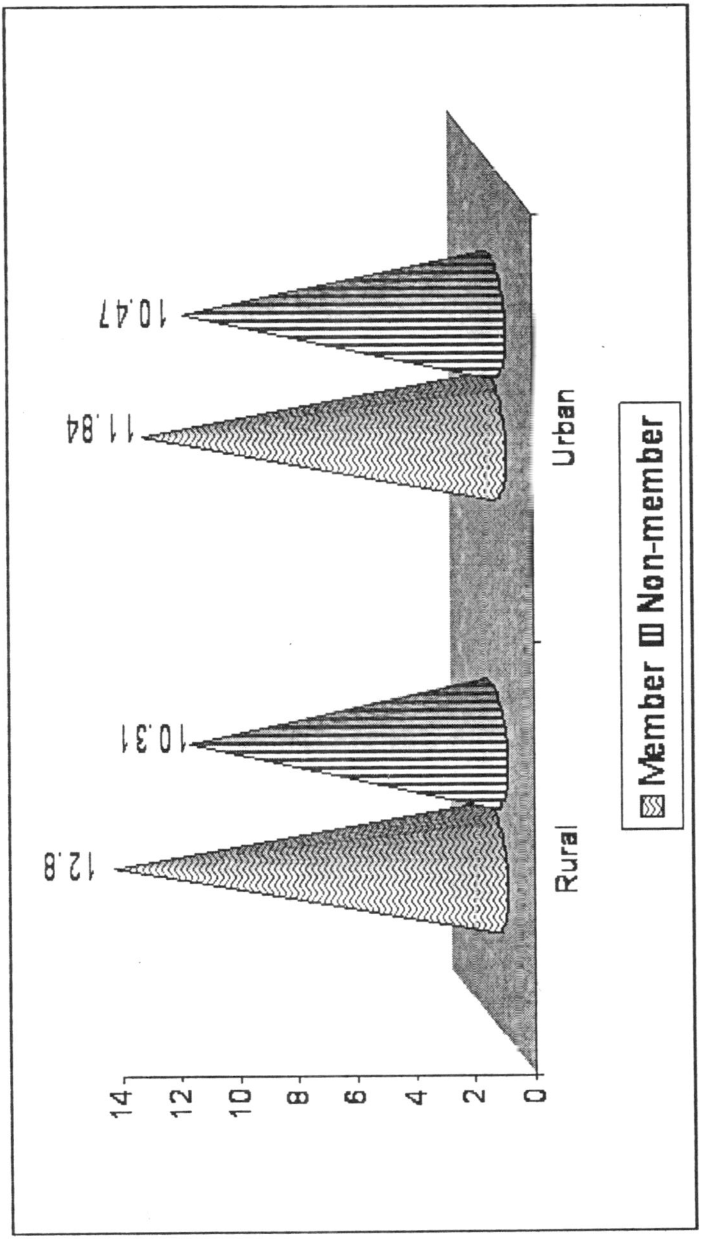

Figure 5.5.3 Autonomy of women on household decisions by membership in SHG

and urban areas (Figure 5.5.3). In both rural and urban areas, members of SHG had significantly more autonomy on household decisions than non-members. In rural areas, members had a mean autonomy score of 12.80 compared to only 10.31 observed for non-members. In urban areas, the members had a mean score of 11.84 compared to the mean score of only 10.47 observed for non-members.

Overall, the results showed that reading newspapers / magazines and membership in self help group had significantly positive effect on the autonomy of women on household decisions in both rural and urban areas. Going to movies and the overall level of exposure to mass media had significantly positive effect only in urban areas.

5.6 Freedom of Choice

The distribution of women by their level of autonomy on freedom of choice in their personal life style and selected background characteristics is presented in Tables 5.6.1 to 5.6.4. On a scale of 0 to 16, the mean autonomy score on freedom of choice was high in both rural (14.63) and urban areas (14.22). The influence of socio-economic, demographic, marital and mass media variables on the autonomy of women on freedom of choice is discussed in the following sections 5.6.1 to 5.6.4.

5.6.1 Women's Autonomy on Freedom of Choice and Socio-Economic Characteristics

The distribution of women by mean autonomy score on freedom of choice and selected socio-economic characteristics is presented in Table 5.6.1. The results indicate that the education of women did not make any significant difference in the autonomy of women on freedom of choice in rural areas. In urban areas, the mean score increased significantly from 13.50 for illiterates to 14.73 for higher secondary and above educated respondents. Education of husband did not show any significant difference in the autonomy of women on freedom of choice in rural areas. However, in urban areas, education of husband showed significant influence on the autonomy of women on freedom of choice. The mean score increased from 13.56 for women who had illiterate husband to 14.49 for women who had husband with education up to higher secondary and above.

Muslim women had significantly lower autonomy on freedom of choice than others in both rural and urban areas. In rural areas, the mean score was lowest at 13.90 for Muslims compared to 14.69 for Hindus and 14.22 for Christians. In urban areas also the mean score was lowest at 13.62 for Muslims compared to 14.27 for Hindus and 14.41 for Christians.

The autonomy of women on freedom of choice varied significantly among women belonging to different caste groups in both rural and urban areas. In rural areas, Most Backward Caste women had more autonomy on freedom of choice than Scheduled Caste / Scheduled Tribe (SC/ST) and Backward Caste women. The mean score was 14.92 for MBC, 14.50 for SC/ST and 14.47 for BC and others. In urban areas, the mean score was significantly highest at 14.33 for BC and others compared to 14.23 for SC/ST and 13.96 for MBC. Standard of living, involvement of women in income earning economic activities, percentage contribution to the total family income and type of family did not show any significant difference in the autonomy of women on freedom of choice in both rural and urban areas.

Overall, the results showed that religion and community were the only socio-economic variables exerting significant influence on the autonomy of women on freedom of choice in both rural and urban areas. Muslim women had significantly lower autonomy than others in both rural and urban areas. Backward caste women in rural areas and most backward caste women in urban areas had significantly lower autonomy than others. Education of women and education of husband had significantly positive effect on women's autonomy on freedom of choice only in urban areas.

Table 5.6.1 Mean autonomy score attained by women on freedom of choice by socio-economic characteristics

Socio-economic characteristics	*Rural*			*Urban*			*Total*		
	Mean	*N*	*SD*	*Mean*	*N*	*SD*	*Mean*	*N*	*SD*
All	**14.63**	**1200**	**2.04**	**14.22**	**1200**	**2.26**	**14.42**	**2400**	**2.16**
Education of woman									
Illiterate	14.23	133	2.76	13.50	124	2.59	13.88	257	2.70
Literate & Primary	14.71	247	1.84	14.06	190	2.18	14.43	437	2.02
Middle (6-8)	14.60	352	1.96	14.02	317	2.32	14.32	669	2.15
High school (9-10)	14.71	310	2.07	14.40	336	2.25	14.55	646	2.17
Higher Sec. & above	14.73	158	1.65	14.73	233	1.94	14.73	391	1.82
		F-1.592	P<0.174		F-7.748	P<0.000		F-7.083	P<0.000
Education of husband									
Illiterate	14.62	117	2.36	13.56	84	2.43	14.18	201	2.44
Literate & Primary	14.60	242	2.00	14.14	173	2.34	14.41	415	2.15
Middle (6-8)	14.68	266	1.91	14.08	275	2.22	14.38	541	2.09
High School (9-10)	14.52	408	2.12	14.30	414	2.33	14.41	822	2.23
Higher Sec. & above	14.83	167	1.83	14.49	254	2.05	14.63	421	1.97
		F-0.761	P<0.551		F-3.164	P<0.013		F-1.649	P<0.159

(Contd.)

(Contd. Table 5.6.1)

Socio-economic characteristics	Rural			Urban			Total		
	Mean	N	SD	Mean	N	SD	Mean	N	SD
Religion									
Hindu	14.69	1082	2.02	14.27	1034	2.20	14.48	2116	2.12
Muslim	13.90	77	2.15	13.62	105	2.64	13.74	182	2.44
Christian	14.22	41	2.00	14.41	61	2.52	14.34	102	2.32
		F-6.208	P<0.002		F-4.143	P<0.016		F-10.023	P<0.000
Community									
SC / ST	14.50	340	2.29	14.23	235	2.45	14.39	575	2.36
MBC	14.92	386	1.87	13.96	304	2.05	14.50	690	2.00
BC & Others	14.47	474	1.96	14.33	661	2.28	14.39	1135	2.15
		F-6.208	P<0.002		F-2.728	P<0.066		F-0.665	P<0.514
Standard of living									
Low	14.56	492	2.23	14.20	337	2.51	14.41	829	2.35
Medium	14.59	379	2.00	14.24	377	1.99	14.41	756	2.00
High	14.77	329	1.76	14.21	486	2.28	14.44	815	2.10
		F-1.149	P<0.317		F-0.021	P<0.980		F-0.027	P<0.973

(Contd.)

(Contd. Table 5.6.1)

Socio-economic characteristics	Rural			Urban			Total		
	Mean	*N*	*SD*	*Mean*	*N*	*SD*	*Mean*	*N*	*SD*
Economic activities									
Yes	14.62	315	2.19	14.10	152	2.37	14.45	467	2.26
No	14.63	885	1.98	14.23	1048	2.25	14.41	1933	2.14
		F-0.005	P<0.945		F-0.472	P<0.492		F-0.100	P<0.752
Contribution to total income									
Nil	14.63	882	1.98	14.23	1045	2.25	14.41	1927	2.14
≤ 25 %	14.58	144	2.10	14.22	100	2.33	14.43	244	2.20
Above 25 %	14.63	174	2.28	13.95	55	2.41	14.47	229	2.33
		F-0.048	P<0.953		F-0.414	P<0.661		F-0.063	P<0.939
Type of family									
Nuclear	14.60	720	2.02	14.26	659	2.12	14.44	1379	2.08
Joint	14.66	480	2.05	14.16	541	2.43	14.40	1021	2.27
		F-0.178	P<0.673		F-0.599	P<0.439		F-0.287	P<0.592

5.6.2 Women's Autonomy on Freedom of Choice and Demographic Characteristics

The mean autonomy score on freedom of choice by selected demographic characteristics of women is presented in Table 5.6.2. Age of women did not make any significant difference in the autonomy of women on freedom of choice in both rural and urban areas. Age at marriage of women showed significantly positive effect on the autonomy of women on freedom of choice in urban areas. However in rural areas, age at marriage of women did not make any significant difference in the autonomy of women on freedom of choice. The mean score for urban women significantly increased from 13.71 for women married at ages 16 years or less to 14.89 for women married at ages 23 years or more. The husband-wife age difference and marital duration did not make any significant difference in the level of autonomy of women on freedom of choice in both rural and urban areas.

Women's autonomy on freedom of choice increased with the number of male children in both rural and urban areas. However, the differences were not statistically significant. The number of female children showed significant difference in the mean score in both rural and urban areas. In rural areas, the mean autonomy score was highest at 14.74 for women who had one female child compared to 14.64 for women who had no female child and 14.37 for women who had two or more female children. In urban areas, the mean autonomy score was significantly highest at 14.33 for women who had no female child compared to those who had one or more female children. The total number of children showed significant difference in the mean score in rural areas. The mean score for rural women on freedom of choice was highest at 14.84 for women who had two living children compared to 14.45 for women who had one living child and 14.35 for women who had three or more number of living children. In urban areas, the total number of children did not make any significant difference in the autonomy of women on freedom of choice.

Table 5.6.2 Mean autonomy score attained by women on freedom of choice by demographic characteristics

Demographic characteristics	*Rural*			*Urban*			*Total*		
	Mean	*N*	*SD*	*Mean*	*N*	*SD*	*Mean*	*N*	*SD*
All	**14.63**	**1200**	**2.04**	**14.22**	**1200**	**2.26**	**14.42**	**2400**	**2.16**
Age (years)									
≤ 19	14.52	50	2.41	13.78	59	3.14	14.12	109	2.84
20 – 24	14.72	478	1.95	14.18	551	2.34	14.43	1029	2.18
25 – 29	14.57	672	2.07	14.30	590	2.08	14.44	1262	2.08
		F-0.783	P<0.457		F-1.571	P<0.208		F-1.129	P<0.324
Age at marriage (years)									
≤ 16	14.41	152	2.55	13.71	100	3.00	14.13	252	2.75
17 – 18	14.81	398	1.96	13.97	316	2.40	14.44	714	2.20
19 – 20	14.63	352	1.90	14.26	418	2.08	14.43	770	2.00
21 – 22	14.41	203	2.02	14.29	234	2.20	14.35	437	2.12
23 +	14.64	95	1.95	14.89	132	1.76	14.79	227	1.84
		F-1.796	P<0.127		F-5.291	P<0.000		F-2.914	P<0.020

(Contd.)

(Contd. Table 5.6.2)

Demographic characteristics	*Rural*			*Urban*			*Total*		
	Mean	*N*	*SD*	*Mean*	*N*	*SD*	*Mean*	*N*	*SD*
Husband-wife age difference (years)									
≤ 4	14.62	417	2.07	14.22	438	2.19	14.41	855	2.14
5 – 8	14.70	499	1.99	14.15	479	2.38	14.43	978	2.21
9 +	14.52	284	2.07	14.33	283	2.18	14.42	567	2.12
		F-0.654	P<0.520		F-0.530	P<0.589		F-0.011	P<0.989
Marital duration (years)									
≤ 3	14.62	223	2.04	14.33	300	2.32	14.46	523	2.07
4 - 6	14.63	376	2.05	14.29	437	2.21	14.45	813	2.14
7 – 9	14.69	347	1.81	14.15	318	2.11	14.43	665	1.97
10+	14.54	254	2.30	13.90	145	2.61	14.31	399	2.44
		F-0.253	P<0.859		F-1.421	P<0.235		F-0.449	P<0.718

(Contd.)

(Contd. Table 5.6.2)

Demographic characteristics	*Rural*			*Urban*			*Total*		
	Mean	*N*	*SD*	*Mean*	*N*	*SD*	*Mean*	*N*	*SD*
Number of male children									
0	14.53	335	1.94	14.15	363	2.32	14.34	698	2.15
1	14.64	596	2.11	14.21	574	2.34	14.43	1170	2.23
2 +	14.71	269	2.00	14.31	263	2.02	14.51	532	2.01
		F-0.061	P<0.516		F-0.340	P<0.712		F-1.046	P<0.351
Number of female children									
0	14.64	357	2.11	14.33	400	2.27	14.48	757	2.20
1	14.74	568	1.93	14.27	558	2.05	14.51	1126	2.0
2 +	14.37	275	2.14	13.88	242	2.68	14.14	517	2.42
		F-3.123	P<0.044		F-3.279	P<0.038		F-5.503	P<0.004
Total No. of children									
1	14.45	345	2.15	14.31	402	2.28	14.37	747	2.22
2	14.84	604	1.87	14.22	605	2.19	14.53	1209	2.06
3 +	14.35	251	2.21	14.00	193	2.45	14.20	444	2.32
		F-7.147	P<0.001		F-1.217	P<0.296		F-4.228	P<0.015

Overall, the results showed that the number of female children had significant influence on the autonomy of women on freedom of choice in both rural and urban areas. Age at marriage showed significant association with the autonomy of women on freedom of choice only in urban areas and the total number of children showed significant association only in rural areas.

5.6.3 Women's Autonomy on Freedom of Choice and Marital Characteristics

In order to assess the influence of the type of marriage on women's autonomy on freedom of choice, the data were analysed according to the type of marriage and autonomy score on freedom of choice. The results are presented in Table 5.6.3. The mean autonomy score on freedom of choice did not vary significantly due to any of the martial characteristics of the women in both rural and urban areas. In both rural and urban areas, women who had consanguineous marriage, women who had married a person from the paternal side and women who had arranged marriage had slightly higher mean autonomy score than others. In the case of inter-caste / inter-religious marriage, the mean autonomy score on freedom of choice was high among women who had same caste marriage in rural areas, whereas it was higher among women who had inter-caste / inter-religious marriage in urban areas. However, the differences were not statistically significant.

The results showed that none of the marital characteristics of women had any significant influence on the autonomy of women on freedom of choice in both rural and urban areas.

5.6.4 Women's Autonomy on Freedom of Choice and Exposure to Mass Media

The results of the analysis of data on the influence of mass media on women's autonomy on freedom of choice are presented in Table 5.6.4. Autonomy of women on freedom of choice was significantly more among women who were listening to radio at least once a week than those who were not having

Table 5.6.3 Mean autonomy score attained by women on freedom of choice by marital characteristics

Marital characteristics	*Rural*			*Urban*			*Total*		
	Mean	*N*	*SD*	*Mean*	*N*	*SD*	*Mean*	*N*	*SD*
All	**14.63**	**1200**	**2.04**	**14.22**	**1200**	**2.27**	**14.42**	**2400**	**2.16**
Type of marriage									
Consanguineous	14.69	399	2.06	14.30	425	2.12	14.49	824	2.09
Non-consanguineous	14.59	801	2.03	14.17	775	2.34	14.39	1576	2.19
		F-0.625	P<0.429		F-0.866	P<0.352		F-1.233	P<0.267
Consanguineous type									
Maternal	14.61	209	2.24	14.29	229	2.13	14.44	438	2.18
Paternal	14.78	190	1.86	14.31	196	2.11	14.54	386	2.00
		F-0.648	P<0.421		F-0.012	P<0.911		F-0.452	P<0.502

(Contd.)

(Contd. Table 5.6.3)

Marital characteristics	*Rural*			*Urban*			*Total*		
	Mean	*N*	*SD*	*Mean*	*N*	*SD*	*Mean*	*N*	*SD*
Kind of marriage									
Arranged marriage	14.64	1078	2.05	14.23	1071	2.23	14.43	2149	1.15
Love marriage	14.54	122	1.90	14.09	129	2.52	14.31	251	2.24
		F-0.235	P<0.628		F-0.486	P<0.486		F-0.785	P<0.376
Inter caste / inter religious marriage									
Same caste marriage	14.63	1128	2.05	14.19	1096	2.29	14.41	2224	2.18
Inter religious / inter caste marriage	14.61	72	1.80	14.54	104	1.98	14.57	176	1.90
		F-0.004	P<0.950		F-2.301	P<0.130		F-0.876	P<0.349

the habit of listening to radio in both rural and urban areas. In rural areas, the mean autonomy score on freedom of choice was highest at 14.75 for women who were listening to radio compared to 14.46 for those who were not listening to radio. In urban areas, the mean score was highest at 14.63 for women who were listening to radio compared to the mean score of 13.76 observed for women who were not listening to radio.

Watching television showed significantly positive effect on the autonomy of women on freedom of choice in rural areas. The mean score was significantly highest at 14.72 for women who were watching television atleast once a week (14.72) compared to 13.96 observed for women who were not watching television. However in urban areas, watching television did not make any significant difference in the mean score on freedom of choice. Going to movies did not make any significant difference in the level of women's autonomy on freedom of choice in rural areas. However, in urban areas, going to movies showed significantly positive effect on the autonomy of women on freedom of choice. In urban areas, the mean score for women going to movies was highest at 14.88 compared to 14.05 for women who were not going to movies.

Reading newspapers / magazines showed significantly positive effect on the autonomy of women on freedom of choice in both rural and urban areas. In rural areas, the mean score was significantly highest at 14.79 for women who were reading newspapers / magazines compared to 14.52 for women who were not having the habit of reading newspapers / magazines. In urban areas, the mean score was highest at 14.64 for women who were reading newspapers / magazines compared to 13.96 for women who were not having the habit of reading newspapers / magazines. The overall level of women's exposure to various mass media showed significantly positive effect on women's autonomy on freedom of choice in both rural and urban areas (Figure 5.6.1). In rural areas, the mean autonomy score on freedom of choice significantly increased from 13.75 for women who had no exposure to mass media to 14.61 for women who had low level of exposure and to 14.84 for women who had a high level of exposure to mass

Table 5.6.4 Mean autonomy score attained by women on freedom of choice by exposure to mass media

Exposure to mass media	*Rural*			*Urban*			*Total*		
	Mean	*N*	*SD*	*Mean*	*N*	*SD*	*Mean*	*N*	*SD*
All	**14.63**	**1200**	**2.04**	**14.22**	**1200**	**2.26**	**14.42**	**2400**	**2.16**
Listening to radio									
Yes	14.75	683	1.92	14.63	630	1.78	14.69	1313	1.85
No	14.46	517	2.17	13.76	570	2.63	14.09	1087	2.45
		F-5.877	P<0.015		F-45.852	P<0.000		F-46.365	P<0.000
Watching television									
Yes	14.72	1050	1.94	14.21	1088	2.25	14.46	2138	2.12
No	13.96	150	2.52	14.28	112	2.45	14.09	262	2.49
		F-18.577	P<0.000		F-0.087	P<0.768		F-6.687	P<0.010
Going to movies									
Yes	14.85	172	1.65	14.88	242	1.65	14.87	414	1.65
No	14.59	1028	2.09	14.05	958	2.37	14.33	1986	2.25
		F-2.536	P<0.112		F-26.227	P<0.000		F-21.433	P<0.000

(Contd.)

(Contd. Table 5.6.4)

Exposure to mass media	*Rural*			*Urban*			*Total*		
	Mean	*N*	*SD*	*Mean*	*N*	*SD*	*Mean*	*N*	*SD*
Reading newspapers / magazines									
Yes	14.79	458	1.86	14.64	456	2.04	14.72	914	1.95
No	14.52	742	2.13	13.96	744	2.36	14.24	1486	2.26
		F-4.848	P<0.028		F-26.275	P<0.000		F-27.616	P<0.000
Mass media index									
No exposure	13.75	76	2.97	13.89	53	2.87	13.81	129	2.92
Low exposure	14.61	752	1.98	13.91	759	2.43	14.26	1511	2.25
High exposure	14.84	372	1.86	14.87	388	1.60	14.86	760	1.73
		F-9.203	P<0.000		F-24.890	P<0.000		F-25.450	P<0.000
Membership in SHG									
Yes	14.83	600	1.81	14.50	304	2.03	14.72	904	1.89
No	14.43	600	2.23	14.12	896	2.33	14.24	1496	2.29
		F-11.765	P<0.001		F-6.549	P<0.011		F-27.572	P<0.000

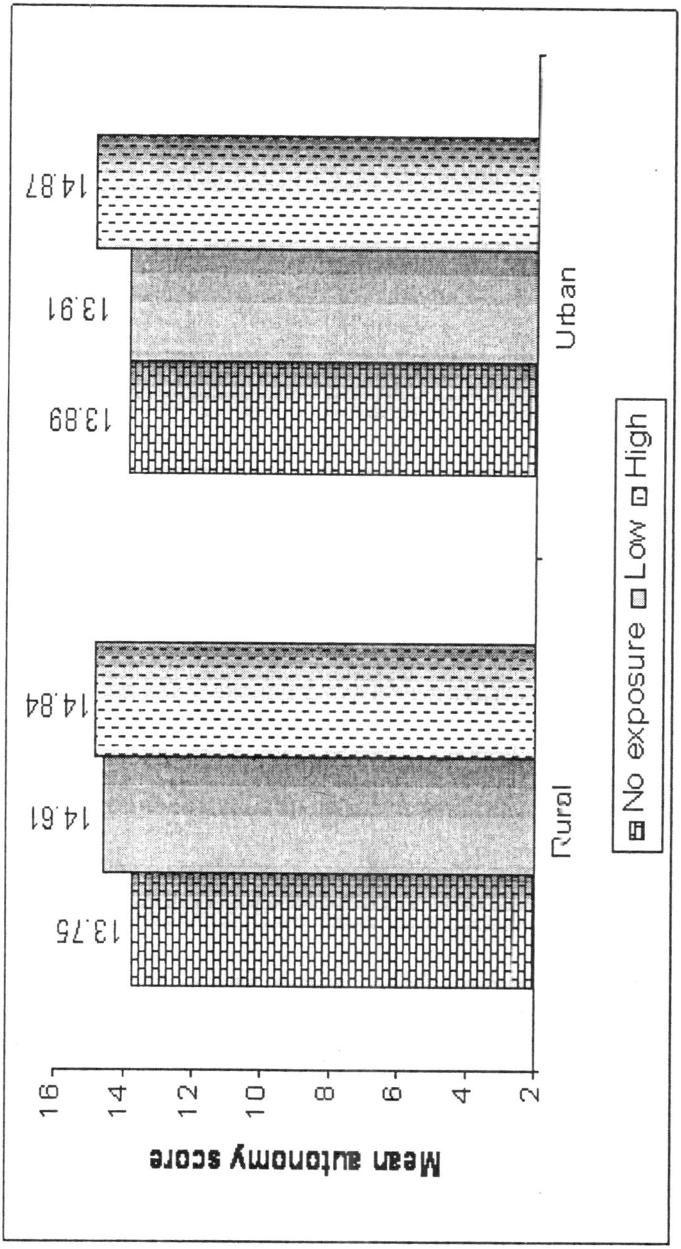

Figure 5.6.1 Autonomy of women on freedom of choice by exposure to mass media

media. In urban areas, the mean score significantly increased from 13.89 for women who had no exposure to mass media to 13.91 for women who had a low level of exposure and to 14.87 for women who had a high level of exposure to mass media.

Membership in SHG showed significantly positive effect on women's autonomy on freedom of choice in both rural and urban areas. In both rural and urban areas, the members of SHG had significantly higher autonomy on freedom of choice than non-members. In rural areas, the members had a mean score of 14.83 compared to 14.43 for non-members. In urban areas, the members had a mean score of 14.50 compared to 14.12 for non-members.

Overall, the results showed that listening to radio, reading newspapers / magazines, overall level of exposure to mass media and membership in SHG had significantly positive effect on the autonomy of women on freedom of choice in both rural and urban areas. Watching television had significantly positive effect only in rural areas and going to movies had significantly positive effect only in urban areas.

5.7 Violence Against Women

The distribution of women by mean autonomy score on violence against women and selected background characteristics is presented in Tables 5.7.1 to 5.7.4. On a scale of 0-20, the mean autonomy score on violence against women was 17.10 for women in rural and 17.16 for women in urban areas. The influence of socio-economic, demographic, marital and mass media variables on the autonomy of women on violence against women is discussed in the following sections 5.7.1 to 5.7.4.

5.7.1 Women's Autonomy on Violence Against Women and Selected Socio-economic Characteristics

The distribution of women by their level of autonomy on violence against women and selected socio-economic characteristics is presented in Table 5.7.1. Education of women showed significantly positive effect on women's autonomy on violence against women in both rural and urban areas. In rural areas, the mean autonomy score increased significantly from 16.48 for illiterates to 17.58 for higher secondary and above educated respondents. In urban areas, the mean score increased from 16.09 for illiterates to 17.95 for higher secondary and above educated respondents. Education of husband also had significantly positive effect on the autonomy of women on violence against women in both rural and urban areas. In rural areas, the mean score significantly increased from 16.80 for women who had illiterate husband to 17.64 for women who had husband with higher secondary and above level of education. In urban areas, the mean score increased from 15.64 for women who had illiterate husband to 17.70 for women who had husband with higher secondary and above level of education. Muslim women had more autonomy on violence against women in both rural and urban areas. However, the differences were statistically significant only for rural areas.

The level of autonomy on violence against women varied significantly among women belonging to different caste groups in both rural and urban areas. Scheduled Caste / Scheduled Tribe (SC/ST) women had a significantly lower level of autonomy than other caste women in both rural and urban areas. In rural areas, the mean autonomy score was significantly lowest at 16.57 for SC/ST women compared to 17.21 for BC and others and 17.45 for the MBC. In urban areas, the mean score was significantly lowest at 16.59 for SC/ST women compared to 17.42 for BC and others and 17.04 for MBC. Standard of living showed significantly positive effect on the autonomy of women on violence against women in both rural and urban areas. In rural areas, the mean score increased significantly from 16.73 for low standard of living to 17.22 for medium and to 17.54 for high standard of living. In urban areas, the mean score increased from 16.47 for low standard of living to 17.09 for medium and to 17.70 for high standard of living.

Surprisingly, involvement in income earning economic activities showed significantly negative effect on the autonomy of women on violence against women in both rural and urban

Table 5.7.1 Mean autonomy Score Attained by Women on Violence Against Women by Socio-Economic Characteristics

Socio-Economic characteristics	*Rural*			*Urban*			*Total*		
	Mean	*N*	*SD*	*Mean*	*N*	*SD*	*Mean*	*N*	*SD*
All	**17.10**	**1200**	**2.32**	**17.16**	**1200**	**2.86**	**17.13**	**2400**	**2.60**
Education of woman									
Illiterate	16.48	133	2.93	16.09	124	3.35	16.30	257	3.14
Literate & Primary	17.07	247	2.35	16.85	190	3.09	16.97	437	2.69
Middle (6-8)	17.13	352	2.10	16.94	317	3.19	17.04	669	2.67
High school (9-10)	17.13	310	2.41	17.39	336	2.57	17.27	646	2.50
Higher Sec. & above	17.58	158	1.80	17.95	233	1.93	17.80	391	1.89
		F-4.161	P<0.002		F-10.642	P<0.000		F-14.482	P<0.000
Education of husband									
Illiterate	16.80	117	2.40	15.64	84	3.79	16.31	201	3.10
Literate & Primary	16.83	242	2.44	16.51	173	2.93	16.69	415	2.66
Middle (6-8)	17.00	266	2.62	17.12	275	2.99	17.06	541	2.81
High school (9-10)	17.20	408	2.16	17.44	414	2.72	17.32	822	2.46
Higher Sec. & above	17.64	167	1.79	17.70	254	2.23	17.67	421	2.06
		F-3.985	P<0.003		F-11.789	P<0.000		F-13.969	P<0.000

(Contd.)

(Contd. Table 5.7.1)

Socio-Economic characteristics	Rural			Urban			Total		
	Mean	*N*	*SD*	*Mean*	*N*	*SD*	*Mean*	*N*	*SD*
Religion									
Hindu	17.12	1082	2.33	17.15	1034	2.79	17.13	2116	2.56
Muslim	17.39	77	2.13	17.53	105	2.79	17.47	182	2.53
Christian	16.27	41	2.16	16.69	61	3.92	16.52	102	3.32
		F-3.281	P<0.038		F-1.732	P<0.177		F-4.398	P<0.012
Community									
SC / ST	16.57	340	2.25	16.59	235	3.31	16.58	575	2.73
MBC	17.45	386	2.18	17.04	304	2.75	17.27	690	2.45
BC & Others	17.21	474	2.41	17.42	661	2.70	17.33	1135	2.59
		F-13.878	P<0.000		F-7.771	P<0.000		F-17.469	P<0.000
Standard of living									
Low	16.73	492	2.76	16.47	337	3.45	16.62	829	3.06
Medium	17.22	379	1.98	17.09	377	2.68	17.15	756	2.35
High	17.54	329	1.81	17.70	486	2.40	17.63	815	2.18
		F-13.009	P<0.000		F-19.196	P<0.000		F-31.931	P<0.000

(Contd.)

(Contd. Table 5.7.1)

Socio-Economic characteristics	*Rural*			*Urban*			*Total*		
	Mean	*N*	*SD*	*Mean*	*N*	*SD*	*Mean*	*N*	*SD*
Economic activities									
Yes	16.79	315	2.63	16.05	152	3.31	16.55	467	2.89
No	17.22	885	2.18	17.32	1048	2.75	17.27	1933	2.50
		F-7.882	P<0.005		F-27.032	P<0.000		F-29.604	P<0.000
Contribution to total income									
Nil	17.21	882	2.18	17.33	1045	2.74	17.28	1927	2.50
Up to 25 %	17.27	144	1.90	16.29	100	3.28	16.87	244	2.59
Above 25 %	16.40	174	3.06	15.44	55	3.37	16.17	229	3.15
		F-9.516	P<0.000		F-17.022	P<0.000		F-20.349	P<0.000
Type of family									
Nuclear	16.95	720	2.38	16.99	659	2.88	16.97	1379	2.63
Joint	17.33	480	2.19	17.37	541	2.82	17.35	1021	2.54
		F-7.736	P<0.005		F-5.464	P<0.020		F-12.898	P<0.000

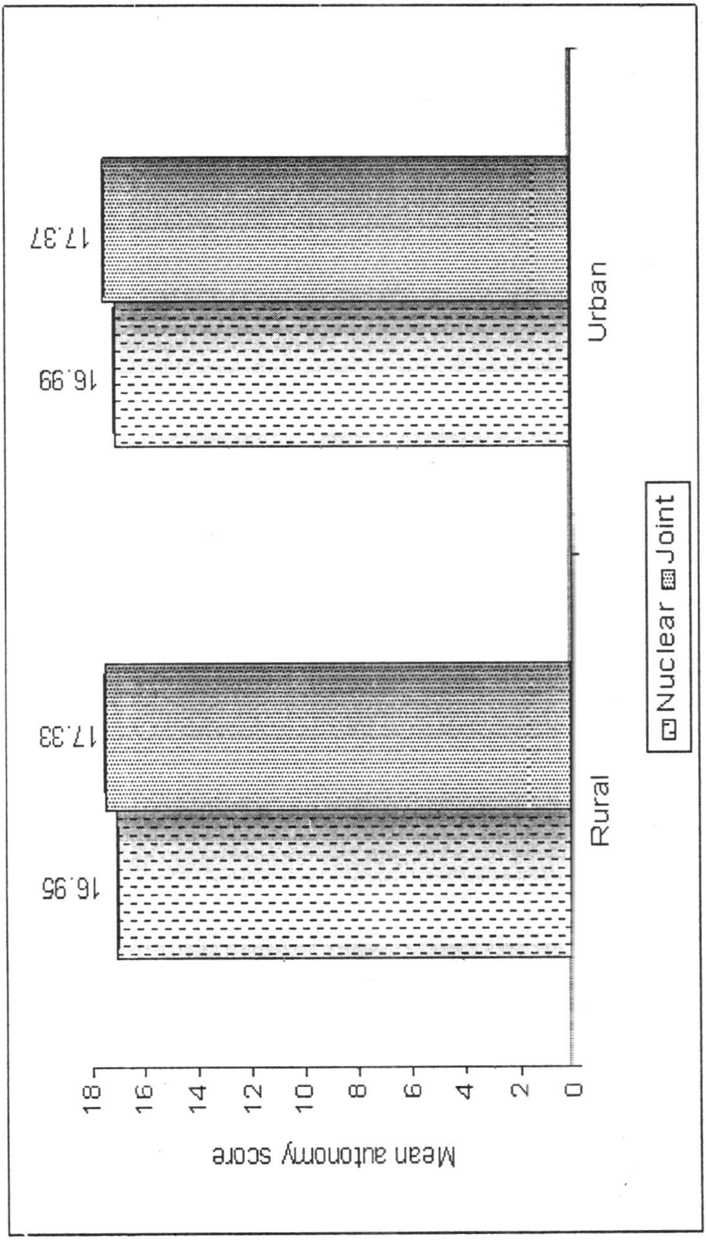

Figure 5.7.1 Autonomy of women on violence against women by type of family

areas. In rural areas, the mean score was higher at 17.22 for women who were not involved in economic activities compared to only 16.79 observed for women involved in economic activities. In urban areas also, women not involved in economic activities had a high mean score of 17.32 compared to only 16.05 observed for women involved in economic activities. Contribution to the total family income also showed significantly negative effect on the autonomy of women on violence against women in both rural and urban areas. Women who contributed more than 25 per cent to the total family income had significantly less autonomy on violence against women than others in both rural and urban areas.

The type of family showed significant effect on the autonomy of women on violence against women in both rural and urban areas (Figure 5.7.1). Women in joint family had a significantly higher autonomy than women in nuclear family in both rural and urban areas. In rural areas, the mean score was significantly highest at 17.33 for women in joint family compared to only 16.95 for women in nuclear family. In urban areas, the mean score was significantly highest at 17.37 for women in joint family compared to 16.99 for women in nuclear family.

Overall, the results showed that education of women and their husband and standard of living had significantly positive effect on women's autonomy on violence against women in both rural and urban areas. Surprisingly, involvement in income earning economic activities and percentage contribution to the total family income had significantly negative effect in both rural and urban areas. Most backward caste women in rural and backward caste women in urban areas had significantly more autonomy than others. Women living in joint family in both rural and urban areas had significantly more autonomy than women living in nuclear family. It is also surprising to note that Muslim women in rural areas had significantly more autonomy on violence against women than others.

5.7.2 Women's Autonomy on Violence Against Women and Demographic Characteristics

The distribution of women by mean autonomy score on violence against women and selected demographic characteristics of women is presented in Table 5.7.2. It is observed that the age of women did not make any significant difference in the level of autonomy of women on violence against women in rural areas. However, in urban areas, women aged 25-29 years had significantly more autonomy than others.

Age at marriage of women showed significantly positive effect on the autonomy of women on violence against women in both rural and urban areas (Figure 5.7.2). In rural areas, the mean score significantly increased from 16.68 for women married at ages 16 years or less to 17.54 for women married at ages 23 years and above. In urban areas, the mean score significantly increased from 15.91 for women married at ages 16 years or less to 18.37 for women married at ages 23 years and above. Husband-wife age difference did not make any significant difference in the level of women's autonomy on violence against women in both rural and urban areas. On the other hand, marital duration showed significantly negative effect on the autonomy of women on violence against women in both rural and urban areas.

The number of male children did not make any significant difference in the mean autonomy score in both rural and urban areas. The number of female children did not make any significant difference in the mean score in rural areas. However, in urban areas, the mean score was significantly high for women who had one female child compared to women who had no female child and women who had two or more female children.

The total number of children did not make any significant difference in the level of autonomy of women in rural areas. In urban areas, the autonomy of women on violence against women significantly decreased with increase in the total number of children. The mean score decreased from 17.46 for women who had one child to 16.65 for women who had three or more children.

Table 5.7.2 Mean autonomy score attained by women on violence against women by demographic characteristics

Demographic characteristics	*Rural*			*Urban*			*Total*		
	Mean	*N*	*SD*	*Mean*	*N*	*SD*	*Mean*	*N*	*SD*
All	**17.10**	**1200**	**2.32**	**17.16**	**1200**	**2.86**	**17.13**	**2400**	**2.60**
Age (years)									
≤ 19	17.64	50	1.98	17.12	59	3.52	17.36	109	2.92
20 – 24	17.15	478	2.32	16.95	551	3.09	17.05	1029	2.76
25 – 29	17.03	672	2.34	17.36	590	2.54	17.18	1262	2.44
		F-1.793	P<0.167		F-2.895	P<0.056		F-1.228	P<0.293
Age at marriage (years)									
≤ 16	16.68	152	2.57	15.91	100	3.87	16.37	252	3.16
17 – 18	17.07	398	2.32	16.84	316	3.12	16.97	714	2.70
19 – 20	17.15	352	2.31	17.15	418	2.69	17.15	770	2.52
21 – 22	17.21	203	2.19	17.47	234	2.57	17.35	437	2.40
23 +	17.54	95	2.08	18.37	132	1.50	18.02	227	1.80
		F-2.290	P<0.058		F-12.900	P<0.000		F-13.795	P<0.000

(Contd.)

(Contd. Table 5.7.2)

Demographic characteristics	*Rural*			*Urban*			*Total*		
	Mean	*N*	*SD*	*Mean*	*N*	*SD*	*Mean*	*N*	*SD*
Husband-wife age difference (years)									
≤ 4	16.99	417	2.44	17.19	438	2.55	17.09	855	2.50
5 – 8	17.10	499	2.27	17.19	479	2.93	17.14	978	2.61
9 +	17.27	284	2.21	17.06	283	3.17	17.17	567	2.73
		F-1.273	P<0.280		F-0.230	P<0.795		F- 0.161	P<0.852
Marital duration (years)									
≤ 3	17.64	223	2.14	17.62	300	2.74	17.63	523	2.50
4 – 6	17.15	376	2.21	17.11	437	2.93	17.13	813	2.62
7 – 9	16.83	347	2.38	16.90	318	2.88	16.86	665	2.63
10+	16.95	254	2.45	16.95	145	2.76	16.95	399	2.56
		F-6.155	P<0.000		F-3.879	P<0.009		F-9.609	P<0.000

(Contd.)

(Contd. Table 5.7.2)

Demographic characteristics	*Rural*			*Urban*			*Total*		
	Mean	*N*	*SD*	*Mean*	*N*	*SD*	*Mean*	*N*	*SD*
Number of male children									
0	17.02	335	2.51	17.28	363	2.82	17.15	698	2.68
1	17.19	596	2.26	17.12	574	2.95	17.15	1170	2.62
2+	17.02	269	2.17	17.08	263	2.70	17.05	532	2.44
		F-0.806	P<0.447		F-0.470	P<0.625		F-0.307	P<0.736
Number of female children									
0	17.29	357	2.18	17.20	400	2.81	17.25	757	2.54
1	17.08	568	2.35	17.32	558	2.74	17.20	1126	2.55
2+	16.91	275	2.40	16.72	242	3.16	16.82	517	2.78
		F-2.183	P<0.113		F-3.768	P<0.023		F-4.725	P<0.009
Total No. of children									
1	17.27	345	2.42	17.46	402	2.85	17.37	747	2.67
2	17.09	604	2.28	17.12	605	2.71	17.11	1209	2.50
3 +	16.92	251	2.24	16.65	193	3.24	16.80	444	2.72
		F-1.657	P<0.191		F-5.338	P<0.005		F-6.770	P<0.001

Figure 5.7.2 Autonomy of women on violence against women by Age at marriage (years)

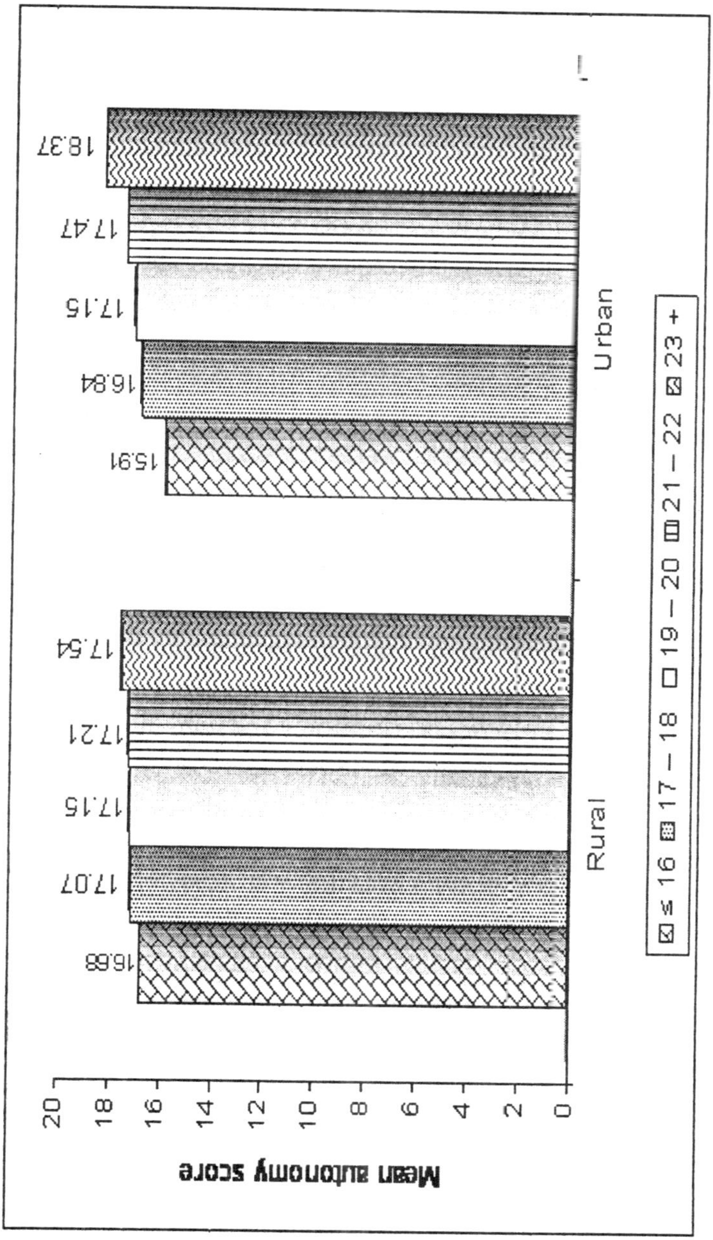

Overall, the results showed that while age at marriage of women had positive influence on the autonomy of women on violence against women, marital duration showed negative influence in both rural and urban areas. The age of women showed positive influence and the number of female children and the total number of children showed negative influence on the autonomy of women on violence against women in urban areas.

5.7.3 Women's Autonomy on Violence Against Women and Marital Characteristics

In order to assess the influence of the type of marriage on women's autonomy on violence against women, the data were analysed according to the type of marriage and autonomy score. The results are presented in Table 5.7.3. Women who had consanguineous type of marriage had significantly more autonomy on violence against women than those who had non-consanguineous marriage in both rural and urban areas. However, the type of consanguineous marriage (maternal / paternal) did not make any significant difference in the mean score in both rural and urban areas. Women who had arranged marriage had significantly more autonomy on violence against women than those who had love marriage in both rural and urban areas (Figure 5.7.3). In rural areas, women who had arranged marriage had a mean score of 17.15 compared to 16.68 observed for women who had love marriage. In urban areas, the mean score was significantly higher at 17.28 for arranged marriage compared 16.20 for love marriage.

Women who had same caste marriage had significantly more autonomy on violence against women than women who had inter-caste/inter-religious marriage in both rural and urban areas. In rural areas, women who had same caste marriage had a high mean score of 17.15 compared to 16.39 observed for inter-caste/ inter-religious marriage. In urban areas, the mean score was significantly highest at 17.21 for same caste marriage

Table 5.7.3 Mean autonomy score attained by women on violence against women by martial characteristics

Marital characteristics	*Rural*			*Urban*			*Total*		
	Mean	*N*	*SD*	*Mean*	*N*	*SD*	*Mean*	*N*	*SD*
All	17.10	1200	2.32	17.16	1200	2.86	17.13	2400	2.60
Type of marriage									
Consanguineous	17.28	399	2.28	17.47	425	2.64	17.37	824	2.48
Non-consanguineous	17.02	801	2.33	16.99	775	2.96	17.01	1576	2.66
		F-3.285	P<0.070		F-7.531	P<0.006		F-10.840	P<0.001
Consanguineous type									
Maternal	17.28	209	2.37	17.45	229	2.67	17.37	438	2.53
Paternal	17.27	190	2.19	17.48	196	2.62	17.38	386	2.41
		F-0.000	P<0.987		F-0.010	P<0.921		F-0.002	P<0.961

(Contd.)

(Contd. Table 5.7.3)

Marital characteristics	*Rural*			*Urban*			*Total*		
	Mean	*N*	*SD*	*Mean*	*N*	*SD*	*Mean*	*N*	*SD*
Kind of marriage									
Arranged marriage	17.15	1078	2.29	17.28	1071	2.76	17.21	2149	2.53
Love marriage	16.68	122	2.50	16.20	129	3.46	16.43	251	3.04
		F-4.563	P<0.033		F-16.480	P<0.000		F-20.359	P<0.000
Inter caste / inter religious marriage									
Same caste marriage	17.15	1128	2.31	17.21	1096	2.84	17.18	2224	2.58
Inter caste / Inter religious marriage	16.39	72	2.34	16.61	104	3.05	16.52	176	2.78
		F-7.346	P<0.007		F-4.303	P<0.038		F-10.674	P<0.001

Figure 5.7.3 Autonomy of women on violence against women by kind of marriage

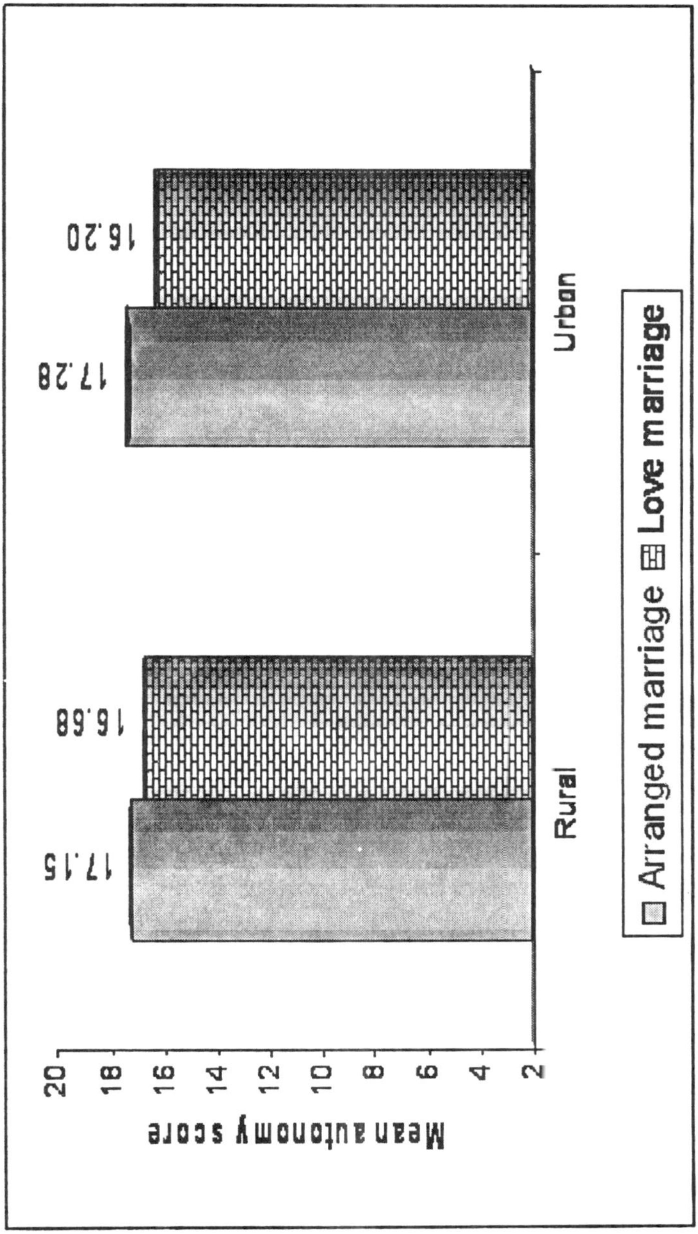

compared to 16.61 for women who had inter-caste / inter-religious marriage.

Overall, the results showed that women who had consanguineous marriage had significantly more autonomy than women who had non-consanguineous marriage in both rural and urban areas. The results also highlighted that women who had love marriage and inter-caste / inter religious marriage had significantly lower autonomy than others in both rural and urban areas.

5.7.4 Women's Autonomy on Violence Against Women and Exposure to Mass Media

The results of the analysis of data on the influence of mass media on women's autonomy on violence against women are presented in Table 5.7.4. Women who were listening to radio at least once a week were having significantly more autonomy on violence against women than those who were not listening to radio in both rural and urban areas. In rural areas, the mean autonomy score was 17.24 for women who had the habit of listening to radio and 16.93 for women who were not having the habit of listening to radio. In urban areas, the mean autonomy score was 17.55 for women who were listening to radio and 16.73 for those who were not listening to radio. Watching television showed significantly positive influence on the autonomy of women on violence against women in both rural and urban areas. In rural areas, the mean autonomy score was highest at 17.17 for women who were watching television once a week compared to 16.64 for women who were not watching television. In urban areas, the mean score was highest at 17.21 for women who were watching television compared to 16.71 for women who were not having the habit of watching television.

Going to movies did not make any significant difference in the level of autonomy of women on violence against women in rural areas. However, in urban areas, going to movies showed

Table 5.7.4 Mean autonomy score attained by women on violence against women by exposure to mass media

Exposure to mass media	*Rural*			*Urban*			*Total*		
	Mean	*N*	*SD*	*Mean*	*N*	*SD*	*Mean*	*N*	*SD*
All	**17.10**	**1200**	**2.32**	**17.16**	**1200**	**2.86**	**17.13**	**2400**	**2.60**
Listening to radio									
Yes	17.24	683	2.05	17.55	630	2.20	17.39	1313	2.12
No	16.93	517	2.62	16.73	570	3.40	16.82	1087	3.05
		F-5.366	P<0.021		F-25.169	P<0.000		F-28.379	P<0.000
Watching television									
Yes	17.17	1050	2.27	17.21	1088	2.82	17.19	2138	2.56
No	16.64	150	2.55	16.71	112	3.23	16.67	262	2.85
		F-6.921	P<0.009		F-3.018	P<0.083		F-9.258	P<0.002
Going to movies									
Yes	17.33	172	1.93	17.73	242	2.10	17.56	414	2.04
No	17.07	1028	2.37	17.02	958	3.00	17.04	1986	2.69
		F-1.935	P<0.165		F-12.000	P<0.001		F-13.762	P<0.000

(Contd.)

(Contd. Table 5.7.4)

Exposure to mass media	*Rural*			*Urban*			*Total*		
	Mean	*N*	*SD*	*Mean*	*N*	*SD*	*Mean*	*N*	*SD*
Reading newspapers / magazines									
Yes	17.23	458	2.05	17.57	456	2.32	17.40	914	2.19
No	17.03	742	2.47	16.91	744	3.12	16.97	1486	2.81
		F-2.163	P<0.142		F-15.420	P<0.000		F-15.757	P<0.000
Level of exposure to mass media									
No exposure	16.26	76	3.01	15.91	53	3.89	16.12	129	3.39
Low	17.14	752	2.38	16.94	759	3.12	17.04	1511	2.77
High	17.21	372	1.98	17.76	388	1.90	17.49	760	1.96
		F-5.515	P<0.004		F-16.051	P<0.000		F-18.150	P<0.000
Membership in SHG									
Yes	17.13	600	2.13	17.12	304	2.49	17.13	904	2.26
No	17.08	600	2.49	17.17	896	2.98	17.13	1496	2.79
		F-.190	P<0.663		F-0.064	P<0.800		F-0.001	P<0.977

Figure 5.7.4 Autonomy of women on violence against women by exposure to mass media

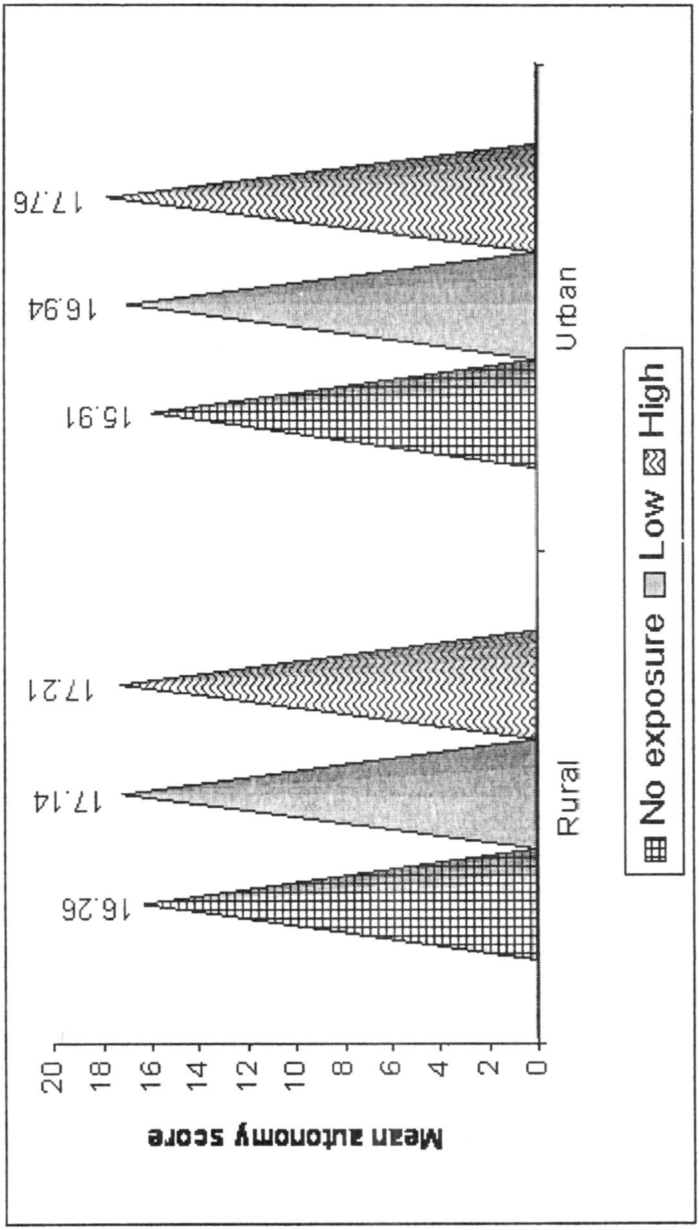

significantly positive influence on the autonomy of women. The mean score for women going to movies was higher at 17.73 compared to 17.02 for women who were not going to movies. Reading newspapers / magazines did not make any significant difference in the autonomy of women in rural areas. However, in urban areas, women who had the habit of reading newspapers/ magazines had a significantly higher mean score of 17.57 compared to 16.91 for women who were not having the habit of reading newspaper / magazines. The overall level of women's exposure to mass media showed significantly positive effect on women's autonomy on violence against women in both rural and urban areas. The increase in the level of exposure to mass media significantly increased the level of women's autonomy on violence against women in both rural and urban areas (Figure 5.7.4). In rural areas, the mean score significantly increased from 16.26 for women who had no exposure to mass media to 17.14 for women who had a low level of exposure and to 17.21 for women who had a high level of exposure to mass media.

In urban areas, the mean score significantly increased from 15.91 for women who had no exposure to 16.94 for women who had a low level of exposure and to 17.76 for women who had a high level of exposure to mass media. Membership in SHG did not make any significant difference in the level of autonomy on violence against women in both rural and urban areas.

The results showed that exposure of women to mass media significantly improved the autonomy of women on violence against women in both rural and urban areas. Listening to radio and watching television were the most effective mass media which significantly improved the autonomy of women in both rural and urban areas. Going to movies and reading newspapers/ magazines had significant effect only in urban areas.

5.8 Decision About Contraception and Fertility

The distribution of women by their level of autonomy on decision about contraception and fertility and selected background characteristics is presented in Tables 5.8.1 to 5.8.4. Overall, the autonomy of women on decision about contraception and fertility was nearly the same for both rural and urban women. On a scale of 0 to 8, the mean autonomy score attained by women in rural areas was 4.22 and the mean score attained by women in urban areas was 4.18. The influence of socio-economic, demographic, marital and mass media variables on the autonomy of women on decision about contraception and fertility is discussed in the following sections 5.8.1 to 5.8.4.

5.8.1 Women's Autonomy on Decision about Contraception and Fertility and Socio-economic Characteristics

The mean autonomy score on decision about contraception and fertility by socio-economic characteristics is presented in Table 5.8.1. Education of women had significant influence on women's autonomy on decision about contraception and fertility in both rural and urban areas. In rural areas, the mean score decreased significantly from 4.62 for illiterates to 4.09 for higher secondary and above educated respondents. However, in urban areas, the mean score increased from 4.11 for illiterates to 4.39 for higher secondary and above educated respondents.

Education of husband showed significant influence on the autonomy of women on decision about contraception and fertility only in rural areas, whereas, in urban areas, education of husband did not make any significant difference in the mean score. In rural areas, the mean score decreased significantly from 5.02 for women who had illiterate husband to 4.08 for women who had husband with higher secondary and above level of education.

Muslim women had lower autonomy on decision about contraception and fertility than others in both rural and urban areas. However, the differences are not statistically significant. The community did not show any significant difference in the level of autonomy of women on decision about contraception and fertility in both rural and urban areas. Standard of living showed significant difference in the level of autonomy on decision about contraception and fertility in both rural and urban areas. While the mean autonomy score was significantly higher among the low standard of living women in rural areas, it was more among high standard of living women in urban areas.

Involvement in income earning economic activities showed significant difference in the level of autonomy on decision about contraception and fertility in rural areas. The mean score was 4.60 for women involved in economic activities whereas it was 4.08 for women not involved in economic activities. In urban areas, the differences in the mean score are not statistically significant.

The extent of contribution to the total family income had significant influence on the level of autonomy on decision about contraception and fertility in rural areas. The mean score was significantly lowest at 4.08 for women who did not contribute anything to the family income compared to the mean score of 4.47 observed for women who contributed up to 25 per cent to the total family income and 4.70 for women who contributed more than 25 per cent to the total family income. The differences in the mean score did not vary significantly among women in urban areas.

Though women in nuclear family had higher autonomy in both rural and urban areas, the differences are statistically significant only for urban areas. In urban areas, the mean autonomy score was significantly highest at 4.26 for women in nuclear family compared to 4.08 observed for women in joint family.

Overall, the results showed that the autonomy of women on decision about contraception and fertility was significantly higher among illiterate women in rural areas and among women who had high school and higher level of education in urban areas. Women who had illiterate husband in rural areas had significantly more autonomy than others. Standard of living had significantly negative effect in rural areas. However, in

Table 5.8.1 Mean autonomy score attained by women on decision about contraception and fertility by socio-economic characteristics

Socio-economic characteristics	*Rural*			*Urban*			*Total*		
	Mean	*N*	*SD*	*Mean*	*N*	*SD*	*Mean*	*N*	*SD*
All	**4.22**	**1200**	**1.58**	**4.18**	**1200**	**1.50**	**4.20**	**2400**	**1.54**
Education of woman									
Illiterate	4.62	133	1.97	4.11	124	1.68	4.38	257	1.85
Literate & Primary	4.06	247	1.62	4.22	190	1.68	4.13	437	1.65
Middle (6-8)	4.13	352	1.64	4.16	317	1.64	4.15	669	1.64
High school (9-10)	4.34	310	1.32	4.04	336	1.25	4.18	646	1.29
Higher sec. & above	4.09	158	1.39	4.39	233	1.36	4.27	391	1.38
		F-3.820	P<0.004		F-1.971	P<0.097		F-1.531	P<0.190
Education of husband									
Illiterate	5.02	117	1.93	4.35	84	1.61	4.74	201	1.83
Literate & Primary	4.17	242	1.65	4.19	173	1.68	4.18	415	1.66
Middle (6-8)	4.15	266	1.52	4.14	275	1.60	4.15	541	1.56
High school (9-10)	4.12	408	1.44	4.24	414	1.42	4.18	822	1.43
Higher sec. & above	4.08	167	1.45	4.04	254	1.36	4.06	421	1.39
		F-8.631	P<0.000		F-1.011	P<0.401		F-7.280	P<0.000

(Contd.)

(Contd. Table 5.8.1)

Socio-economic characteristics	Rural			Urban			Total		
	Mean	*N*	*SD*	*Mean*	*N*	*SD*	*Mean*	*N*	*SD*
Religion									
Hindu	4.21	1082	1.55	4.18	1034	1.52	4.20	2116	1.54
Muslim	4.09	77	1.91	4.08	105	1.51	4.08	182	1.69
Christian	4.68	41	1.69	4.21	61	1.07	4.40	102	1.37
		F-2.047	P<0.130		F-0.267	P<0.766		F-1.406	P<0.245
Community									
SC / ST	4.28	340	1.77	4.11	235	1.74	4.21	575	1.76
MBC	4.19	386	1.30	4.25	304	1.47	4.21	690	1.38
BC & others	4.20	474	1.64	4.17	661	1.43	4.18	1135	1.52
		F-0.327	P<0.721		F-0.595	P<0.552		F-0.107	P<0.898
Standard of living									
Low	4.37	492	1.68	4.20	337	1.75	4.30	829	1.71
Medium	4.13	379	1.64	4.02	377	1.33	4.08	756	1.49
High	4.10	329	1.32	4.28	486	1.43	4.21	815	1.39
		F-3.797	P<0.023		F-3.259	P<0.039		F-4.207	P<0.015

(Contd.)

(Contd. Table 5.8.1)

Socio-economic characteristics	Rural			Urban			Total		
	Mean	*N*	*SD*	*Mean*	*N*	*SD*	*Mean*	*N*	*SD*
Economic activities									
Yes	4.60	315	1.63	4.36	152	1.59	4.52	467	1.62
No	4.08	885	1.54	4.15	1048	1.49	4.12	1933	1.51
		F-25.055	P<0.000		F-2.647	P<0.104		F-25.723	P<0.000
Contribution to total income									
Nil	4.08	882	1.54	4.15	1045	1.49	4.12	1927	1.51
≤25 %	4.47	144	1.52	4.28	100	1.56	4.39	244	1.53
Above 25 %	4.70	174	1.70	4.56	55	1.68	4.66	229	1.69
		F-13.173	P<0.000		F-2.278	P<0.103		F-15.133	P<0.000
Type of family									
Nuclear	4.27	720	1.61	4.26	659	1.50	4.26	1379	1.56
Joint	4.15	480	1.53	4.08	541	1.50	4.11	1021	1.51
		F-1.689	P<0.194		F-4.454	P<0.035		F-5.913	P<0.015

urban areas, high standard of living women had significantly more autonomy than others. Involvement of women in income earning economic activities and contribution to the total family income significantly improved the autonomy of women in both rural and urban areas. Women in nuclear family had significantly more autonomy on decision about contraception than women in joint family in both rural and urban areas.

5.8.2 Women's Autonomy on Decision about Contraception and Fertility and Demographic Characteristics

The mean autonomy score on decision about contraception and fertility by selected demographic characteristics are presented in Table 5.8.2. The age of women did not make any significant difference in the level of autonomy of women on decision about contraception and fertility in rural areas. However, in urban areas, the mean autonomy score significantly increased with the age of women. It increased from 3.80 for women aged 19 years or less to 4.04 for women aged 20-24 years and to 4.34 for women aged 25-29 years. Age at marriage of women did not make any significant difference in the autonomy of women in rural areas. However, it showed significant effect in urban areas. While women's autonomy increased with age at marriage for women married up to 20 years of age, it showed a declining trend for women married at ages 21 years or more. The husband-wife age difference did not make any significant difference in the level of autonomy of women on decision about contraception and fertility in both rural and urban areas.

Autonomy of women on decision about contraception and fertility increased significantly with marital duration in both rural and urban areas. In rural areas, the mean score increased from 4.12 for women who had a marital duration of three years or less to 4.39 for women who had a marital duration of ten years or more. In urban areas, the mean score increased from 4.14 for women who had a marital duration of three years or less to 4.38 for women who had a marital duration of ten years or more.

Table 5.8.2 Mean autonomy score attained by women on decision about contraception and fertility by demographic characteristics

Demographic characteristics	*Rural*			*Urban*			*Total*		
	Mean	*N*	*SD*	*Mean*	*N*	*SD*	*Mean*	*N*	*SD*
All	4.22	1200	1.58	4.18	1200	1.50	4.20	2400	1.54
Age (years)									
≤ 19	3.96	50	1.74	3.80	59	1.55	3.87	109	1.64
20 – 24	4.16	478	1.49	4.04	551	1.53	4.10	1029	1.51
25 – 29	4.28	672	1.63	4.34	590	1.46	4.31	1262	1.55
		F-1.567	P<0.209		F-7.575	P<0.001		F-7.969	P<0.000
Age at marriage (years)									
≤ 16	4.25	152	1.90	3.96	100	1.76	4.14	252	1.85
17 – 18	4.18	398	1.63	4.00	316	1.54	4.10	714	1.59
19 – 20	4.20	352	1.50	4.35	418	1.50	4.28	770	1.50
21 – 22	4.36	203	1.47	4.24	234	1.46	4.30	437	1.46
23 +	4.10	95	1.32	4.10	132	1.24	4.10	227	1.27
		F-0.636	P<0.637		F-3.221	P<0.012		F-2.071	P<0.082

(Contd.)

(Contd. Table 5.8.2)

Demographic characteristics	*Rural*			*Urban*			*Total*		
	Mean	*N*	*SD*	*Mean*	*N*	*SD*	*Mean*	*N*	*SD*
Husband-wife age difference (years)									
≤ 4	4.20	417	1.62	4.20	438	1.58	4.20	855	1.60
5 – 8	4.22	499	1.57	4.21	479	1.42	4.21	978	1.50
9 +	4.25	284	1.53	4.09	283	1.52	4.17	567	1.53
		F-0.096	P<0.908		F-0.645	P<0.525		F-0.149	P<0.862
Marital duration (years)									
≤ 3	4.12	223	1.52	4.14	300	1.41	4.13	523	1.46
4 – 6	4.11	376	1.44	4.01	437	1.59	4.05	813	1.52
7 – 9	4.28	347	1.63	4.35	318	1.35	4.32	665	1.50
10+	4.39	254	1.76	4.38	145	1.70	4.38	399	1.73
		F-.2.093	P<0.099		F-4.4281	P<0.005		F-6.026	P<0.000

(Contd.)

(Contd. Table 5.8.2)

Demographic characteristics	Rural			Urban			Total		
	Mean	N	SD	Mean	N	SD	Mean	N	SD
Number of male children									
0	4.23	335	1.86	4.08	363	1.53	4.15	698	1.69
1	4.24	596	1.41	4.17	574	1.43	4.21	1170	1.42
2 +	4.17	269	1.56	4.32	263	1.61	4.24	532	1.59
		F-0.210	P<0.810		F-1.881	P<0.153		F-0.514	P<0.598
Number of female children									
0	4.28	357	1.45	4.26	400	1.55	4.27	757	1.50
1	4.16	568	1.51	4.17	558	1.39	4.16	1126	1.45
2 +	4.27	275	1.86	4.07	242	1.67	4.17	517	1.77
		F-0.780	P<0.458		F-1.204	P<0.300		F-1.132	P<0.323
Total Number of children									
1	4.25	345	1.54	4.12	402	1.41	4.18	747	1.47
2	4.27	604	1.51	4.21	605	1.52	4.24	1209	1.53
3 +	4.06	251	1.71	4.09	193	1.63	4.07	444	1.67
		F-1.611	P<0.200		F-1.217	P<0.296		F-2.329	P<0.098

Neither the number of male children nor the number of female children showed any significant difference in the level of women's autonomy on decision about contraception and fertility in both rural and urban areas. The total number of children also did not make any significant difference in the mean score in both rural and urban areas.

Overall, the results showed that the age of women increased the autonomy of women on decision about contraception and fertility in both rural and urban areas. But the differences are significant only in urban areas. Marital duration significantly improved the autonomy of women in both rural and urban areas.

5.8.3 Women's Autonomy on Decision about Contraception and Fertility and Marital Characteristics

In order to assess the influence of the type of marriage on women's autonomy on decision about contraception and fertility, the data were analysed according to the type of marriage and autonomy score. The results are presented in Table 5.8.3. The type of marriage did not make any significant difference in the mean score on decision about contraception and fertility in rural areas. However, in urban areas, the mean score was significantly higher at 4.24 for women who had non-consanguineous marriage compared to 4.06 observed for women who had consanguineous marriage.

The type of consanguineous marriage (maternal/paternal) did not make any significant difference in the mean autonomy score of women on decision about contraception and fertility in both rural and urban areas. Love marriage did not show any significant difference in the mean score in rural areas, whereas in urban areas the mean score was significantly higher at 4.47 for love marriage compared to 4.14 for arranged marriage. Inter-caste/ inter-religious marriage did not make any significant difference in the mean score of women on decision about contraception and fertility in rural areas. However, in urban areas, women who had same caste marriage had significantly lower autonomy than women

Table 5.8.3 Mean autonomy score attained by women on decision about contraception and fertility by marital characteristics

Marital characteristics	*Rural*			*Urban*			*Total*		
	Mean	*N*	*SD*	*Mean*	*N*	*SD*	*Mean*	*N*	*SD*
All	**4.22**	**1200**	**1.58**	**4.18**	**1200**	**1.50**	**4.20**	**2400**	**1.54**
Type of marriage									
Consanguineous	4.18	399	1.52	4.06	425	1.59	4.12	824	1.55
Non-consanguineous	4.24	801	1.61	4.24	775	1.45	4.24	1576	1.53
		F-0.441	P<0.507		F-3.740	P<0.053		F-3.368	0.067
Consanguineous type									
Maternal	4.20	209	1.60	3.95	229	1.64	4.07	438	1.63
Paternal	4.15	190	1.43	4.14	196	1.50	4.17	386	1.47
		F-0.123	P<0.726		F-2.473	P<0.117		F-0.853	P<0.356

(Contd.)

(Contd. Table 5.8.3)

Marital characteristics	*Rural*			*Urban*			*Total*		
	Mean	*N*	*SD*	*Mean*	*N*	*SD*	*Mean*	*N*	*SD*
Kind of marriage									
Arranged marriage	4.20	1078	1.56	4.14	1071	1.48	4.17	2149	1.52
Love marriage	4.37	122	1.73	4.47	129	1.67	4.41	251	1.70
		F-1.104	P<0.294		F-5.347	P<0.021		F-5.563	P<0.018
Inter caste / inter religious marriage									
Same caste	4.20	1128	1.56	4.15	1096	1.51	4.18	2224	1.54
Inter caste / inter religious	4.52	72	1.88	4.42	104	1.45	4.46	176	1.64
		F-2.690	P<0.101		F-2.833	P<0.093		F-5.296	P<0.021

who had inter-caste/inter-religious marriage. The mean autonomy score was 4.15 for women who had same caste marriage and it was 4.42 for women who had inter-caste/inter-religious marriage.

Overall, the results showed that the autonomy of women on decision about contraception and fertility was higher among women who had non-consanguineous marriage, who had love marriage and women who had inter-caste / inter religious marriage in both rural and urban areas. However, the differences are significant only for women in urban areas.

5.8.4 Women's Autonomy on Decision about Contraception and Fertility by Exposure to Mass Media

The results of the analysis of data on the influence of mass media on women's autonomy on decision about contraception and fertility are presented in Table 5.8.4. None of the mass media variables showed any significant influence on the autonomy of women on decision about contraception and fertility in both rural and urban areas. Membership in self help group showed significantly positive effect. Members of Self Help Group had more autonomy on decision about contraception and fertility in both rural and urban areas (Figure 5.8.1). In rural areas, members had a mean score of 4.34 and non-members had a mean score of 4.10. In urban areas, the members had a mean score of 4.33 and non-members had a mean score of 4.13.

Overall, the results showed that members of self help group had significantly more autonomy on decision about contraception and fertility in both rural and urban areas. None of the mass media variables had any significant influence on the autonomy of women in both rural and urban areas.

5.9 Total Autonomy

In order to assess the overall autonomy status of women, the total score attained by women for all the eight dimensions of autonomy was taken into consideration. The results of the analysis of data combining all the eight dimensions of autonomy

Table 5.8.4 Mean autonomy score attained by women on decision about contraception and fertility by exposure to mass media

Exposure to mass media	*Rural*			*Urban*			*Total*		
	Mean	*N*	*SD*	*Mean*	*N*	*SD*	*Mean*	*N*	*SD*
All	**4.22**	**1200**	**1.58**	**4.18**	**1200**	**1.50**	**4.20**	**2400**	**1.54**
Listening to radio									
Yes	4.17	683	1.59	4.16	630	1.42	4.17	1313	1.51
No	4.29	517	1.56	4.19	570	1.59	4.24	1087	1.58
		F-1.684	P<0.195		F-0.102	P<0.750		F-1.269	P<0.260
Watching television									
Yes	4.20	1050	1.54	4.19	1088	1.47	4.19	2138	1.50
No	4.34	150	1.84	4.09	112	1.78	4.23	262	1.81
		F-1.019	P<0.313		F-0.507	P<0.476		F-0.123	P<0.726
Going to movies									
Yes	4.06	172	1.39	4.18	242	1.45	4.13	414	1.42
No	4.25	1028	1.61	4.18	958	1.52	4.21	1986	1.56
		F-2.070	P<0.150		F-0.000	P<0.991		F-1.018	P<0.313

(Contd.)

(Contd. Table 5.8.4)

Exposure to mass media	Rural			Urban			Total		
	Mean	*N*	*SD*	*Mean*	*N*	*SD*	*Mean*	*N*	*SD*
Reading newspapers/ magazines									
Yes	4.29	458	1.49	4.16	456	1.33	4.22	914	1.41
No	4.18	742	1.63	4.19	744	1.60	4.19	1486	1.61
		F-1.363	P<0.243		F-0.089	P<0.765		F-0.410	P<0.522
Mass media index									
No exposure	4.37	76	1.98	4.02	53	2.16	4.22	129	2.05
Low exposure	4.21	752	1.60	4.19	759	1.51	4.20	1511	1.55
High exposure	4.20	372	1.45	4.18	388	1.38	4.19	760	1.41
		F-0.382	P<0.682		F-0.315	P<0.730		F-0.048	P<0.954
Membership in SHG									
Yes	4.34	600	1.52	4.33	304	1.57	4.33	904	1.53
No	4.10	600	1.63	4.13	896	1.48	4.12	1496	1.54
		F-6.971	P<0.008		F-4.014	P<0.045		F-11.445	P<0.001

Figure 5.8.1 Autonomy of women on decision about contraception and fertility by membership in SHG

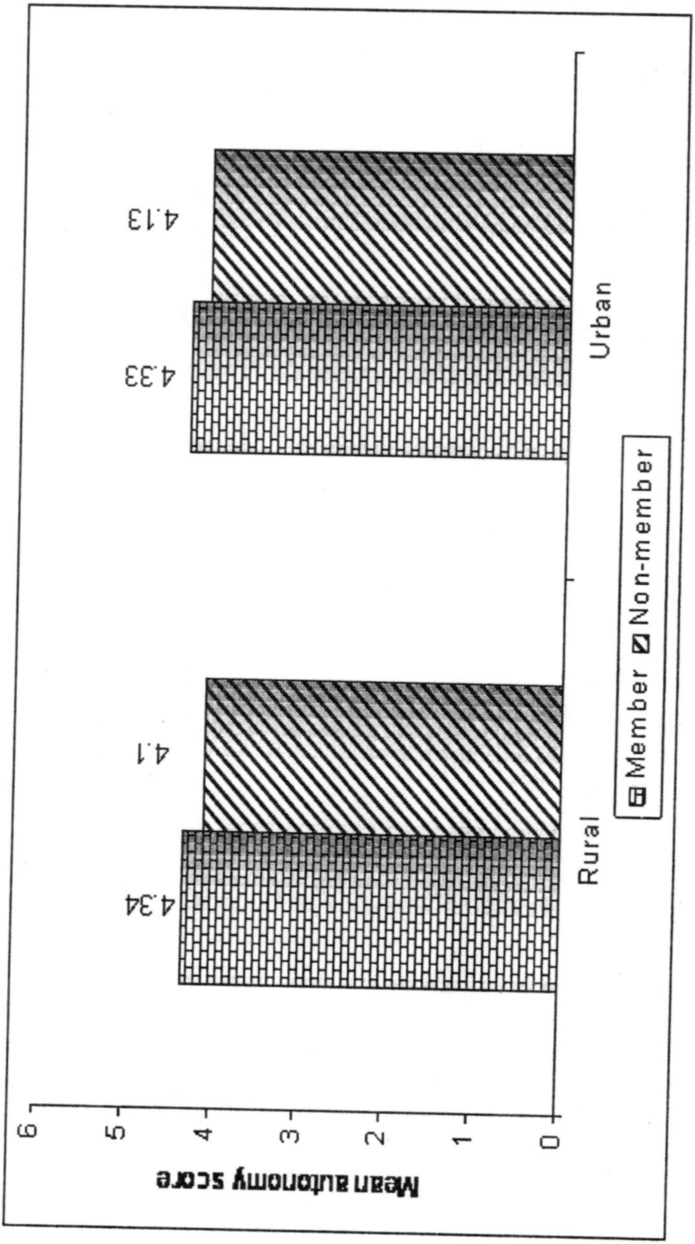

score by selected background characteristics of the respondents are discussed in this section. The combined total score for all the eight dimensions of autonomy is 128. The results of the analysis of data on the total autonomy of women by selected background characteristics are presented in Tables 5.9.1 to 5.9.4. It is found that rural women had more autonomy than urban women as measured by their total mean autonomy score which was 81.05 for rural and 76.47 for urban women. The influence of socio-economic, demographic, marital and mass media variables on the autonomy of women is discussed in the following sections 5.9.1 to 5.9.4.

5.9.1 Women's Autonomy and Socio-economic Characteristics

The distribution of women by their mean autonomy score and selected socio-economic characteristics is presented in Table 5.9.1. The mean autonomy score increased with the education of women in both rural and urban areas (Figure 5.9.1). In rural areas, the mean autonomy score significantly increased from 77.49 for illiterates to 84.22 for higher secondary and above educated respondents. In urban areas, the mean autonomy score increased from 72.05 for illiterates to 80.54 for higher secondary and above educated respondents. It is to be noted that the mean score among women in rural areas was higher at all levels of education than among women in urban areas. Education of husband did not make any significant difference in the mean autonomy score in rural areas. However, in urban areas, education of husband showed significantly positive effect on women's autonomy.

Muslim women had significantly lower autonomy than others in both rural and urban areas. The level of autonomy varied significantly among women belonging to different caste groups in both rural and urban areas. Most Backward Caste women had significantly more autonomy than others in both rural and urban areas. In rural areas, the mean autonomy score was highest at

82.27 for MBC, 81.71 for SC/ST, and 79.59 for BC and others. In urban areas, the mean autonomy score was highest at 78.10 for MBC compared to 75.06 for SC/ST and 76.23 for BC and others.

Standard of living did not make any significant difference in the level of autonomy in rural areas. The mean autonomy score was staggering around 80 to 81 at all levels of standard of living. However, in urban areas, standard of living showed significant influence on the autonomy of women. The mean autonomy score was significantly low est at 72.84 for low standard of living women compared with 77.97 for medium and 77.83 for high standard of living women. It is also to be noted that there was not much difference in the mean autonomy score between medium and high standard of living.

Involvement in income earning economic activities showed significantly positive effect on the autonomy of women in rural areas. The mean autonomy score was significantly higher at 86.80 for women involved in economic activities compared to 79.01 observed for women not involved in economic activities. In urban areas, though involvement of women in economic activities showed higher autonomy, the differences are not statistically significant. The mean autonomy score for women in urban areas was 77.64 for women involved in economic activities and 76.30 for women who were not involved in any economic activities.

Contribution to the total family income showed significantly positive influence on the autonomy of women in rural areas. The mean autonomy score was significantly lowest at 79.03 for women who did not contribute anything to the family income compared to the mean autonomy score of 86.53 for women who contributed up to 25 per cent of the total family income and 86.80 for women who contributed more than 25 per cent to the total family income. In urban areas, though the level of autonomy increased with increase in the level of contribution to the total family income, the differences are not statistically significant. The mean autonomy score increased

Table 5.9.1 Mean autonomy score attained by women aged 15-29 years by socio-economic characteristics

Socio-economic characteristics	*Rural*			*Urban*			*Total*		
	Mean	*N*	*SD*	*Mean*	*N*	*SD*	*Mean*	*N*	*SD*
All	**81.05**	**1200**	**14.84**	**76.47**	**1200**	**14.73**	**78.76**	**2400**	**14.96**
Education of woman									
Illiterate	77.49	133	15.16	72.05	124	15.83	74.86	257	15.70
Literate & Primary	80.13	247	14.19	74.47	190	12.97	77.67	437	13.94
Middle (6-8)	80.76	352	15.26	75.05	317	15.08	78.05	669	15.43
High school (9-10)	82.05	310	14.65	77.77	336	14.77	79.82	646	14.86
Higher Secondary & above	84.22	158	14.36	80.54	233	13.83	82.02	391	14.14
		F-4.388	P<0.002		F-9.774	P<0.000		F-10.962	P<0.000
Education of husband									
Illiterate	83.87	117	15.35	74.21	84	15.95	79.84	201	16.28
Literate & Primary	81.68	242	15.13	75.40	173	14.71	79.06	415	15.26
Middle (6-8)	79.86	266	14.38	75.00	275	14.23	77.39	541	14.50
High school (9-10)	80.67	408	15.24	78.21	414	15.20	79.43	822	15.26
Higher Secondary & above	81.03	167	13.62	76.72	254	13.85	78.43	421	13.91
		F-1.663	P<0.156		F-2.875	P<0.022		F-1.899	P<0.108

(Contd.)

(Contd. Table 5.9.1)

Socio-economic characteristics	*Rural*			*Urban*			*Total*		
	Mean	*N*	*SD*	*Mean*	*N*	*SD*	*Mean*	*N*	*SD*
Religion									
Hindu	81.60	1082	14.73	76.89	1034	14.81	79.30	2116	14.96
Muslim	72.99	77	15.17	71.72	105	14.27	72.26	182	14.64
Christian	81.78	41	12.76	77.64	61	12.78	79.30	102	12.87
		F-12.390	P<0.000		F-6.105	P<0.000		F-18.897	P<0.000
Community									
SC / ST	81.71	340	14.53	75.06	235	15.62	78.99	575	15.33
MBC	82.27	386	14.95	78.10	304	14.32	80.43	690	14.81
BC & others	79.59	474	14.88	76.23	661	14.55	77.63	1135	14.77
		F-3.955	P<0.019		F-3.044	P<0.048		F-7.663	P<0.000
Standard of living									
Low	80.50	492	15.18	72.84	337	14.42	77.39	829	15.34
Medium	81.92	379	14.41	77.97	377	14.32	79.95	756	14.49
High	80.89	329	14.81	77.83	486	14.86	79.07	815	14.91
		F-1.001	P<0.368		F-14.579	P<0.000		F-6.073	P<0.002

(Contd.)

(Contd. Table 5.9.1)

Socio-economic characteristics	*Rural*			*Urban*			*Total*		
	Mean	*N*	*SD*	*Mean*	*N*	*SD*	*Mean*	*N*	*SD*
Economic activities									
Yes	86.80	315	14.72	77.64	152	16.59	83.82	467	15.93
No	79.01	885	14.34	76.30	1048	14.44	77.54	1933	14.46
		F-67.582	P<0.000		F-1.090	P<0.297		F-68.047	P<0.008
Percent contribution to total income									
Nil	79.03	882	14.33	76.26	1045	14.44	77.53	1927	14.45
25 %	86.53	144	14.39	76.99	100	15.77	82.62	244	15.66
Above 25 %	86.80	174	15.20	79.60	55	17.95	85.07	229	16.16
		F-32.739	P<0.000		F-1.412	P<0.244		F-36.108	P<0.008
Type of family									
Nuclear	83.04	720	14.19	78.67	659	14.02	80.95	1379	14.27
Joint	78.07	480	15.30	73.80	541	15.15	75.81	1021	15.36
		F-33.150	P<0.000		F-33.284	P<0.000		F-71.334	P<0.000

Figure 5.9.1 Total autonomy of women by education

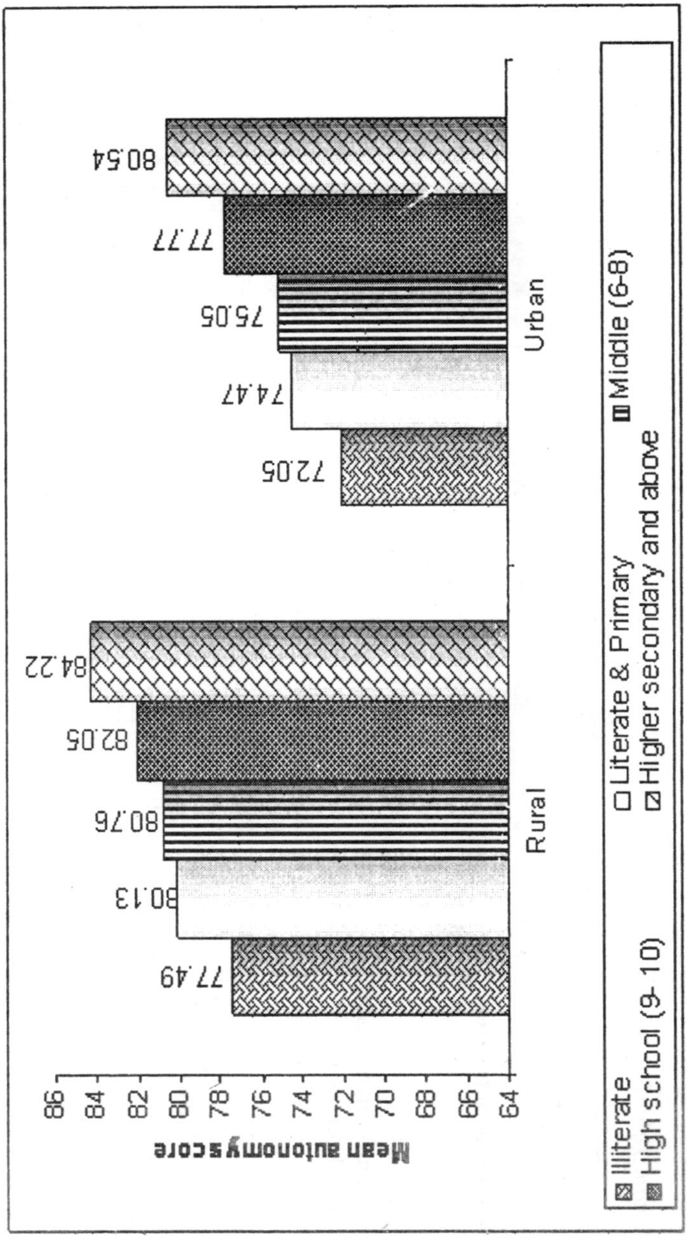

Figure 5.9.2 Total autonomy of women by type of family

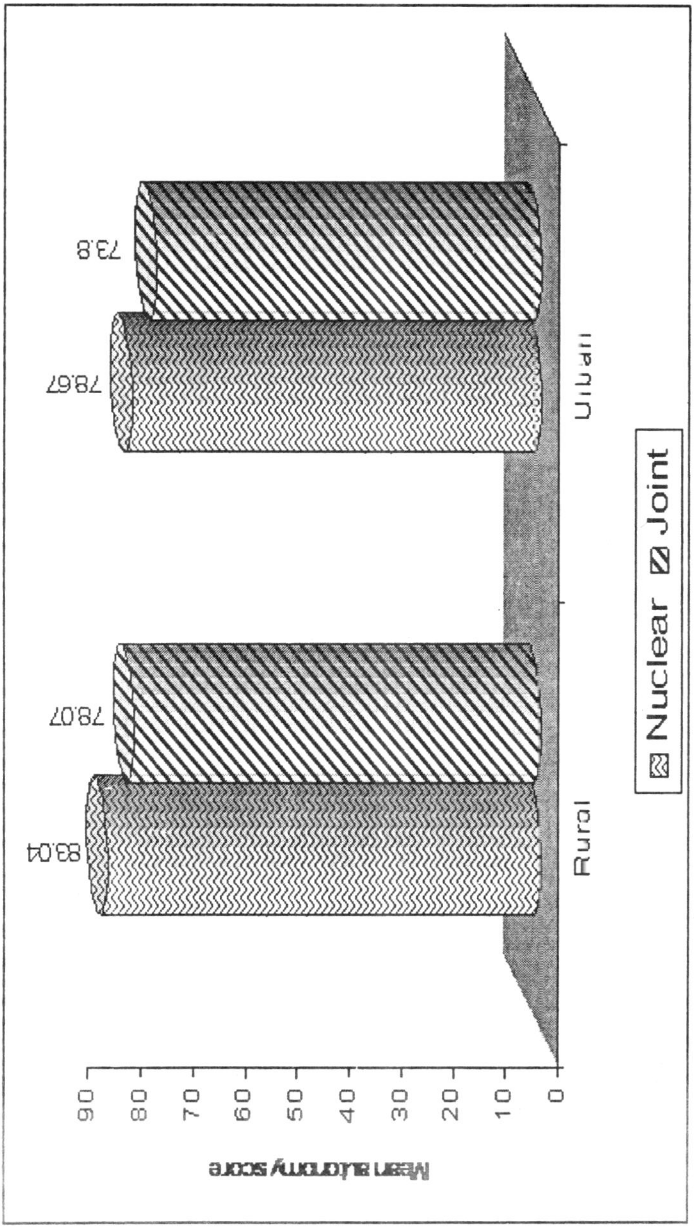

from 76.26 for women who made no contribution to the total family income to 76.99 for women who contributed up to 25 per cent and to 79.60 for women who contributed more than 25 per cent to total family income.

The type of family showed significant influence on the autonomy of women in both rural and urban areas (Figure 5.9.2). Women in nuclear family had significantly higher autonomy than women in joint family. In rural areas, the mean autonomy score was significantly higher at 83.04 for women in nuclear family compared to 78.07 for women in joint family. In urban areas, the mean autonomy score was significantly higher at 78.67 for women in nuclear families compared to 73.80 for women in joint family.

Overall, the results showed that education of women had significantly improved the autonomy of women in both rural and urban areas. Muslim women had significantly less autonomy than others in both rural and urban areas. Backward caste women in rural areas and SC/ST women in urban areas had significantly less autonomy than others. Standard of living showed significantly positive influence on the autonomy of women only in urban areas. Involvement in income earning economic activities and contribution to the total family income had significantly positive influence on the autonomy of women only in rural areas. Women in nuclear family had significantly more autonomy than women in joint family in both rural and urban areas.

5.9.2 Women's Autonomy and Demographic Characteristics

The distribution of women by their mean autonomy score and demographic characteristics is presented in Table 5.9.2. Increase in age significantly improved the autonomy of women in both rural and urban areas (Figure 5.9.3). In rural areas, the mean autonomy score increased significantly from 73.20 for women aged 19 years or less to 78.37 for women aged 20–24 years and to 83.54 for women aged 25-29 years. In urban areas also, the mean autonomy score increased significantly from 66.68 for women aged 19 years or less to 79.92 for women aged 25-29 years.

Age at marriage of women did not make any significant difference in the level of autonomy of women in rural areas. However, in urban areas, age at marriage showed significant influence on the autonomy of women. The mean autonomy score for women in urban areas significantly increased from 73.05 for women married at ages 16 years or less to 77.33 for women married at ages 23 years or more. The husband-wife age difference did not make any significant difference in the level of women's autonomy in both rural and urban areas. Marital duration showed significantly positive effect on the autonomy of women in both rural and urban areas. The mean autonomy score significantly increased with marital duration in both rural and urban areas (Figure 5.9.4). In rural areas, the mean score increased from 74.96 for women who had marital duration of three years or less to 86.67 for women who had marital duration of ten years or more. In urban areas, the mean score increased from 72.63 for women who had marital duration of three years or less to 80.25 for women who had marital duration of ten years or more.

The autonomy of women increased with the number of male children in both rural and urban areas. However, the differences are statistically significant only for women in rural areas. In rural areas, the mean autonomy score significantly increased from 79.32 for women who had no male child to 82.88 for women who had two or more male children. In urban areas, though the mean autonomy score increased with the number of male children, the differences are not statistically significant. It is also observed that the number of female children did not make any significant difference in the level of women's autonomy in both rural and urban areas.

Women who had a total of two living children had significantly more autonomy than women who had one child or three or more children in both rural and urban areas. In rural areas, the mean autonomy score was highest at 82.99 for women who had two children compared to 77.18 for women who had one living child and 81.73 for women who had three or more children. In urban areas, the mean autonomy score was highest at 78.54 for women

Table 5.9.2 Mean autonomy score attained by women aged 15-29 years by demographic characteristics

Demographic characteristics	*Rural*			*Urban*			*Total*		
	Mean	*N*	*SD*	*Mean*	*N*	*SD*	*Mean*	*N*	*SD*
All	**81.05**	**1200**	**14.84**	**76.48**	**1200**	**14.73**	**78.76**	**2400**	**14.95**
Age (years)									
≤ 19	73.20	50	13.67	66.68	59	14.89	69.67	109	14.65
20 – 24	78.37	478	13.99	73.82	551	14.38	75.94	1029	14.38
25 – 29	83.54	672	14.99	79.92	590	14.09	81.85	1262	14.69
		F-25.238	P<0.000		F-40.612	P<0.000		F-69.057	P<0.000
Age at marriage (years)									
≤ 16	81.01	152	16.54	73.05	100	16.32	77.85	252	16.88
17 – 18	81.80	398	15.02	75.14	316	15.09	78.85	714	15.41
19 – 20	81.55	352	14.47	77.71	418	14.86	79.46	770	14.79
21 – 22	80.38	203	14.36	77.04	234	14.02	78.59	437	14.26
23 +	77.62	95	13.22	77.33	132	12.85	77.45	227	12.98
		F-1.729	P<0.141		F-2.951	P<0.019		F-1.113	P<0.349

(Contd.)

(Contd. Table 5.9.2)

Demographic characteristics	*Rural*			*Urban*			*Total*		
	Mean	*N*	*SD*	*Mean*	*N*	*SD*	*Mean*	*N*	*SD*
Husband-wife age difference (years)									
≤ 4	80.96	417	15.18	76.34	438	14.42	78.59	855	14.97
5 – 8	80.98	499	14.00	77.22	479	14.83	79.14	978	14.53
9 +	81.32	284	15.79	75.41	283	15.03	78.37	567	15.68
		F-0.061	P<0.940		F-1.378	P<0.253		F-0.554	P<0.576
Marital duration(years)									
≤ 3	74.96	223	13.94	72.63	300	13.86	73.63	523	13.93
4 – 6	79.36	376	13.66	75.61	437	14.46	77.35	813	14.21
7 – 9	82.69	347	14.24	79.56	318	14.06	81.19	665	14.23
10+	86.67	254	15.72	80.25	145	16.46	84.34	399	16.27
		F-29.664	P<0.000		F-15.670	P<0.000		F 50.203	P<0.000

(Contd.)

(Contd. Table 5.9.2)

Demographic characteristics	*Rural*			*Urban*			*Total*		
	Mean	*N*	*SD*	*Mean*	*N*	*SD*	*Mean*	*N*	*SD*
Number of male children									
0	79.32	335	14.81	75.63	363	14.47	77.40	698	14.74
1	81.20	596	14.73	76.53	574	14.91	78.91	1170	14.99
2 +	82.88	269	14.84	77.49	263	14.68	80.22	532	15.04
		F-4.390	P<0.013		F-1.235	P<0.291		F-5.501	P<0.004
Number of female children									
0	80.55	357	14.67	76.10	400	15.24	78.19	757	15.13
1	80.73	568	14.84	77.00	558	14.15	78.88	1126	14.62
2 +	82.39	275	15.02	75.87	242	15.20	79.33	517	15.44
		F-1.452	P<0.234		F-0.687	P<0.503		F-0.949	P<0.387
Total No. of children									
1	77.18	345	14.62	74.26	402	14.45	75.61	747	14.59
2	82.99	604	14.30	78.54	605	14.53	80.76	1209	14.58
3 +	81.73	251	15.45	74.62	193	15.08	78.64	444	15.68
		F-17.608	P<0.000		F-12.248	P<0.000		F-28.027	P<0.000

Figure 5.9.3 Total autonomy of women by age (years)

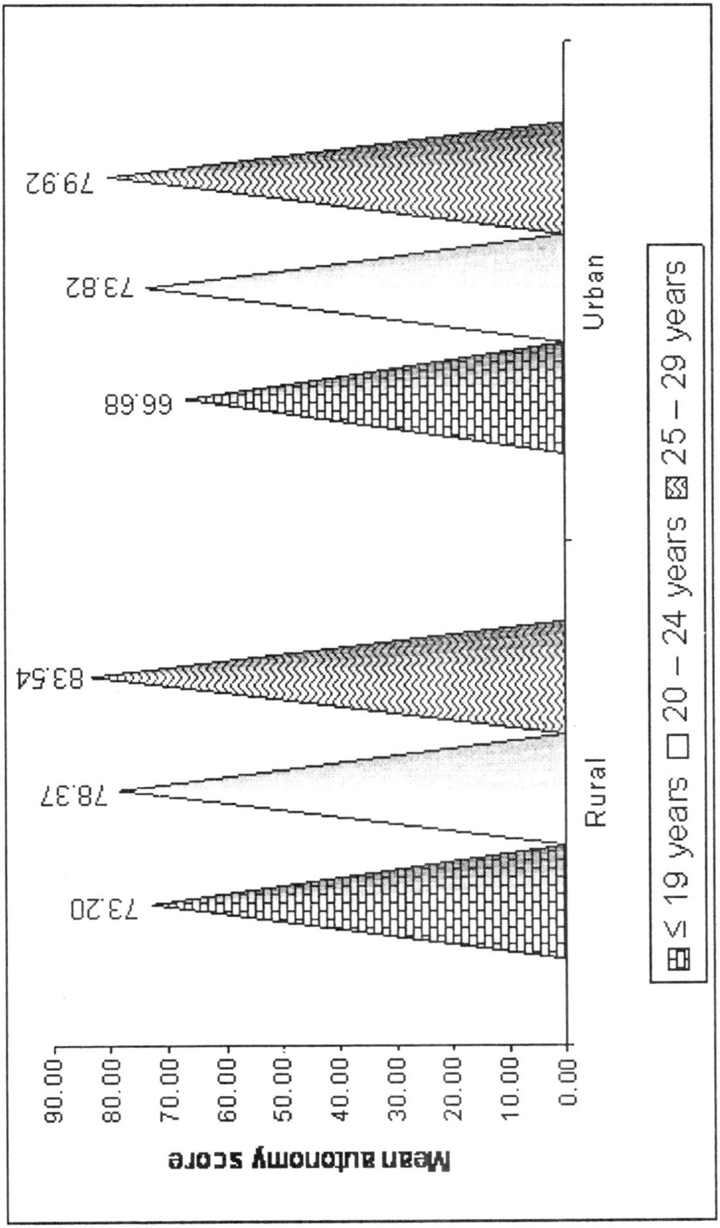

Figure 5.9.4 Total autonomy of women by marital duration (years)

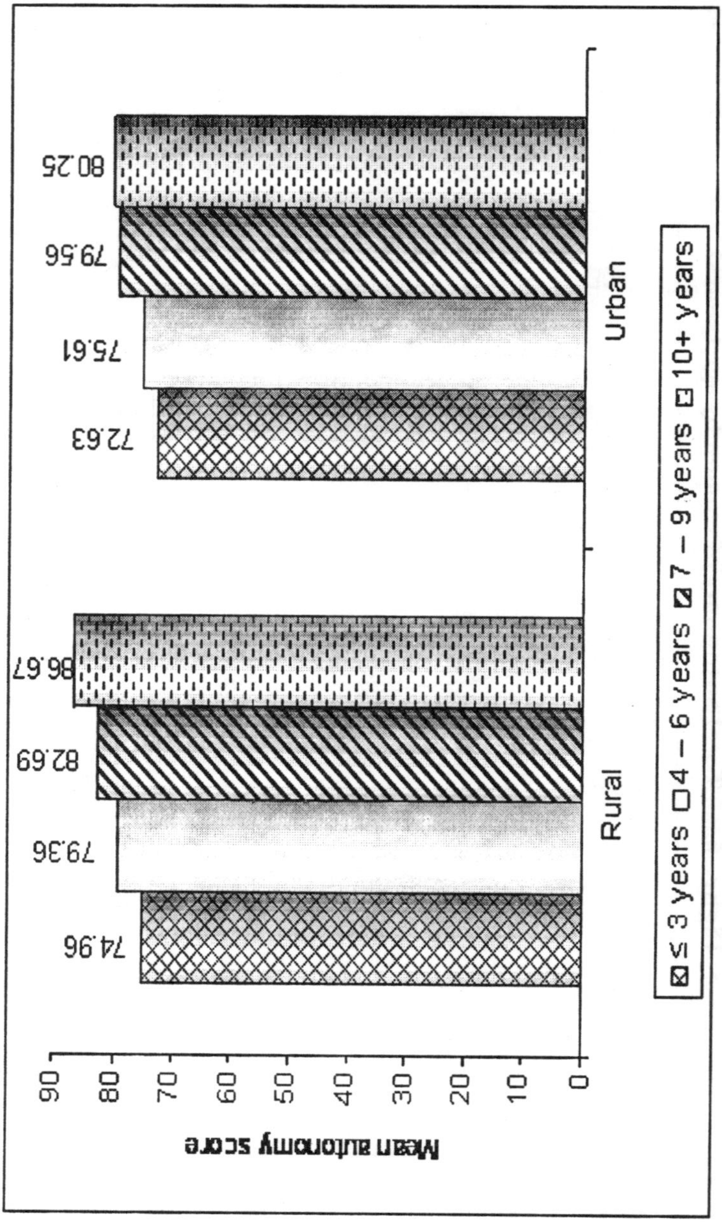

who had two living children compared to 74.26 for women who had one living child and 74.62 for women who had three or more children.

Overall, the results showed that the autonomy of women increased significantly with the age and marital duration in both rural and urban areas. Women who had two children had significantly more autonomy than women who had one child and three or more number of children in both rural and urban areas. Autonomy also increased significantly with the number of male children for women in rural areas.

5.9.3 Women's Autonomy and Marital Characteristics

In order to assess the influence of the type of marriage on women's autonomy, the data were analyzed according to the type of marriage and mean autonomy score. The results are presented in Table 5.9.3.

The mean autonomy score was slightly higher among women who had consanguineous marriage than those who had non-consanguineous marriage in both rural and urban areas. However, the differences are not statistically significant for both rural and urban areas.

Women who had married a person from paternal side had slightly more autonomy than those who had married a person from maternal side in both rural and urban areas. However, the differences are not statistically significant. Women who had love marriage had significantly higher autonomy than those who had arranged marriage in both rural and urban areas (Figure 5.9.5). Similarly, women who had inter-caste / inter-religious marriage had more autonomy than those who had same caste marriage in both rural and urban areas. However, the differences are significant only for urban areas.

Overall, the results showed that women who had love marriage had significantly more autonomy than women who had arranged marriage in both rural and urban areas. It is also observed that the autonomy of women was significantly more

Table 5.9.3 Mean autonomy score attained by women aged 15-29 years by marital characteristics

Marital characteristics	*Rural*			*Urban*			*Total*		
	Mean	*N*	*SD*	*Mean*	*N*	*SD*	*Mean*	*N*	*SD*
All	**81.05**	**1200**	**14.84**	**76.60**	**425**	**14.44**	**78.76**	**2400**	**14.96**
Type of marriage									
Consanguineous	81.51	399	15.39	76.60	425	14.44	78.98	824	15.10
Non-consanguineous	80.83	801	14.56	76.40	775	14.90	78.65	1576	14.89
		F-0.567	P<0.452		F-0.047	P<0.828		F-0.256	P<0.613
Consanguineous type									
Maternal	80.78	209	15.94	76.41	229	15.14	78.49	438	15.66
Paternal	82.32	190	14.76	76.82	196	13.62	79.53	386	14.44
		F-0.991	P<0.320		F-0.087	P<0.768		F-0.960	P<0.328

(Contd.)

(Contd. Table 5.9.3)

Marital characteristics	Rural			Urban			Total		
	Mean	N	SD	Mean	N	SD	Mean	N	SD
Kind of marriage									
Arranged marriage	80.80	1078	14.84	76.09	1071	14.58	78.45	2149	14.89
Love marriage	83.33	122	14.67	79.62	129	15.63	81.42	251	15.25
		F-3.194	P<0.074		F-6.629	P<0.010		F-8.885	P<0.003
Inter caste / inter religious marriage									
Same caste marriage	81.00	1128	14.86	76.13	1096	14.77	78.60	2224	15.01
Inter caste / inter religious marriage	81.86	72	14.66	80.07	104	13.85	80.80	176	14.18
		F-0.226	P<0.634		F-6.813	P<0.009		F-3.528	P<0.060

Figure 5.9.5 Total autonomy of women by kind of marriage

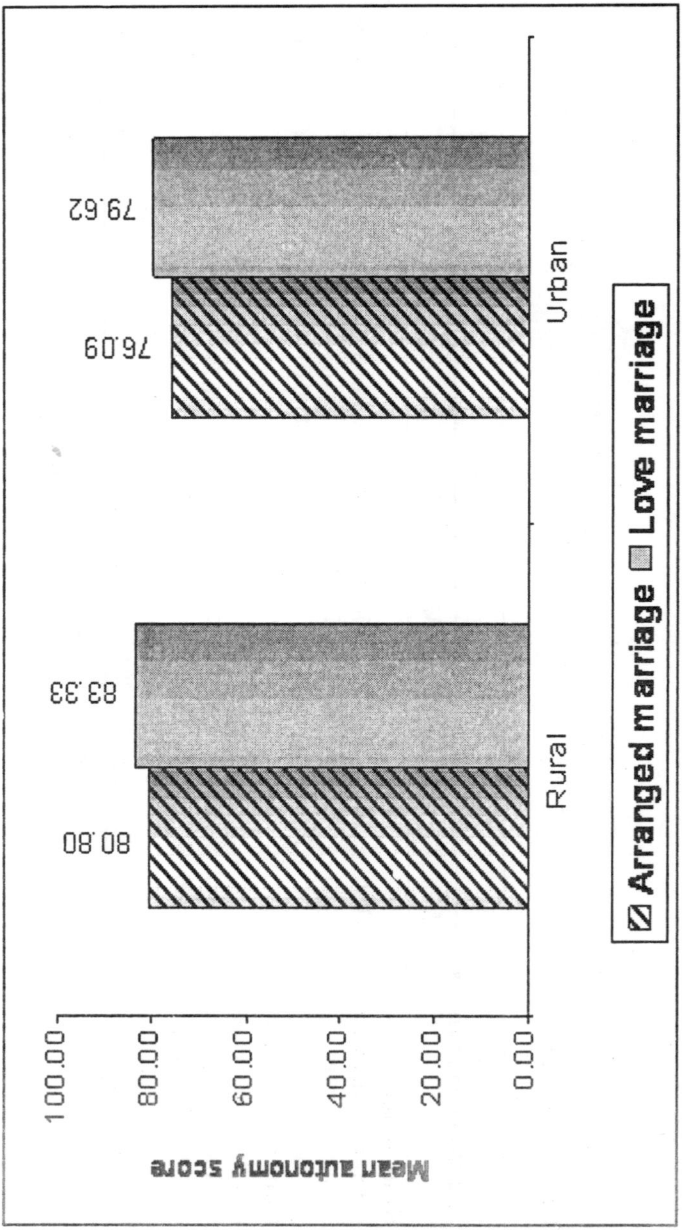

for those who had inter-caste / inter religious marriage than those who had same caste marriage in urban areas.

5.9.4 Women's Autonomy and Exposure to Mass Media

The results of the analysis of data on the influence of mass media on women's autonomy are presented in Table 5.9.4. Women who had the habit of listening to radio at least once a week had significantly more autonomy than those who were not having the habit of listening to radio in both rural and urban areas. In rural areas, the mean autonomy score was higher at 81.85 for women who were having the habit of listening to radio compared to 80.00 for women who were not having the habit. In urban areas, the mean autonomy score was higher at 78.02 for women who were listening to radio compared to 74.76 observed for women who were not listening to radio. Watching television showed significant influence on women's autonomy in both rural and urban areas. In rural areas, the mean autonomy score was significantly higher for women who were watching television once a week (81.60) than those who were not watching television (77.21). In urban areas, the mean autonomy score was significantly higher at 76.95 for women who were watching television compared to 71.82 for women who were not having the habit of watching television.

Going to movies did not make any significant difference in the level of women's autonomy in rural areas. However, in urban areas, going to movies showed significant influence on the autonomy of women. The mean autonomy score for women in urban areas was higher at 80.74 for women going to movies compared to 75.40 for women who were not going to movies. Reading newspapers / magazines showed significantly positive effect on women's autonomy in both rural and urban areas. In rural areas, the mean autonomy score was significantly higher at 84.16 for women who were reading newspapers / magazines compared to 79.14 for women who were not having the habit of reading newspapers / magazines. In urban areas, the mean

Table 5.9.4 Mean autonomy score attained by women aged 15-29 years by level of exposure to mass media

Marital characteristics	*Rural*			*Urban*			*Total*		
	Mean	*N*	*SD*	*Mean*	*N*	*SD*	*Mean*	*N*	*SD*
All	**81.05**	**1200**	**14.84**	**76.47**	**1200**	**14.73**	**78.76**	**2400**	**14.95**
Listening to radio									
Yes	81.85	683	14.37	78.02	630	13.23	80.01	1313	13.96
No	80.00	517	15.39	74.76	570	16.07	77.25	1087	15.96
		F-4.580	P<0.033		F-14.816	P<0.000		F-20.392	P<0.000
Watching television									
Yes	81.60	1050	14.67	76.95	1088	14.67	79.24	2138	14.85
No	77.21	150	15.49	71.82	112	14.63	74.90	262	15.33
		F-11.625	P<0.001		F-12.430	P<0.000		F-19.721	P<0.000
Going to movies									
Yes	82.03	172	13.45	80.74	242	13.51	81.28	414	13.49
No	80.89	1028	15.06	75.40	958	14.84	78.24	1986	15.19
		F-0.877	P<0.349		F-25.911	P<0.000		F-14.185	P<0.000

(Contd.)

(Contd. Table 5.9.4)

Marital characteristics	*Rural*			*Urban*			*Total*		
	Mean	*N*	*SD*	*Mean*	*N*	*SD*	*Mean*	*N*	*SD*
Reading newspapers / magazines									
Yes	84.16	458	14.15	79.65	456	14.67	81.91	914	14.58
No	79.14	742	14.94	74.53	744	14.44	76.83	1486	14.87
		F-33.255	P<0.000		F-35.122	P<0.000		F-66.981	P<0.000
Mass media index									
No exposure	74.53	76	17.64	67.92	53	15.82	71.81	129	17.17
Low exposure	80.22	752	14.49	75.13	759	14.79	77.66	1511	14.86
High exposure	84.08	372	14.31	80.27	388	13.50	82.13	760	14.02
		F-16.712	P<0.000		F-25.996	P<0.000		F-38.480	P<0.000
Membership in SHG									
Yes	87.55	600	13.38	83.32	304	13.74	86.13	904	13.64
No	74.56	600	13.32	74.15	896	14.34	74.31	1496	13.93
		F-283.857	P<0.000		F-94.020	P<0.000		F-411.262	P<0.000

Figure 5.9.6 Total autonomy of women by level of exposure to mass media

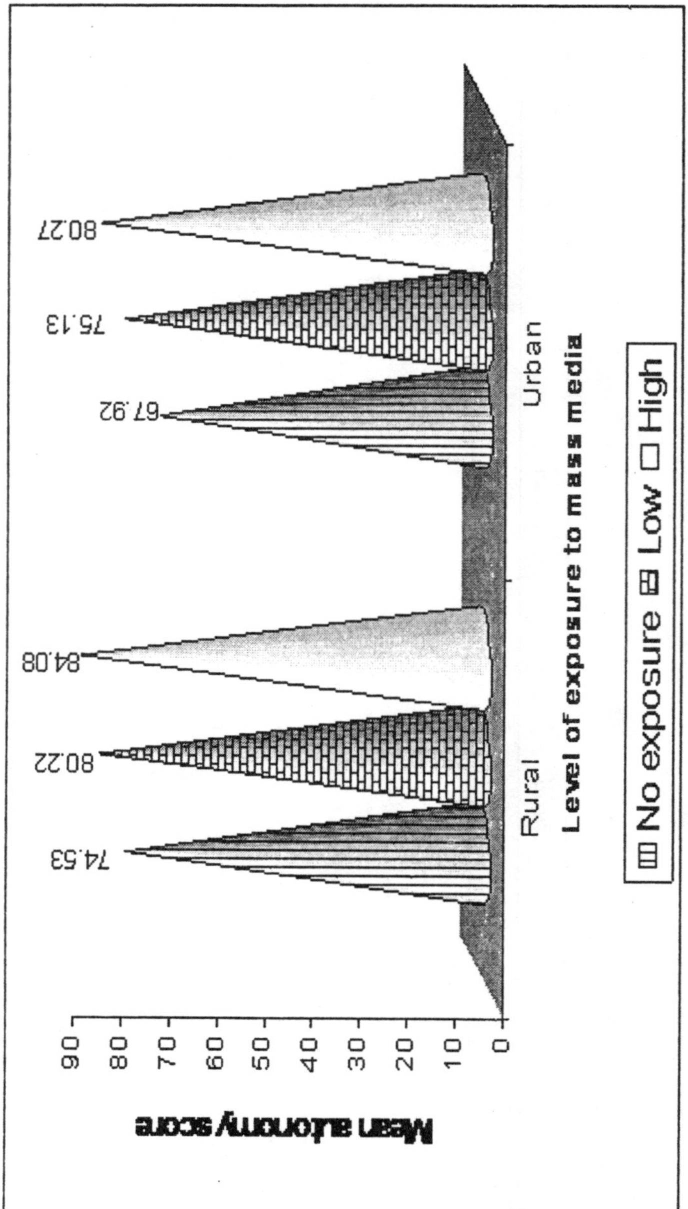

Figure 5.9.7 Total autonomy of women by membership in SHG

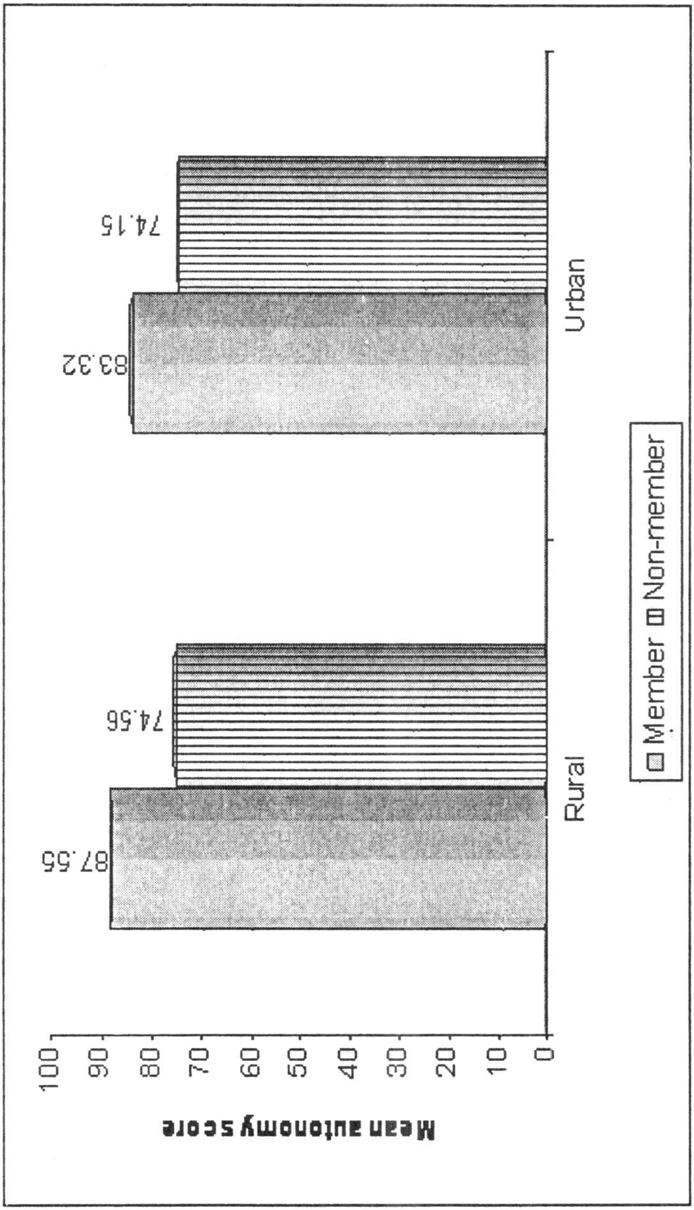

autonomy score was 79.65 for women reading newspapers / magazines compared to 74.53 for women who were not having the habit of reading newspapers / magazines.

The overall exposure of women to various mass media was scored and a combined mass media index was developed based on the total score attained by women for all the four mass media variables. The mass media index was classified into three groups as no exposure, low level of exposure and high level of exposure.

Increase in the level of exposure to mass media increased the level of women's autonomy in both rural and urban areas (Figure 5.9.6). In rural areas, the mean autonomy score significantly increased from 74.53 for women who had no exposure to mass media to 80.22 for women who had low level of exposure and to 84.08 for women who had high level of exposure. In urban areas, the mean autonomy score significantly increased from 67.92 for those who had no exposure to 75.13 for those who had low level of exposure and to 80.27 for those who had high level of exposure to mass media.

Membership in self help group had significantly positive effect on women's autonomy in both rural and urban areas (Figure 5.9.7). In rural areas, members had a mean autonomy score of 87.55 and non-members had a mean autonomy score of only 74.56. In urban areas, members had a mean autonomy score of 83.32 and non-members had a mean autonomy score of only 74.15.

Overall, the results showed that the exposure of women to mass media and membership in self help group significantly improved the autonomy of women in both rural and urban areas.

6

Level of Autonomy and Factors Associated with Women's Autonomy

A summary of the level of autonomy attained by women on each of the eight dimensions of autonomy and total autonomy and also the factors significantly associated with the women's autonomy are presented in the following sections.

6.1 Level of Autonomy

The level of autonomy attained by women on each of the eight dimensions of autonomy is estimated based on the percent score. The results are presented in Table 6.1.1. and Figure 6.1. The mean autonomy score attained by women on sex-segregated interaction was 76.19 per cent of the total expected score of 16. Rural women attained slightly more autonomy on sex-segregated interaction (76.31 per cent) than their urban counterparts (76.13 per cent). The mean score attained by women on freedom of movement was only 51.35 per cent of the total expected score of 26. Autonomy on freedom of movement was substantially more among women in rural areas (54.07 per cent) than among women

Table 6.1.1 Mean autonomy score and percent score attained by women in rural and urban areas

Autonomy variables	*Total score*	*Mean score*			*Percent score*		
		Rural	*Urban*	*Total*	*Rural*	*Urban*	*Total*
1. Sex-segregated interaction	16	12.21	12.18	12.19	76.31	76.13	76.19
2. Freedom of movement	26	14.06	12.63	13.35	54.07	48.58	51.35
3. Freedom to participation in social and political activities	14	4.24	2.56	3.39	30.29	18.29	24.22
4. Financial management	6	3.07	2.76	2.91	51.17	46.00	48.50
5. Household decisions	22	11.56	10.81	11.18	52.55	49.14	50.82
6. Freedom of choice	16	14.63	14.22	14.42	91.44	88.88	90.13
7. Violence against women	20	17.10	17.16	17.13	85.50	85.80	85.65
8. Decision about contraception and fertility	8	4.22	4.18	4.19	52.75	52.25	52.38
Total autonomy (1–8)	128	81.05	76.47	78.76	63.32	59.74	61.53

Figure 6.1 Percent score attained by women on various dimensions of autonomy in rural and urban areas

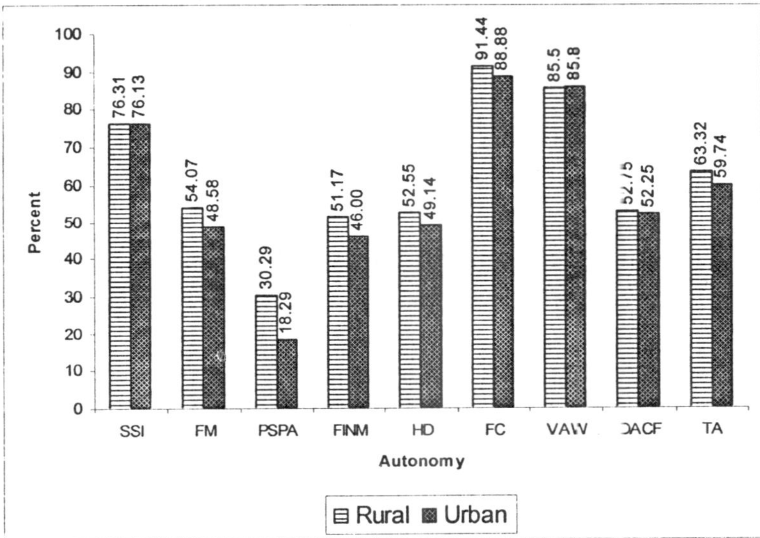

1. SSI - Sex-segregated interaction
2. FM - Freedom of Movement
3. PSPA - Participation in Social and Political Activities
4. FINM - Financial Management
5. HD - Household Decisions
6. FC - Freedom of Choice
7. VAW - Violence Against Women
8. DACF- Decision About Contraception and Fertility
9. TA - Total Autonomy

in urban areas (48.58 per cent). The mean score attained by women on freedom to participate in social and political activities was very low at 24.22 per cent of the total expected score of 14.

Rural women had more autonomy on freedom to participate in social and political activities than urban women. It was 30.29 per cent for women in rural areas compared to only 18.29 per cent for women in urban areas. The per cent score attained by women on financial management was only

48.5 per cent of the total expected score of 6. Rural women had more control over finance than urban women. The mean score attained by women on financial management was 51.17 per cent in rural and 46 per cent in urban areas.

The mean score attained by women on household decisions was only 50.82 per cent of the total expected score of 22. Again, rural women had more autonomy on household decisions than their urban counterparts. The mean score attained by women was 52.55 per cent in rural and 49.14 per cent in urban areas.

Autonomy of women on freedom of choice in their life style behaviour was substantially more at 90.13 per cent of the total expected score of 16. Autonomy of women on freedom of choice was more for women in rural than for women in urban areas. It was 91.44 per cent for women in rural and 88.88 per cent for women in urban areas. The percent score on violence against women was also substantially high at 85.65 per cent of the total expected score of 20. There was not much difference between rural and urban women in the autonomy on violence against women. It was 85.5 per cent for women in rural and 85.8 per cent for women in urban areas. The percent score on decision about contraception and fertility was only 52.38 per cent of the total expected score of 8. The percent score on decision about contraception and fertility did not vary much between rural and urban areas. It was 52.75 per cent for women in rural and 52.25 per cent for women in urban areas.

The overall total autonomy score attained by women was only 61.53 per cent of the total expected score of 128. Surprisingly, rural women had more autonomy than urban women. It was 63.32 per cent for women in rural and 59.74 per cent for women in urban areas. Overall, the results indicate that women attained significantly high level of autonomy (more than 75 per cent of the expected level) only on sex-segregated interaction, freedom of choice and violence against women in both rural and urban areas (Table 6.1.2). The results suggest

Table 6.1.2 Percent score attained by women on various dimensions of autonomy and total autonomy in rural and urban areas

Autonomy	*Rural*				*Urban*			
	≤25%	*26–50%*	*51–74%*	*75%*	*≤25%*	*26–50%*	*51–74%*	*75%*
1. Sex-segregated interaction				?				?
2. Freedom of movement			?			?		
3. Freedom to participation in social and political activities		?			?			
4. Financial management			?			?		
5. Household decisions			?			?		
6. Freedom of choice				?				?
7. Violence against women				?				?
8. Decision about contraception and fertility			?				?	
Total autonomy			?				?	

the need for an improvement in the level of autonomy of women on all the dimensions in both rural and urban areas.

6.2 Factors Associated with Women's Autonomy

Among the various socio-economic, demographic, marital and mass media variables examined in this study, factors which are significantly associated with women's autonomy are presented in the following sections.

6.2.1 Sex-segregated Interaction

The factors which are significantly associated with women's autonomy on sex-segregated interaction in both rural and urban areas are presented in Table 6.2.1. The results showed that among the various socio-economic variables examined in this study, education of women, education of husband and standard of living had significantly positive influence on women's autonomy on sex-segregated interaction in both rural and urban areas. Community variable showed significantly positive effect (higher caste women had high autonomy) on women's autonomy only in urban areas. Surprisingly, involvement of women in income earning economic activities showed significantly negative effect on women's autonomy in urban areas. Though contribution to the total family income showed significant effect in urban areas, it did not show any systematic pattern of relationship with women's autonomy on sex-segregated interaction.

The age of women showed significantly positive effect on women's autonomy on sex-segregated interaction in both rural and urban areas. Age at marriage of women showed significantly positive effect only in urban areas. Similarly, husband-wife age difference, the number of female children and the total number of children had significant association with women's autonomy in urban areas. While the number of male children showed significantly positive effect, the number of female children showed significantly negative effect on women's autonomy in rural areas. Women who had a total of two children had significantly more autonomy than women who had one child and three or more number of children in both rural and urban areas.

Table 6.2.1 Factors associated with women's autonomy on sex-segregated interaction

Factors	*Nature of relationship*	
	Rural	*Urban*
Socio-economic factors		
Education of women	+	+
Education of husband	+	+
Standard of living	+	+
Community (caste)	NS	+
Involvement in income earning economic activities	NS	-
Contribution to total family income	NS	v
Demographic factors		
Age of women	–	+
Age at marriage	NS	+
Husband-wife age difference	NS	^
Number of male children	+	NS
Number of female children	-	^
Total number of children	^	^
Mass media factors		
Exposure to mass media	+	+
Membership in SHG	+	+

Note: + – positive – – negative; ^ – initially increased and then deceased; v – Initially decreased and then increased; NS – Not significant

Exposure of women to mass media and membership in SHG had significantly positive influence on women's autonomy on sex-segregated interaction in both rural and urban areas. Overall, education of women and their husband, standard of living, age of women, exposure of women to mass media and membership in SHG showed significantly positive effect on the autonomy of women on sex-segregated interaction in both rural and urban areas. While the number of male children showed significantly positive effect, the number of female children showed significantly negative effect in rural areas.

6.2.2 Freedom of Movement

The factors associated with women's autonomy on freedom of movement in rural and urban areas are presented in Table 6.2.2. The results showed that education of women,

Table 6.2.2 Factors associated with women's autonomy on freedom of movement

Factors	*Nature of relationship*	
	Rural	*Urban*
Socio-economic factors		
Education of women	+	+
Religion	Muslim (Low)	Muslim (Low)
Community (caste)	BC (Low)	BC (Low)
Standard of living	NS	^
Involvement in income earning economic activities	+	+
Contribution to total family income	+	+
Type of family	Nuclear (High)	Nuclear (High)
Demographic factors		
Age of women	+	+
Age at marriage	^	^
Marital duration	+	+
Number of female children	+	+
Total number of children	^	^
Marital factors		
Love marriage	NS	+
Inter-caste / inter-religious marriage	NS	+
Mass media factors		
Exposure to mass media	+	+
Membership in SHG	+	+

Note: + – positive; ^ – initially increased and then deceased; NS – Not significant involvement of women in income earning economic activities, contribution to the total family income were the socio-economic variables exerting significantly positive effect on the autonomy of women on freedom of movement in both rural and urban areas. Muslim women and backward caste women in both rural and urban areas had significantly low autonomy on freedom of movement. Women in nuclear family had significantly more autonomy on freedom of movement than women in joint family in both rural and urban areas.

The age of women, marital duration and the number of female children were the demographic variables showing significantly positive influence on the autonomy of women on freedom of movement in both rural and urban areas. Autonomy of women increased with age at marriage of women up to 20 years of age and then showed a declining trend in both rural and urban areas. Thus the results showed that women who married at younger ages (d"18 years) and later ages (21+) had significantly lower autonomy than women who married at 19-20 years in both rural and urban areas. Women who had a total of two children had significantly more autonomy than women who had one child and three or more number of children in both rural and urban areas.

Love marriage and inter-caste/inter religious marriage showed significantly positive influence on women's autonomy only in urban areas. Exposure of women to mass media and membership in SHG had significantly positive influence on women's autonomy on freedom of movement in both rural and urban areas.

Overall, the results showed that higher caste women, Muslim women and women living in joint family had significantly low autonomy on freedom of movement in both rural and urban areas. Educated women, working women, higher age women, women who had longer period of marital duration, women who had more exposure to mass media and members of SHG had significantly more autonomy on freedom of movement in both rural and urban areas.

6.2.3 Freedom to Participate in Social and Political Activities

Factors associated with women's autonomy on freedom to participate in social and political activities in both rural and urban areas are presented in Table 6.2.3. Education of women, involvement of women in income earning economic activities and contribution of women to the total family income were the

Table 6.2.3 Factors associated with women's autonomy on freedom to participate in social and political activities

Factors	*Nature of relationship*	
	Rural	*Urban*
Socio-economic factors		
Education of women	+	+
Religion	Muslim (Low)	Muslim (Low)
Community (caste)	BC (Low)	BC (Low)
Standard of living	NS	^
Involvement in income earning economic activities	+	+
Contribution to total family income	+	+
Type of family	Nuclear (High)	Nuclear (High)
Demographic factors		
Age of women	+	+
Age at marriage	^	NS
Marital duration	+	+
Total number of children	^	^
Marital factors		
Love marriage	+	+
Mass media factors		
Exposure to mass media	+	+
Membership in SHG	+	+

Note: + – positive; ^ – initially increased and then deceased; NS – Not significant socio-economic variables showing significantly positive influence on the autonomy of women on freedom to participate in social and political activities in both rural and urban areas. Higher caste women (BC) and Muslim women had significantly low autonomy in both rural and urban areas. At the same time women in nuclear family had significantly higher autonomy than women in joint family in both rural and urban areas.

Age of women and marital duration were the demographic variables showing significantly positive influence on women's autonomy in both rural and urban areas. Women who had love marriage had significantly more autonomy than women who had arranged marriage in both rural and urban areas. Women who had more exposure to mass media had significantly more autonomy than others in both rural and urban areas. Members of SHG had significantly more autonomy than non-members in both rural and urban areas. Though age at marriage showed significant association in rural areas, the relationship was not systematic. Similarly, the significant association of the total number of children with women's autonomy in urban areas also did not show a systematic relationship. At the same time the total number of children showed significantly positive influence on women's autonomy in rural areas.

Overall, the results showed that Muslim women, higher caste women and women living in joint family had significantly low autonomy in both rural and urban areas. Educated women, working women and women who contributed more to the family income had significantly more autonomy in both rural and urban areas. Age, marital duration, total number of children, love marriage, exposure to mass media and membership in SHG showed significant association with women's autonomy on freedom to participate in social and political activities in both rural and urban areas.

6.2.4 Financial Management

The factors associated with women's autonomy on financial management in both rural and urban areas are presented in Table 6.2.4. Education of husband showed significantly negative effect on women's autonomy on financial management in both rural and urban areas. Involvement of women in income earning economic activities and contribution to the total family income had significantly positive effect on women's autonomy on financial management in both rural and urban areas. Women in nuclear family had significantly more autonomy on financial management than women in joint family

Table 6.2.4 Factors associated with women's autonomy on financial management in rural and urban areas

Factors	*Nature of relationship*	
	Rural	*Urban*
Socio-economic factors		
Education of husband	-	-
Community (caste)	SC/ST (High)	NS
Standard of living	^	NS
Involvement in income earning economic activities	+	+
Contribution to total family income	+	+
Type of family	Nuclear (High)	Nuclear (High)
Demographic factors		
Age	+	+
Age at marriage	-	NS
Marital duration	+	+
Number of male children	+	NS
Number of female children	V	NS
Total number of children	+	^
Marital factors		
Non-consanguineous marriage	NS	+
Love marriage	+	+
Inter-caste / inter-religious marriage	NS	+
Membership in SHG	+	+

Note: + – positive; – – negative; ^ – initially increased and then deceased; v – Initially decreased and then increased; NS – Not significant in both rural and urban areas. SC/ST women had significantly more autonomy than others only in rural areas.

Age of women and marital duration showed significantly positive influence on women's autonomy on financial management in both rural and urban areas. Total number of children showed significantly positive influence only in rural areas. Women who had love marriage and members of SHG had significantly more autonomy than others in both rural and urban areas. Inter-caste / inter religious marriage had significantly positive effect on women's autonomy on financial management only in urban areas.

Overall, the results showed that involvement of women in income earning economic activities, contribution to the total family income, age of women, marital duration, love marriage and membership in SHG showed significantly positive influence on women's autonomy on financial management in both rural and urban areas. Education of husband showed significantly negative effect. SC/ST women had significantly more autonomy only in rural areas. While age at marriage showed significantly negative effect, the total number of children showed significantly positive effect on women's autonomy in rural areas.

6.2.5 Household Decisions

The factors associated with women's autonomy on household decisions in rural and urban areas are presented in Table 6.2.5. Women in nuclear family had significantly more autonomy on household decisions than women in joint family in both rural and urban areas. Age of women and marital duration showed significantly positive influence on women's autonomy in both rural and urban areas. Women who had love marriage had significantly more autonomy than women who had arranged marriage in both rural and urban areas. Similarly women who had inter-caste / inter religious marriage had significantly more autonomy than women who had same caste marriage in both rural and urban areas. Members of SHG also had significantly more autonomy than non-members in both rural and urban areas. Involvement of women in income earning economic activities and contribution to the total family income showed significantly positive effect only in rural areas. Education of husband showed significantly negative effect on women's autonomy mainly in rural areas. While Muslim women had low autonomy, SC/ST women had significantly high autonomy on

Table 6.2.5 Factors associated with women's autonomy on household decisions

Factors	*Nature of relationship*	
	Rural	*Urban*
Socio-economic factors		
Education of husband	-	NS
Religion	Muslim (Low)	NS
Community (caste)	SC/ST (High)	NS
Involvement in income earning economic activities	+	NS
Contribution to total family income	+	NS
Type of family	Nuclear (High)	Nuclear (High)
Demographic factors		
Age	+	+
Marital duration	+	+
Number of male children	NS	+
Number of female children	+	NS
Total number of children	+	^
Marital factors		
Love marriage	+	+
Inter-caste / inter-religious marriage	+	+
Mass media factors		
Exposure to mass media	NS	+
Membership in SHG	+	+

Note: + – positive; – – negative; ^ – initially increased and then deceased; NS – Not significant household decisions in rural areas. Exposure of women to mass media showed significantly positive effect only in urban areas.

Overall, the results showed that age of women, marital duration, love marriage, inter-caste / inter religious marriage and membership in SHG showed significantly positive effect on women's autonomy on household decisions in both rural and urban areas. Women in nuclear family had significantly high autonomy in both rural and urban areas. While education of husband showed negative effect, involvement in income earning economic activities, contribution to the total family income, the number of female children and the total number of children showed significantly positive influence in rural areas. While Muslim women had significantly low autonomy, SC/ST women had significantly high autonomy in rural areas. The number of male children and exposure of women to mass media showed significantly positive effect only in urban areas.

6.2.6 Freedom of Choice

The factors associated with women's autonomy on freedom of choice on their personal life style behaviour in rural and urban areas are presented in Table 6.2.6. Education of women and education of husband had significantly positive effect on women's autonomy on freedom of choice only in urban areas. Exposure of women to mass media and membership in SHG showed significantly positive effect on the autonomy of women on freedom of choice in both rural and urban areas. Muslim women had significantly low autonomy on freedom of choice in both rural and urban areas. While MBC women had significantly high autonomy in rural areas, backward caste women had significantly high autonomy in urban areas. Age at marriage showed significantly positive effect and the number of female children showed significantly negative effect on women's autonomy in urban areas.

Overall the results showed that religion, community, number of female children, exposure of women to mass media

Table 6.2.6 Factors associated with women's autonomy on freedom of choice

Factors	*Nature of relationship*	
	Rural	*Urban*
Socio-economic factors		
Education of women	NS	+
Education of Husband	NS	+
Religion	Muslim (Low)	Muslim (Low)
Community (Caste)	MBC (High)	BC (High)
Demographic factors		
Age at marriage	NS	+
Number of female children	^	-
Total number of children	^	NS
Mass media factors		
Exposure to mass media	+	+
Membership in SHG	+	+

Note: + – positive; – – negative; ^ – initially increased and then deceased; NS – Not significant

and membership in SHG had significant association with women's autonomy on freedom of choice in both rural and urban areas. Education of women, education of husband, and age at marriage had significant association with women's autonomy on freedom of choice only in urban areas.

6.2.7 Violence Against Women

The factors associated with women's autonomy on violence against women in rural and urban areas are presented in Table 6.2.7. Education of women, education of husband, standard of living were the socio-economic variables showing significantly positive influence on women's autonomy on violence against women in both rural and urban areas. Surprisingly, involvement of women in income earning economic activities and contribution of women to the total family income showed significantly negative effect on women's autonomy in both rural and urban areas. Women in joint family had significantly high autonomy on violence against women in both rural and urban areas and SC/ST women had significantly low autonomy in both

Table 6.2.7 Factors associated with women's autonomy on violence against women

Factors	*Nature of relationship*	
	Rural	*Urban*
Socio-economic factors		
Education of women	+	+
Education of husband	+	+
Religion	Muslim (High)	NS
Community (caste)	SC/ST (Low)	SC/ST (Low)
Standard of living	+	+
Involvement in income earning economic activities	-	-
Contribution to total family income	-	-
Type of family	Joint (High)	Joint (High)
Demographic factors		
Age	NS	v
Age at marriage	+	+
Marital duration	-	-
Number of female children	NS	^
Total number of children	NS	-
Marital factors		
Consanguineous marriage	+	+
Arranged marriage	+	+
Same caste marriage	+	+
Mass media factors		
Exposure to mass media	+	+

Note: + – positive; – – negative; ^ – initially increased and then deceased; V – Initially decreased and then increased; NS – Not significant rural and urban areas. Muslim women had significantly high autonomy only in rural areas.

While age at marriage showed significantly positive effect on the autonomy of women on violence against women, marital duration showed significantly negative effect in both rural and urban areas. The total number of children showed significantly negative effect only in urban areas.

Women who had consanguineous marriage, women who had arranged marriage and women who had same caste marriage had significantly more autonomy than others in both rural and urban areas. Exposure of women to mass media significantly increased the autonomy of women on violence against women in both rural and urban areas.

Overall, the results showed that education of women and their husband standard of living, age at marriage, consanguineous marriage, arranged marriage, same caste marriage and exposure to mass media had significantly positive association with women's autonomy on violence against women in both rural and urban areas. Involvement in income earning economic activities, contribution to the total family income and marital duration had significantly negative association with women's autonomy on violence against women. While SC/ST women had significantly low autonomy, women in joint family had significantly high autonomy on violence against women in both rural and urban areas.

6.2.8 Decision about Contraception and Fertility

The factors associated with women's autonomy on decision about contraception and fertility are presented in Table 6.2.8. While the education of husband and standard of living showed significantly negative effect, involvement in income earning economic activities and contribution to the total family income showed significantly positive effect on women's autonomy on decision about contraception and fertility in rural areas. Women's autonomy significantly increased with marital duration in both rural and urban areas. Women who had non-consanguineous marriage, women who had love marriage, women who had inter-caste / inter religious marriage had significantly positive effect only in urban areas. It is also found that autonomy increased significantly with the age of women only in urban areas. Members of SHG had significantly more autonomy on decision about contraception and fertility than non-members in both rural and urban areas.

Overall, the results showed that women's autonomy on decision about contraception and fertility significantly associated with marital duration and membership in SHG in both rural and urban areas. Education of husband, standard of living,

Table 6.2.8 Factors associated with women's autonomy on decision about contraception and fertility

Factors	*Nature of relationship*	
	Rural	*Urban*
Socio-economic factors		
Education of women	-	+
Education of husband	-	NS
Standard of living	-	v
Involvement in income earning economic activities	+	NS
Contribution to total family income	+	NS
Type of family	NS	Nuclear (High)
Demographic factors		
Age	NS	+
Age at marriage	NS	^
Marital duration	+	+
Marital factors		
Non-consanguineous marriage	NS	+
Love marriage	NS	+
Inter-caste / inter-religious marriage	NS	+
Membership in SHG	+	+

Note: + – positive; – - negative; ^ – initially increased and then deceased; v – Initially decreased and then increased; NS – Not significant involvement in income earning economic activities and contribution to the total family income had significant association with women's autonomy only in rural areas.

Age, age at marriage, non-consanguineous marriage, love marriage and inter-caste / inter religious marriage had significant association with women's autonomy on decision about contraception and fertility only in urban areas.

6.2.9 Total Autonomy

The factors associated with women's total autonomy in rural and urban areas are presented in Table 6.2.9. Education of women showed significantly positive effect on women's autonomy in both rural and urban areas. While Muslim women had significantly low autonomy, MBC women had significantly high autonomy in both rural and urban areas. Women in nuclear family had significantly more autonomy than women in joint family in both rural and urban areas. Involvement of women in income earning economic activities and contribution of women to total family income showed significantly positive effect on women's autonomy only in rural areas. Standard of living showed significantly positive effect only in urban areas.

Age of women and marital duration showed significantly positive effect on women's autonomy in both rural and urban areas. Age at marriage showed significantly positive effect only in urban areas. The number of male children showed significantly positive effect only in rural areas. Women who had a total of two children had significantly more autonomy than women who had one child and two or more number of children in both rural and urban areas.

Women who had love marriage, women who had more exposure to mass media and members of SHG had significantly more autonomy in both rural and urban areas. Women who had inter-caste / inter religious marriage had significantly more autonomy only in urban areas.

Table 6.2.9 Factors associated with women's autonomy (total)

Factors	*Nature of relationship*	
	Rural	*Urban*
Socio-economic factors		
Education of women	+	+
Education of husband	NS	^
Religion	Muslim (Low)	Muslim (Low)
Community (caste)	MBC (High)	MBC (High)
Standard of living	NS	+
Involvement in income earning economic activities	+	NS
Contribution to total family income	+	NS
Type of family	Nuclear (High)	Nuclear (High)
Demographic factors		
Age	+	+
Age at marriage	NS	+
Marital duration	+	+
Number of male children	+	NS
Total number of children	^	^
Marital factors		
Love marriage	+	+
Inter-caste / inter-religious marriage	NS	+
Mass media factors		
Exposure to mass media	+	+
Membership in SHG	+	+

Note: + – positive; ^ – initially increased and then deceased; NS – Not significant.

6.3 Regression Analysis

The results of the regression analysis on the effect of various socio-economic demographic and mass media variables on women's autonomy are presented in Table 6.3 In rural areas, education of women, work status, age at marriage, marital duration, love marriage, exposure to mass media and

Table 6.3 Regression analysis showing the effect of various background characteristics of women on autonomy

Background characteristics	*Rural*			*Urban*			*Total*		
	Parameter Estimate	*Standard error*	*P-value*	*Parameter Estimate*	*Standard error*	*P-value*	*Parameter Estimate*	*Standard error*	*P-value*
(Constant) p	48.430	4.460	**0.000**	38.460	4.654	**0.000**	43.209	3.222	**0.000**
Education of women	2.399	0.385	**0.000**	1.676	0.393	**0.000**	2.008	0.275	**0.000**
Education of husband	-0.813	0.351	**0.021**	-0.393	0.381	0.303	-0.652	0.259	**0.012**
Work status	5.513	2.337	**0.018**	-1.843	3.160	0.560	1.516	1.872	0.418
Percent to total income	-0.587	1.405	0.676	1.683	2.175	0.439	1.240	1.178	0.293
Standard of living	-0.9157	0.050	**0.065**	.0326	0.047	0.486	- 0.024	0.034	0.479
Age at marriage	0.684	0.192	**0.000**	1.016	0.201	**0.000**	0.850	0.139	**0.000**

(Contd.)

(Contd. Table 6.3)

Background characteristics	*Rural*			*Urban*			*Total*		
	Parameter Estimate	*Standard error*	*P-value*	*Parameter Estimate*	*Standard error*	*P-value*	*Parameter Estimate*	*Standard error*	*P-value*
Husband-wife age difference	0.127	0.104	0.223	-.0234	0.120	0.845	0.060	0.079	0.444
Marital duration(years)	1.158	0.169	**0.000**	1.486	0.184	**0.000**	1.353	0.124	**0.000**
Total number of children	-1.189	0.660	**0.072**	-0.853	0.707	0.228	-0.997	0.483	**0.039**
Whether love marriage	3.299	1.441	**0.022**	4.312	1.505	**0.004**	3.785	1.044	**0.000**
Whether inter-caste / inter religious	-1.309	1.791	0.465	1.126	1.625	0.489	0.006	1.201	0.996
Exposure to mass media	3.616	0.726	**0.000**	4.164	0.802	**0.000**	3.973	0.541	**0.000**
Membership in SHG	10.734	0.777	**0.000**	7.824	0.914	**0.000**	9.723	0.584	**0.000**

a. Dependent Variable: Total autonomy of women

membership in self help group showed significantly positive effect on women's autonomy. Education of husband, total number of children and standard of living showed significantly negative effect on women's autonomy.

In urban areas, education of women, age at marriage, level of exposure to mass media and marital duration showed significantly positive effect on women's autonomy. Women who had love marriage and women who were members of self help group had significantly more autonomy than others.

The results showed that in rural areas, autonomy of women was significantly more for educated women, working women, women married at later ages, women who had longer duration of marital life, women who had love marriage, women who had higher level of exposure to mass media and women who were members of self help group. At the same time, autonomy of women decreased significantly for women who had educated husband, women who had more number of children and women who had high standard of living.

In urban areas, autonomy of women was significantly more for women who had higher level of education, women who had later marriage, women who had higher level of exposure to mass media, women who had longer duration of marital life, women who had love marriage and women who were members of self help group.

In sum, it is inferred that women's autonomy hinges on the education of women, age at marriage of women, exposure to mass media and participation in self help group activities in both rural and urban areas. Work opportunities for women improve their autonomy only in rural areas.

7

Women's Autonomy and Reproductive Behaviour

In this study, women's autonomy is related to their reproductive behaviour such as starting, spacing and stopping of reproduction in order to assess the impact of women's autonomy on their reproductive behaviour. The analysis of data on the reproductive behaviour of women was restricted only to those women who had reported to have completed their fertility at the time of the interview. Of the 1200 women in rural areas, 794 reported to have completed their fertility and, in the urban areas, 684 of the 1200 women had reported to have completed their fertility. The results of the analysis of data on the impact of women's autonomy on their reproductive behaviour are presented in the following sections.

7.1 Women's Autonomy and Fertility Completion Status

The fertility completion status as reported by the women according to their level of autonomy and place of residence is presented in Table 7.1 and Figure 7.1 The results show that 66.2 per cent of women in rural and 57 per cent of women in urban areas reported to have completed their fertility at the

Table 7.1 Percent distribution of women who had completed their fertility at the time of interview by their level of autonomy and place of residence

Autonomy	*Fertility completion status*					
	Rural		*Urban*		*Total*	
	N	*% completed*	*N*	*% completed*	*N*	*% completed*
N	1200	66.2	1200	57.0	2400	61.6
Low	371	54.2	457	49.9	828	51.8
Medium	383	66.6	440	55.7	823	60.8
High	446	75.8	303	69.6	749	73.3
	χ^2-42.279 DF=2 P<0.000		χ^2-29.478 DF=2 P<0.000		χ^2-77.103 DF=2 P<0.000	

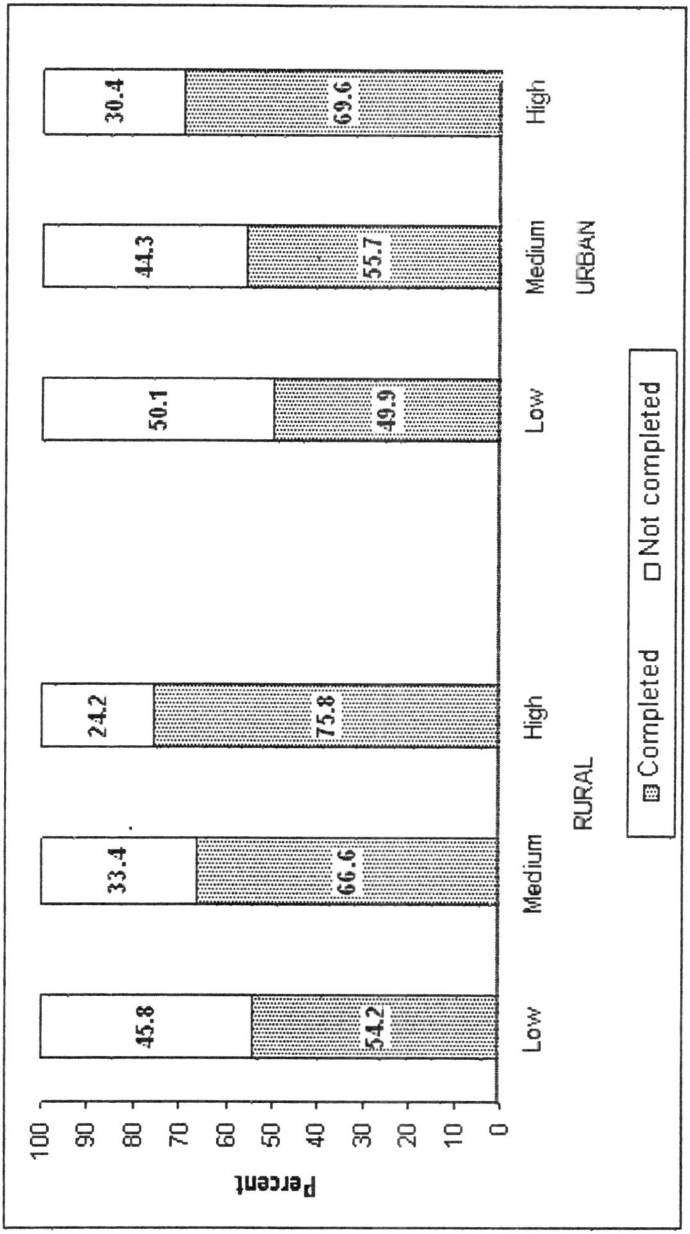

Figure 7.1 Fertility completion status of women by level of autonomy

time of the survey. Women's autonomy showed significantly positive effect on the fertility completion status of women in both rural and urban areas. It is found that in rural areas, the proportion of women who had completed their fertility increased from 54.2 per cent for low autonomy to 75.8 per cent for high autonomy women. In urban areas, the proportion of women who had completed their fertility increased from 56.9 per cent for low autonomy to 69.6 per cent for high autonomy women. The results show that the ability of women to take early decision about the number of children and adoption of family planning methods was significantly more among high autonomy women than others in both rural and urban areas.

7.2 Women's Autonomy, Fertility and Socio-economic Characteristics

In this study, the level of fertility is measured by the mean number of children ever born to women aged 15-29 years who reported to have completed their fertility by the time of the interview.

The mean number of children ever born to women who had completed their fertility by their level of autonomy and selected socio-economic characteristics are presented in Table 7.2.

The mean number of children ever born (CEB) was slightly higher in rural than in urban areas. It was 2.35 in rural and 2.31 in urban areas. Further, it is observed that, in rural areas, the mean number of CEB was comparatively low at 2.32 for women who had high autonomy compared to women who had low (2.36) and medium (2.38) autonomy. In urban areas also, the mean number of children ever born was low at 2.23 for high autonomy women compared to 2.28 for medium and 2.40 for low autonomy women (Figure 7.2). Though women's autonomy showed differences in the level of fertility in both rural and urban areas, the differences are more pronounced only in urban areas. The overall total sample also showed the influence of women's autonomy on fertility. The level of fertility consistently declined

Table 7.2 Mean number of children ever born to women aged 15-29 years who had completed their fertility by their level of autonomy and socio-economic characteristics

Socio-economic characteristics	*Rural*				*Urban*				*Total*			
	L-201	*M-255*	*H-338*	*T-794*	*L-228*	*M-245*	*H-211*	*T-684*	*L-429*	*M-500*	*H-549*	*T-1478*
All	**2.36**	**2.38**	**2.32**	**2.35**	**2.40**	**2.28**	**2.23**	**2.31**	**2.38**	**2.33**	**2.29**	**2.33**
Education of woman												
Illiterate	2.49	2.66	2.43	2.52	2.53	2.32	2.50	2.45	2.51	2.48	2.46	2.49
Literate & Primary	2.49	2.46	2.47	2.47	2.64	2.34	2.30	2.44	2.56	2.40	2.43	2.46
Middle (6-8)	2.39	2.32	2.29	2.32	2.33	2.23	2.33	2.29	2.36	2.27	2.30	2.31
High school (9-10)	2.14	2.38	2.31	2.29	2.29	2.28	2.19	2.25	2.22	2.33	2.26	2.27
Higher secondary & above	1.86	2.07	2.11	2.07	2.25	2.21	2.07	2.15	2.16	2.14	2.09	2.12
	F=267.120			P<0.000	F=5.579		P<0.000		F=12.776		P<0.000	
Education of husband												
Illiterate	2.47	2.35	2.50	2.45	2.50	2.43	2.31	2.42	2.49	2.38	2.46	2.44
Literate & Primary	2.41	2.48	2.39	2.42	2.54	2.31	2.32	2.39	2.47	2.40	2.37	2.41
Middle	2.26	2.39	2.42	2.36	2.47	2.32	2.14	2.33	2.37	2.36	2.31	2.35
High school (9-10)	2.40	2.43	2.19	2.32	2.38	2.29	2.22	2.29	2.39	2.36	2.20	2.31
Higher secondary & above	2.30	2.11	2.24	2.20	2.20	2.08	2.28	2.18	2.23	2.09	2.26	2.19
	F=2.291		P<0.058		F=2.657		P<0.032		F=5.170		P<0.000	

(Contd.)

(Contd. Table 7.2)

Socio-economic characteristics	*Rural*				*Urban*				*Total*			
	L-201	*M-255*	*H-338*	*T-794*	*L-228*	*M-245*	*H-211*	*T-684*	*L-429*	*M-500*	*H-549*	*T-1478*
Religion												
Hindu	2.37	2.39	2.32	2.36	2.41	2.26	2.23	2.30	2.39	2.33	2.28	2.33
Muslim	2.44	2.25	2.75	2.44	2.53	2.38	2.33	2.44	2.49	2.33	2.64	2.44
Christian	1.80	2.10	2.31	2.16	2.11	2.33	2.33	2.27	2.00	2.24	2.32	2.22
	F=1.619		P<0.199		F=1.324		P<0.267		F=2.292		P<0.101	
Community												
SC / ST	2.56	2.58	2.54	2.56	2.61	2.39	2.51	2.51	2.59	2.51	2.53	2.54
MBC	2.27	2.36	2.24	2.28	2.41	2.35	2.19	2.31	2.33	2.36	2.22	2.29
BC & others	2.30	2.23	2.23	2.25	2.31	2.20	2.15	2.22	2.31	2.21	2.19	2.24
	F=16.808		P<0.000		F=13.316		P<0.000		F=30.885		P<0.000	
Standard of living Index (SLI)												
Low	2.46	2.46	2.48	2.47	2.51	2.43	2.34	2.45	2.48	2.45	2.45	2.46
Medium	2.31	2.38	2.23	2.29	2.50	2.22	2.29	2.33	2.41	2.29	2.26	2.31
High	2.22	2.25	2.19	2.22	2.18	2.18	2.14	2.17	2.20	2.21	2.17	2.19
	F=10.126		P<0.000		F=14.522		P<0.000		F=24.039		P<0.000	

(Contd.)

(Contd. Table 5.7.2)

Socio-economic characteristics	Rural				Urban				Total			
	L-201	*M-255*	*H-338*	*T-794*	*L-228*	*M-245*	*H-211*	*T-684*	*L-429*	*M-500*	*H-549*	*T-1478*
Work status												
Not working	2.32	2.34	2.30	2.32	2.39	2.28	2.23	2.30	2.36	2.31	2.27	2.31
Working	2.50	2.54	2.36	2.43	2.47	2.23	2.24	2.31	2.49	2.43	2.34	2.39
	F=4.211		P<0.040		F=0.024		P<0.876		F=4.355		P<0.037	
Percent contribution to total income												
Nil	2.33	2.34	2.30	2.32	2.39	2.29	2.23	2.31	2.36	2.31	2.27	2.31
≤ 25 %	2.65	2.50	2.51	2.53	2.54	2.06	2.17	2.29	2.58	2.33	2.42	2.44
Above 25 %	2.36	2.58	2.25	2.34	2.17	2.43	2.29	2.32	2.32	2.53	2.26	2.33
	F=4.539		P<0.011		F=0.033		P<0.967		F=3.087		P<0.046	
Type of family												
Nuclear	2.38	2.43	2.33	2.38	2.46	2.34	2.25	2.34	2.42	2.39	2.30	2.36
Joint	2.34	2.27	2.31	2.32	2.33	2.19	2.21	2.24	2.34	2.23	2.27	2.28
	F=.1.879		P<0.171		F=4.974		P<0.026		F=6.407		P<0.011	

Figure 7.2 Mean number of children ever-born by level of autonomy

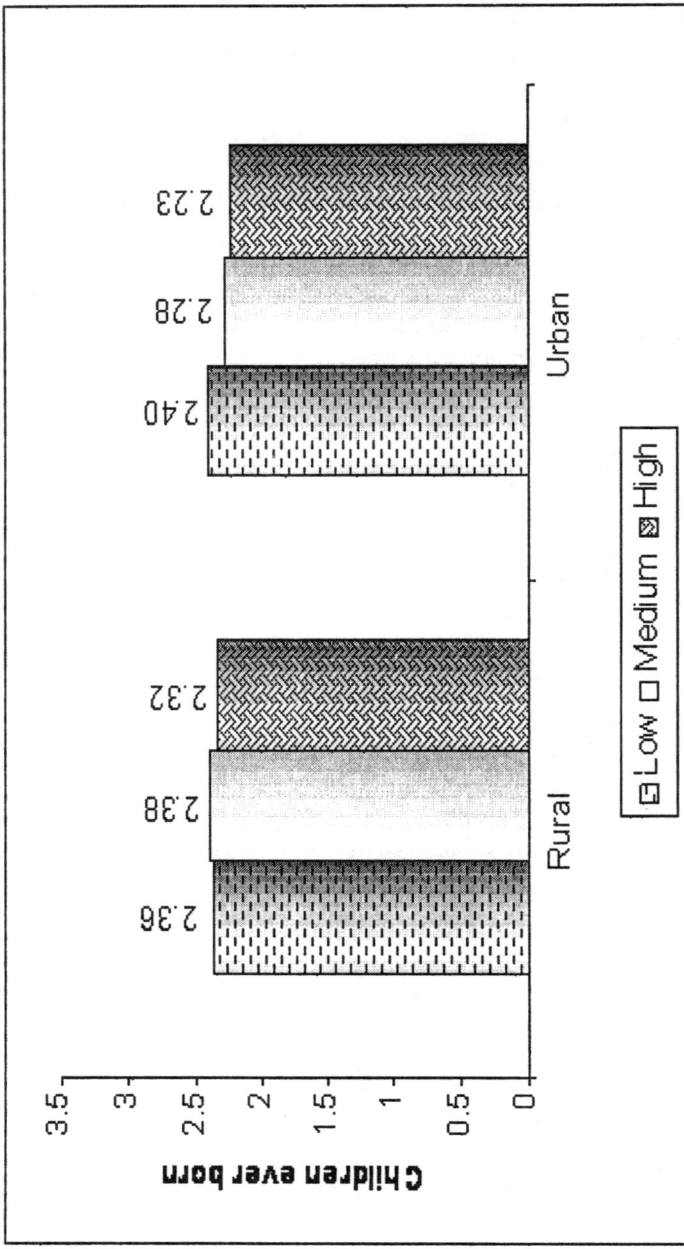

with increase in women's autonomy. The level of fertility measured based on the mean number of CEB was comparatively low at 2.29 for high autonomy women compared to 2.33 for medium and 2.38 for low autonomy women.

The results show that, in general, the level of fertility was comparatively low in urban than in rural areas. However, the difference is very negligible at 0.04 points. Autonomy of women showed negative effect on fertility in both rural and urban areas. But the effect of autonomy is more pronounced in urban than in rural areas.

Irrespective of the level of autonomy, education of women played an important role in reducing fertility in both rural and urban areas. In rural areas, the mean number of children ever born declined from 2.52 for illiterates to 2.07 for higher secondary and above educated respondents. In urban areas, the mean number of CEB significantly declined from 2.45 for illiterates to 2.15 for higher secondary and above educated respondents. The effect of education in reducing fertility was more in rural than in urban areas. The reduction of fertility was 0.45 points in rural compared to only 0.30 points in urban areas for the same level of education. In rural areas, low autonomy women with higher level of education had lower fertility whereas in urban areas high autonomy women with high level of education had lower fertility. In fact the level of fertility increased with autonomy among women who had higher secondary and above level of education in rural areas. On the other hand, the level of fertility declined with increase in autonomy among women who had higher secondary and above level of education in urban areas.

Education of husband showed significantly reducing effect on fertility in both rural and urban areas. In rural areas, the mean number of CEB declined from 2.45 for women who had illiterate husband to 2.20 for women who had husband with educational level of higher secondary and above. In urban areas, the mean number of CEB declined from 2.42 for women who had illiterate husband to 2.18 for women who had husband with educational level of higher secondary and above. Autonomy of women did not show any consistent relationship with fertility in rural areas. However, in urban areas, women's autonomy showed negative effect on fertility among all women except for those who had husband with educational level of higher secondary and above. At the higher secondary level, women's autonomy did not show any consistent pattern of relationship.

The mean number of CEB to women in rural areas was lowest at 2.16 for Christians compared to 2.36 for Hindus and 2.44 for Muslims. In urban areas also, Christians had lower fertility (2.27) than Hindus (2.30) and Muslims (2.44). High autonomy women among Hindus, medium autonomy women among Muslims and low autonomy women among Christians had significantly low fertility when compared to others in rural areas. In urban areas, the level of fertility declined with increase in the autonomy among Hindu and Muslim women. However, among Christian women, low autonomy women had significantly lower fertility than medium and high autonomy women.

Lower caste women (SC/ST) had higher fertility in both rural and urban areas. In rural areas, the mean number of CEB was significantly highest at 2.56 for SC/ST women compared to 2.28 for most backward caste women and 2.25 for backward and other caste women. In urban areas, the mean number of CEB was highest at 2.51 for SC/ST compared to 2.31 for Most Backward Caste (MBC) and 2.22 for backward and other caste women. High autonomy women had lower fertility among all caste groups in rural areas. However, in urban areas, it is true only for MBC and BC. Women's autonomy did not show any significant influence on fertility among SC/ST women in urban areas.

Improvement in standard of living is generally believed to effect lower fertility. The results of the study confirmed the notion of 'the higher the socio-economic status, the lower the fertility'. The mean number of CEB declined with the increase in the Standard of Living Index (SLI). In rural areas, the mean number of CEB was highest at 2.47 for women who had low SLI compared to 2.29 for medium and 2.22 for high SLI. In urban areas also, standard of living played a vital role in reducing fertility. The mean number of CEB declined significantly from 2.45 for low SLI to 2.17 for high SLI. High autonomy women had lower fertility only among those who had medium and high standard of living in rural areas and among low and high standard of living women in urban areas. Though the level of autonomy showed significant association with standard of living index, no systematic pattern of relationship is observed between them in rural areas.

Women's involvement in income earning economic activities showed significant influence on fertility. Women involved in income earning economic activities had more number of CEB than those who were not involved in any economic activities in both rural and urban areas. In rural areas, the mean number of CEB was 2.43 for women involved in economic activities compared to only 2.32 observed for women not involved in economic activities. In rural areas, irrespective of the work status, high autonomy women had lower fertility than the low and medium autonomy women. In urban areas, women's autonomy did not make any significant difference in the level of fertility among working and non-working women. Irrespective of the work status, low autonomy women in urban areas had significantly higher fertility than medium and high autonomy women.

The contribution of women to the total family income showed significant difference in the mean number of CEB in rural areas. The mean number of CEB was lowest at 2.32 for women who did not contribute anything to family income compared to women who contributed up to 25 per cent to the total income (2.53) and women who contributed more than 25 per cent to the total family income (2.34). In urban areas, the mean number of CEB was slightly higher at 2.32 for women who contributed more than 25 per cent to the total family income compared to 2.29 for women who contributed up to 25 per cent to the total income and 2.31 for women who did not contribute anything to the family income. In rural areas, high autonomy women had lower fertility among those who did not contribute anything to the family income and among those who contributed more than 25 per cent to the total family income. In urban areas, autonomy of women did not show any consistent relationship with the level of fertility.

Women in nuclear family had more number of CEB compared to women in joint family in both rural and urban areas. In rural areas, the mean number of CEB was 2.38 for women in nuclear family compared to 2.32 for women in joint family. In urban areas, the mean number of children ever born was higher at 2.34 for women in nuclear family compared to 2.24 for women in joint family. High autonomy women in nuclear family had lower fertility than low and medium autonomy women in rural and urban areas. Thus autonomy of women showed significant influence on fertility among women in nuclear family in both rural and urban areas.

The results indicate that education of women is an important and independent factor in reducing fertility in both rural and urban areas. Women's autonomy did not make significant difference in the level of fertility in rural areas. However, in urban areas, women's autonomy showed significantly negative effect on fertility. Muslim women had higher fertility than others in both rural and urban areas. Lower caste women (SC/ST) in both rural and urban areas had high fertility compared to others. Standard of living showed negative effect on fertility in both rural and urban areas. Surprisingly, working women had higher fertility in rural areas while not much difference is observed in urban areas. Women in nuclear family had higher fertility than women in joint family in both rural and urban areas. High autonomy women in nuclear family had lower fertility in both rural and urban areas.

7.3 Women's Autonomy, Fertility and Demographic Characteristics

The mean number of children ever born to women who had completed their fertility by their level of autonomy and

Table 7.3 Mean number of children ever born to women aged 15-29 years who had completed their fertility by their level of autonomy and demographic characteristics

Demographic characteristics	*Rural*				*Urban*				*Total*			
	L	*M*	*H*	*T*	*L*	*M*	*H*	*T*	*L*	*M*	*H*	*T*
All	**2.36**	**2.38**	**2.33**	**2.35**	**2.40**	**2.28**	**2.23**	**2.31**	**2.38**	**2.33**	**2.29**	**2.33**
Age (years)												
≤ 19	1.75	2.00	2.33	2.00	2.14	2.00	2.00	2.11	2.00	2.00	2.25	2.06
20 – 24	2.18	2.16	2.12	2.15	2.31	2.27	2.26	2.28	2.25	2.21	2.17	2.22
25 – 29	2.49	2.51	2.40	2.45	2.50	2.29	2.23	2.32	2.49	2.40	2.33	2.40
	F=19.645		P<0.000		F=0.945		P<0.389		F=15.605		P<0.000	
Age at marriage (years)												
≤ 16	2.81	2.46	2.60	2.62	2.80	2.50	2.44	2.60	2.81	2.47	2.56	2.62
17 – 18	2.27	2.59	2.47	2.46	2.55	2.33	2.33	2.41	2.41	2.46	2.43	2.44
19 – 20	2.37	2.26	2.17	2.25	2.27	2.29	2.25	2.27	2.31	2.28	2.21	2.26
21 – 22	2.15	2.26	2.04	2.15	2.31	2.18	2.07	2.18	2.25	2.22	2.05	2.16
23 +	1.91	1.80	2.00	1.89	2.00	1.88	2.06	1.98	1.97	1.84	2.04	1.94
	F=16.416		P<0.000		F=13.431		P<0.000		F=20.315		P<0.000	

(Contd.)

(Contd. Table 7.3)

Demographic characteristics	*Rural*				*Urban*				*Total*			
	L	*M*	*H*	*T*	*L*	*M*	*H*	*T*	*L*	*M*	*H*	*T*
Husband-wife age difference (years)												
≤ 4	2.26	2.40	2.34	2.34	2.47	2.39	2.21	2.36	2.38	2.39	2.29	2.35
5 – 8	2.48	2.36	2.33	2.38	2.43	2.26	2.24	2.31	2.45	2.32	2.29	2.35
9 +	2.30	2.39	2.30	2.33	2.29	2.16	2.25	2.23	2.29	2.27	2.28	2.28
	F=0.417		P<0.659		F=2.722		P<0.066		F=1.527		P<0.218	
Number of male children												
0	2.25	2.21	2.14	2.19	2.38	2.13	2.11	2.21	2.31	2.17	2.13	2.20
1	2.27	2.29	2.27	2.28	2.34	2.17	2.20	2.24	2.31	2.24	2.25	2.26
2+	2.60	2.61	2.51	2.57	2.51	2.52	2.35	2.46	2.55	2.56	2.45	2.56
	F=19.508		P<0.000		F=13.284		P<0.000		F=32.259		P<0.000	
Number of female children												
0	2.14	2.11	2.06	2.10	2.10	2.07	2.17	2.12	2.12	2.09	2.11	2.11
1	2.20	2.23	2.21	2.21	2.31	2.28	2.14	2.24	2.26	2.25	2.18	2.23
2+	2.81	2.83	2.74	2.79	2.81	2.45	2.50	2.60	2.81	2.65	2.66	2.70
	F=85.867		P<0.000		F=38.531		P<0.000		F=123.021		P<0.000	

selected demographic characteristics is presented in Table 7.3. The mean number of children ever born increased with age in both rural and urban areas. In rural areas, the mean number of CEB increased from 2.00 for women aged 19 years or less to 2.45 for women aged 25-29 years. In urban areas, the mean number of CEB increased from 2.11 for women aged 19 years or less to 2.32 for women aged 25-29 years. The results indicate that younger women had lower fertility than older women in both rural and urban areas. In rural areas, among women aged 19 years or less, low autonomy women had lower fertility than medium and high autonomy women. However, among women aged 20-24 and 25-29 years, high autonomy women had lower fertility than low and medium autonomy women. In urban areas, high autonomy women among all age groups had lower fertility than others. However, the differences are not statistically significant. Increase in age at marriage significantly decreased fertility in both rural and urban areas. In rural areas, the mean number of CEB declined from 2.62 for women married at ages 16 years or less to 1.89 for women married at ages 23 years or more. In urban areas also, the mean number of CEB declined significantly from 2.60 for women married at ages 16 years or less to 1.98 for women married at ages 23 years or more. In rural areas, high autonomy women had lower fertility than low and medium autonomy women only among those who had married at ages 19-20 and 21-22 years. In urban areas, high autonomy women had lower fertility among women married at all ages except among those who had married at ages 23 years or more.

Husband-wife age difference did not make any significant difference in the level of fertility in rural areas. However, in urban areas, the mean number of CEB declined consistently with increase in husband-wife age difference. It decreased from 2.36 for the age difference of 4 years or less to 2.23 for the age difference of 9 years or more. While the autonomy of women did not make significant difference in the level of fertility among women in rural areas, it had significantly negative effect on fertility in urban areas among women who had the husband-wife age difference of 4 years or less and 5-8 years.

The number of CEB increased with the number of male children in both rural and urban areas. Among those who had no male child, the mean number of children ever born decreased with increase was autonomy in both rural and urban areas. High autonomy women had lower fertility only among those who had no male child and among those who had two or more number of male children in both rural and urban areas.

The number of children ever born increased with the number of female children in both rural and urban areas. The increase was observed to be more for female children compared to the increase observed for male children in both rural and urban areas. Autonomy of women showed negative effect on fertility only for those who had no female child in rural areas. In urban areas, autonomy of women showed negative effect on fertility only for those who had one female child.

Overall, the results indicate that among the women who had completed their fertility, younger women (aged 19 years or less) had lower fertility than older women (aged 20-29 years) in both rural and urban areas. Increase in age at marriage decrease fertility in both rural and urban areas. Women's autonomy showed significant influence on fertility only among women who got married at ages 19-20 and 21-22 years in rural areas. While the husband-wife age difference did not make any difference in the level of fertility in rural areas, it had negative effect on fertility in urban areas. Women who had more number of female children (2+) had higher fertility compared to women who had more number of male children (2+).

7.4 Women's Autonomy, Fertility and Marital Characteristics

The mean number of CEB by their level of autonomy and marital characteristics is presented in Table 7.4. The level of fertility was slightly higher among women who had

Table 7.4 Mean number of children ever born to women aged 15-29 years who had completed their fertility by their level of autonomy and Marital characteristics

Marital characteristics	*Rural*				*Urban*				*Total*			
	L	*M*	*H*	*T*	*L*	*M*	*H*	*T*	*L*	*M*	*H*	*T*
All	**2.36**	**2.38**	**2.33**	**2.35**	**2.40**	**2.28**	**2.23**	**2.31**	**2.38**	**2.33**	**2.29**	**2.33**
Type of marriage												
Consanguineous	2.43	2.41	2.29	2.36	2.43	2.33	2.20	2.32	2.43	2.37	2.26	2.34
Non-consanguineous	2.33	2.36	2.35	2.35	2.39	2.25	2.25	2.30	2.36	2.31	2.31	2.32
	F=0.068		P<0.794		F=0.357		P< 0.550		F=0.299		P<0.585	
Consanguineous type												
Maternal	2.47	2.42	2.29	2.37	2.30	2.30	2.13	2.23	2.38	2.35	2.22	2.31
Paternal	2.37	2.41	2.29	2.35	2.58	2.36	2.32	2.42	2.48	2.38	2.30	2.38
	F=0.089		P<0.766		F=6.296		P<0.013		F=1.826		P<0.177	

(Contd.)

(Contd. Table 5.7.4)

Marital characteristics	*Rural*				*Urban*				*Total*			
	L	*M*	*H*	*T*	*L*	*M*	*H*	*T*	*L*	*M*	*H*	*T*
Kind of marriage												
Love marriage	2.50	2.70	2.43	2.53	2.32	2.43	2.31	2.36	2.40	2.56	2.39	2.45
Arranged marriage	2.35	2.34	2.31	2.33	2.41	2.26	2.22	2.30	2.38	2.30	2.28	2.32
	F=6.939		P<0.009		F=0.641		P< 0.424		F=6.556		P<0.011	
Inter caste / inter religious marriage												
Same caste	2.36	2.37	2.34	2.36	2.42	2.26	2.22	2.30	2.39	2.32	2.30	2.33
Inter-caste / inter-religious marriages	2.36	2.48	2.15	2.31	2.20	2.43	2.30	2.32	2.27	2.45	2.22	2.31
	F=0.322		P<0.571		F=0.053		P< 0.818		F=0.097		P<0.755	

L: Low M: Medium H: High T: Total

consanguineous marriage than among those who had non-consanguineous marriage in both rural and urban areas. Autonomy of women showed negative effect on fertility only among women who had consanguineous marriage in both rural and urban areas. However, the differences are not significant in both rural and urban areas.

Women who had married a person from the maternal side had slightly higher fertility than those who had married a person from the paternal side in rural areas. However, the differences are not statistically significant. In urban areas, women who had married a person from the paternal side had significantly higher fertility than those who had married a person from the maternal side. Women's autonomy showed negative effect on fertility only among women who had married a person from the maternal side in rural areas. However, in urban areas, women's autonomy showed significantly negative effect on fertility among women who had married a person from the paternal side.

Women who had arranged marriage had less number of CEB compared to those who had love marriage in both rural and urban areas. Irrespective of the kind of marriage, high autonomy women in both rural and urban areas had lower fertility than others. However, the differences are significant only in rural areas.

While fertility was more among women who had same caste marriage in rural areas, it was more among women who had inter-caste / inter-religious marriage in urban areas. High autonomy women had lower fertility among all women in rural areas. In urban areas, high autonomy women had lower fertility only among women who had same caste marriage.

Overall, the results showed that in rural areas women's autonomy did not make any significant difference in fertility for any of the marital characteristics variables except for the kind of marriage where women who had arranged marriage had lower fertility than women who had love marriage and high autonomy women had lower fertility than low and medium autonomy women for both love marriage and arranged marriage. In urban areas, autonomy of women did not make any significant difference in fertility for any of the marital characteristics variables except for consanguineous type where the fertility was significantly high among women who had married a person from the paternal side compared to women who had married a person from the maternal side and the fertility was also negatively associated with autonomy of women.

7.5 Women's Autonomy, Fertility and Exposure to Mass Media

The mean number of children ever born to women by their level of autonomy and exposure to mass media is presented in Table 7.5. Exposure of women to various mass media such as listening to radio at least once a week, watching television at least once a week, going to movies at least once a month and reading newspapers / magazines showed profound negative effect on fertility in both rural and urban areas. The overall combined index of mass media indicates that women who had high level of exposure to mass media had lower fertility compared to those who had no exposure or low level of exposure in both rural and urban areas. Autonomy of women showed negative effect on fertility among women who had the habit of listening to radio and watching television in both rural and urban areas. In general, women's autonomy showed significant difference in the level of fertility among women who had exposure to various mass media in both rural and urban areas.

The mean number of children ever born was more among members of SHG than non-members in both rural and urban areas. However, the differences are significant only for women in rural areas. Autonomy of women showed negative effect on fertility in both rural and urban areas. However, the effect is significant only for rural areas.

Table 7.5 Mean number of children ever born to women aged 15-29 years who had completed their fertility by their level of autonomy and exposure to mass media

Exposure to mass media	*Rural*				*Urban*				*Total*			
	L	*M*	*H*	*T*	*L*	*M*	*H*	*T*	*L*	*M*	*H*	*T*
All	**2.36**	**2.38**	**2.33**	**2.35**	**2.40**	**2.28**	**2.23**	**2.31**	**2.38**	**2.33**	**2.29**	**2.33**
Listening to radio												
Yes	2.33	2.31	2.28	2.30	2.33	2.21	2.18	2.23	2.33	2.26	2.24	2.27
No	2.34	2.49	2.40	2.43	2.46	2.36	2.30	2.38	2.43	2.42	2.36	2.40
	F=6.972		P<0.008		F=11.493		P<0.001		F=16.605		P<0.000	
Watching television												
Yes	2.37	2.34	2.34	2.35	2.38	2.28	2.23	2.29	2.37	2.31	2.30	2.32
No	2.32	2.63	2.24	2.37	2.65	2.30	2.23	2.41	2.47	2.48	2.24	2.40
	F=0.423		P<0.516		F=2.422		P<0.120		F=2.251		P<0.134	
Going to movies												
Yes	2.50	2.08	2.24	2.23	2.23	2.35	2.19	2.25	2.33	2.22	2.21	2.24
No	2.35	2.42	2.34	2.37	2.43	2.26	2.25	2.32	2.39	2.35	2.31	2.35
	F=3.796		P<0.052		F=1.249		P<0.264		F=5.141		P<0.024	

(Contd.)

(Contd. Table 7.5)

Exposure to mass media	Rural				Urban				Total			
	L	*M*	*H*	*T*	*L*	*M*	*H*	*T*	*L*	*M*	*H*	*T*
Reading newspapers / magazines												
Yes	2.29	2.18	2.25	2.23	2.21	2.16	2.17	2.18	2.25	2.17	2.21	2.21
No	2.39	2.49	2.38	2.42	2.47	2.33	2.29	2.37	2.43	2.40	2.35	2.40
	F=13.956		P<0.000		F=18.463		P<0.000		F=31.050		P<0.000	
Mass media index												
No exposure	2.11	2.75	2.37	2.36	2.85	2.38	2.50	2.60	2.41	2.56	2.40	2.45
Low exposure	2.41	2.47	2.37	2.41	2.42	2.30	2.25	2.33	2.41	2.38	2.32	2.37
High exposure	2.31	2.14	2.25	2.22	2.24	2.19	2.20	2.21	2.27	2.16	2.23	2.22
	F=6.667		P<0.001		F=7.168		P<0.001		F=11.048		P<0.000	
Membership in SHG												
Yes	2.46	2.43	2.35	2.39	2.49	2.30	2.27	2.33	2.47	2.39	2.33	2.37
No	2.32	2.32	2.25	2.31	2.38	2.29	2.20	2.30	2.36	2.29	2.22	2.30
	F=2.741		P<0.098		F=0.313		P<0.576		F=4.118		P<0.043	

L: Low M: Medium H: High T: Total

7.6 Age at First Birth

The percent distribution of women who had completed their fertility by age at first birth and level of autonomy is presented in Table 7.6. Substantially higher proportion of women in rural areas had their first birth at younger ages (19 years or less) compared to urban women. The proportion of women who had their first birth at ages 19 years or less was substantially higher at 43.6 per cent in rural compared to only 33.8 per cent in urban areas.

In rural areas, the level of autonomy did not show any systematic variation in the proportion of women who had their first birth at ages 19 years or less. In fact, a higher proportion of high autonomy women in rural areas (45.8 per cent) had their first birth at 19 years or less. In urban areas, the proportion of women who had their first birth at younger ages (d"19 years) decreased significantly with the increase in the level of autonomy of women. It decreased from 39.1 per cent for low autonomy women to 25.1 per cent for high autonomy women. While the mean age at first birth was staggering around 20 years for all women in rural areas, it increased from 20.37 years for low autonomy women to 20.71 years for high autonomy women in urban areas.

Overall, the results showed that women's autonomy significantly reduced child birth at younger ages in urban areas and it did not show any systematic pattern in rural areas.

7.7 Age at Last Birth

The percent distribution of women by their age at last birth and autonomy status is presented in Table 7.7. The majority of women in both rural and urban areas had completed their fertility by the age of 24 years. The proportion of women who had completed their fertility by the age of 24 years was comparatively higher in rural (69.8 per cent) than in urban areas (62.8 per cent). While the autonomy of women did not show any significant association with age at last birth in rural areas, it

Table 7.6 Percent distribution of women aged 15-29 years by their age at first birth and level of autonomy

Age at first birth (years)	*Rural*				*Urban*				*Total*			
	L-201	*M-255*	*H-338*	*T-794*	*L-228*	*M-245*	*H-211*	*T-684*	*L-429*	*M-500*	*H-549*	*T-1478*
? 19	44.3	40.0	45.8	43.6	39.1	36.4	25.1	33.8	41.5	38.2	37.9	39.0
20+	55.7	60.0	54.2	56.5	61.0	63.7	74.6	62.7	56.5	61.8	62.1	60.9
Mean	19.86	20.09	19.87	19.94	20.37	20.38	20.71	20.48	20.13	20.24	20.19	20.19
Significance	χ^2=10.90 DF-6 P<0.091				χ^2=12.519 DF-6 P<0.051				χ^2=6.104 DF-6 P<0.412			

L: Low M: Medium H: High T: Total

Table 7.7 Percent distribution of women who had completed their fertility according to their level of autonomy and age at last birth

Age at last birth (years)	*Rural*				*Urban*				*Total*			
	L-201	*M-255*	*H-338*	*T-794*	*L-228*	*M-245*	*H-211*	*T-684*	*L-429*	*M-500*	*H-549*	*T-1478*
≤ 19	7.5	6.3	4.7	5.9	2.2	2.0	2.8	2.3	4.7	4.2	4.0	4.3
20 - 24	63.2	60.8	66.6	63.9	63.6	64.9	52.1	60.5	63.4	62.8	61.0	62.3
25 – 29	29.4	32.9	28.7	30.2	34.2	33.1	45.0	37.1	31.9	33.0	35.0	33.4
Mean	23.13	23.41	23.21	23.26	23.59	23.51	24.02	23.69	23.38	23.46	23.52	23.46
Significance	χ^2=3.380 DF-4 P<0.496				χ^2= 9.084 DF-4 P<0.059				χ^2=1.203 DF-4 P<0.878			

L: Low M: Medium H: High T: Total

showed significant influence on the age at last birth in urban areas.

The mean age at last birth did not vary much due to the autonomy of women in rural areas and it was staggering around 23 years for women at all levels of autonomy. However in urban areas, significantly higher proportion of low (65.8 per cent) and medium (66.9 per cent) autonomy women had completed their fertility by the age of 24 years than those who had high level of autonomy (54.9 per cent). The mean age at last birth was significantly high at 24.02 years for high autonomy women compared to 23.59 years for low and 23.51 years for medium autonomy women.

7.8 Number of Living Children

The percent distribution of women who had completed their fertility by number of living children and level of autonomy is presented in Table 7.8. The proportion of women who had three or more number of living children was comparatively higher in rural (29.7 per cent) than in urban areas (26 per cent). The proportion of women who had only one living child was also higher in rural (4.7 per cent) than in urban areas (2.5 per cent). Women's autonomy did not make any significant difference in the number of living children in rural areas. However, in urban areas, the proportion of women who had three or more number of living children decreased significantly with the increase in autonomy. It decreased from 32.9 per cent for women who had low level of autonomy to 19.9 per cent for high autonomy women. The results indicate a comparatively lower level of fertility among high autonomy women in urban areas. While the mean number of living children did not vary much due to autonomy of women in rural areas, it decreased significantly from 2.29 for low autonomy to 2.18 for high autonomy women in urban areas.

Overall, the results showed that women's autonomy was having significantly negative effect on higher order births (3+) only in urban areas. It also showed significantly negative effect on the total number of living children in urban areas.

Table 7.8 Percent distribution of women by number of living children and their level of autonomy

Number of living children	*Rural*				*Urban*				*Total*			
	L-201	*M-255*	*H-338*	*T-794*	*L-228*	*M-245*	*H-211*	*T-684*	*L-429*	*M-500*	*H-549*	*T-1478*
1	5.5	4.7	4.1	4.7	3.1	2.0	2.4	2.5	4.2	3.4	3.5	3.7
2	64.7	65.9	66.0	65.6	64.0	73.1	77.7	71.5	64.3	69.4	70.5	68.3
3 +	29.9	29.4	29.9	29.7	32.9	24.9	19.9	26.0	31.5	27.2	26.0	28.0
Mean	2.24	2.25	2.26	2.25	2.29	2.22	2.18	2.24	2.27	2.23	2.22	2.24
Significance	χ^2=0.529 DF-4 P<0.971				χ^2=10.815 DF-4 P<0.029				χ^2=4.654 DF-4 P<0.325			

L: Low M: Medium H: High T: Total

7.9 Number of Male Children

The results of the analysis of data on the number of male children by the level of autonomy of women are presented in Table 7.9. The results show that in both rural and urban areas, a substantially higher proportion of women (around 16 per cent) had completed their fertility without a male child. The results indicated that irrespective of the level of autonomy, women's desire for male child decreased significantly in both rural and urban areas. The proportion of women who had completed their fertility without a male child decreased with the increase in the level of women's autonomy in rural areas. However, no such trend was observed in urban areas.

7.10 Number of Abortions

The percent distribution of women by number of abortions and level of autonomy is presented in Table 7.10. The results show that the proportion of women who had experienced at least one abortion was more in rural than in urban areas. The proportion of women who reported to have had at least one abortion was 19.6 per cent in rural and 17.1 per cent in urban areas. A higher proportion of high autonomy women in both rural and urban areas had experienced abortion than others. The mean number of abortions was also higher among high autonomy women than among those who had low and medium level of autonomy. However, the differences are not statistically significant in both rural and urban areas.

7.11 Induced Abortion

The percent distribution of women who had completed their fertility according to number of induced abortions and autonomy status is presented in Table 7.11. The proportion of women who had at least one induced abortion was nearly the same (around 8 per cent) in both rural and urban areas. It was more among high autonomy women compared to low and medium autonomy women in both rural and urban areas. In

Table 7.9 Percent distribution of women by number of male children and their level of autonomy

Number of male children	*Rural*				*Urban*				*Total*			
	L-201	*M-255*	*H-338*	*T-794*	*L-228*	*M-245*	*H-211*	*T-684*	*L-429*	*M-500*	*H-549*	*T-1478*
0	18.9	16.5	14.8	16.4	14.9	18.4	16.1	16.5	16.8	17.4	15.3	16.4
1	48.3	49.8	53.3	50.9	48.7	48.2	48.8	48.5	48.5	49.0	51.5	49.8
2	27.9	27.8	27.8	27.8	31.1	29.4	30.3	30.3	29.6	28.6	28.8	29.0
3 +	32.9	33.7	31.9	32.7	36.4	33.5	35.0	35.0	34.7	33.6	33.2	33.8
Mean	**1.10**	**1.14**	**1.16**	**1.14**	**1.18**	**1.14**	**1.16**	**1.16**	**1.14**	**1.14**	**1.16**	**1.15**
Significance	χ^2=2.907	DF-6	P<0.820		χ^2=1.371	DF-6	P<0.968		χ^2=1.732	DF= 6	P<0.94	

L: Low M: Medium H: High T: Total

Table 7.10 Percent distribution of women by total number of abortions and their level of autonomy

Total number of abortions	*Rural*				*Urban*				*Total*			
	L=201	*M=255*	*H=338*	*T=794*	*L=228*	*M=245*	*H=211*	*T=684*	*L=429*	*M=500*	*H=549*	*T=1478*
0	82.6	82.7	77.2	80.4	83.3	84.5	80.6	82.9	83.0	83.6	78.5	81.5
1	15.4	12.5	17.5	15.4	14.5	12.7	16.1	14.3	14.9	12.6	16.9	14.9
2	1.5	4.3	4.7	3.8	1.8	2.4	2.8	2.3	1.6	3.4	4.0	3.1
3 +	0.5	0.4	0.6	0.5	0.4	0.4	0.5	0.4	0.5	4.0	0.5	0.5
Mean	**0.20**	**0.22**	**0.29**	**0.25**	**0.19**	**0.19**	**0.23**	**0.21**	**0.20**	**0.20**	**0.27**	**0.23**
Significance	χ^2=6.902	DF-6	P<0.330		χ^2=1.758	DF -6	P<0.941		χ^2=8.988	DF-6	P<0.174	

L: Low M: Medium H: High T: Total

Table 7.11 Percent distribution of women by number of induced abortion and their level of autonomy

Number of induced abortion	*Rural*				*Urban*				*Total*			
	L-201	*M-255*	*H-338*	*T-794*	*L-228*	*M-245*	*H-211*	*T-684*	*L-429*	*M-500*	*H-549*	*T-1478*
0	92.5	92.9	89.9	91.6	91.7	93.5	90.0	91.8	92.1	93.2	90.0	91.7
1	7.0	5.5	8.0	6.9	7.9	5.7	7.6	7.0	7.5	5.6	7.8	7.0
2 +	0.5	1.6	2.1	1.5	0.4	0.8	2.4	1.10	0.5	1.2	2.2	1.4
Mean	**0.08**	**0.09**	**0.12**	**0.10**	**0.09**	**0.08**	**0.12**	**0.10**	**0.08**	**0.08**	**0.12**	**0.10**
Significance	χ^2=3.554	DF -4		P<0.470	χ^2=4.986		DF -4	P<0.289	χ^2=7.77	DF- 4		P<0.100

L: Low M: Medium H: High T: Total

general, high autonomy women had more number of induced abortions than others in both rural and urban areas.

7.12 Spontaneous Abortion

The percent distribution of women who had experienced spontaneous abortion by their level of autonomy is presented in Table 7.12. The proportion of women who had experienced spontaneous abortion was higher in rural (12.3 per cent) than in urban areas (9.5 per cent). A higher proportion of high autonomy women had experienced spontaneous abortion than others in both rural and urban areas. It was highest at 14.5 per cent for high autonomy women compared to 10.4 per cent for low and 11 per cent for medium autonomy women in rural areas. In urban areas, it was highest at 12.8 per cent for high autonomy women compared to 10.8 per cent for low autonomy and 10.2 per cent for medium autonomy women.

7.13 Reproductive Span

In this study the reproductive span is defined as the diffference between age at marriage and age at last birth of a woman who had completed her fertility on the date of survey. The percent distribution of women by their reproductive span (child bearing years) and autonomy status is presented in Table 7.13. The proportion of women who had longer period of child bearing (7 years or more) was higher in rural (19.0 per cent) than in urban areas (13.3 per cent). The mean duration of child bearing was 4.74 years in rural and 4.51 years in urban areas. The mean duration of child bearing increased with women's autonomy in both rural and urban areas. However, the differences are not significant in both rural and urban areas.

7.14 Birth Interval

The mean duration of birth interval between different orders of birth by women's autonomy is presented in Table 7.14. The mean duration of birth interval between different orders of birth did not vary much in both rural and urban areas. The

Table 7.12 Percent distribution of women by number of spontaneous abortion by their level of autonomy

Number of spontaneous abortion	*Rural*				*Urban*				*Total*			
	L-201	*M-255*	*H-338*	*T-794*	*L-228*	*M-245*	*H-211*	*T-684*	*L-429*	*M-500*	*H-549*	*T-1478*
0	89.6	89.0	85.5	87.7	90.8	90.6	90.0	90.5	90.2	89.8	87.2	89.0
1	9.5	8.3	12.4	10.2	8.3	7.8	8.5	8.2	8.9	8.0	10.9	9.3
2 +	1.0	2.7	2.1	2.1	0.8	1.6	1.4	1.3	1.0	2.2	1.9	1.7
Mean	**0.12**	**0.13**	**0.17**	**0.15**	**0.11**	**0.11**	**0.12**	**0.11**	**0.14**	**0.14**	**0.17**	**0.15**
Significantly	χ^2=4.704 DF-4 P<0.319				χ^2=0.638 DF-4 P<0.959				χ^2=5.129 DF-4 P<0.274			

L: Low M: Medium H: High T: Total

Table 7.13 Percent distribution of women by number of years of child bearing and level of autonomy

Reproductive span (years)	*Rural*				*Urban*				*Total*			
	L-201	*M-255*	*H-338*	*T-794*	*L-228*	*M-245*	*H-211*	*T-684*	*L-429*	*M-500*	*H-549*	*T-1478*
≤ 3	29.4	30.2	31.4	30.5	34.2	35.5	31.3	33.8	31.9	32.8	31.3	32.0
4 – 6	53.7	50.6	48.5	50.5	51.3	54.3	53.1	52.9	52.4	52.4	50.3	51.6
7 – 9	14.4	17.3	17.5	16.6	13.2	8.6	14.2	11.8	13.8	13.0	16.2	14.4
10+	2.5	2.0	2.7	2.4	1.3	1.6	1.4	1.5	1.9	1.8	2.2	2.0
Mean (years)	4.66	4.76	4.77	4.74	4.50	4.48	4.62	4.51	4.58	4.60	4.72	4.64
Significance	χ^2= 3.148 DF-4 P<0.533				χ^2 = 4.445 DF-6 P<0.615				χ^2 = 2.768 DF-6 P<0.837			

L: Low M: Medium H: High T: Total

Table 7.14 Mean duration of birth interval by women's autonomy

Birth order	*Rural*				*Urban*				*Total*			
	L	*M*	*H*	*T*	*L*	*M*	*H*	*T*	*L*	*M*	*H*	*T*
1st and 2nd birth	28.52	28.38	28.39	28.42	26.76	29.35	21.25	29.58	27.58	28.86	29.50	28.73
2nd and 3rd birth	29.94	26.57	29.55	28.71	26.58	26.97	28.48	27.19	28.13	26.73	29.22	28.07
3rd and 4th birth	24.70	27.33	26.09	26.31	27.10	21.33	26.50	25.11	25.90	25.83	26.15	25.93
4th and 5th birth	23.00	27.33	27.50	26.67	27.50	24.00	----	26.33	26.00	26.50	27.50	28.56

L: Low M: Medium H: High T: Total

mean duration of birth interval was more than 24 months for all births in both rural and urban areas. Women's autonomy did not make significant difference in the mean duration of birth interval in both rural and urban areas.

7.15 Child Loss

The child loss experience of women by their level of autonomy is presented in Table 7.15. The child loss experienced by women was assessed based on the difference between the mean number of children ever born and surviving. The mean number of children died was higher in rural than in urban areas. It was 0.12 per woman in rural and 0.07 per woman in urban areas. Women's autonomy did not make any difference in the mean number of children died in rural areas whereas in urban areas low autonomy women had experienced more child loss than medium and high autonomy women.

7.16 Effect of Selected Background Characteristics of Women on Number of Children Ever Born

The results of the regression analysis showing the effect of various background characteristics of women on the number of children ever born and selected background characteristics of the women are presented in Table 7.16. In rural areas, the number of children ever born was positively affected by marital duration and love marriage and negatively affected by percent contribution to the total family income, standard of living and autonomy of women. In urban areas, the number of children ever born was positively affected by marital duration and negatively affected by per cent contribution to the total family income, husband-wife age difference, exposure to mass media, standard of living and autonomy of women. The analysis of the overall total sample showed that the number of children ever born was positively affected by marital duration and love marriage and negatively affected by percent contribution to the total family income, husband-wife age difference, exposure to mass media, standard of living and the autonomy of women.

Table 7.15 Mean number of children ever born and surviving to women who had completed their fertility according to their level of autonomy

Mean	*Rural*				*Urban*				*Total*			
	L-201	*M-255*	*H-338*	*T-794*	*L-228*	*M-245*	*H-211*	*T-684*	*L-429*	*M-500*	*H-549*	*T-1478*
Children ever born	2.36	2.37	2.38	2.37	2.40	2.28	2.23	2.31	2.38	2.33	2.29	2.33
Children surviving	2.24	2.25	2.26	2.25	2.30	2.23	2.18	2.24	2.27	2.24	2.26	2.24
Child loss	**0.12**	**0.12**	**0.12**	**0.12**	**0.10**	**0.05**	**0.05**	**0.07**	**0.11**	**0.09**	**0.03**	**0.09**

L: Low M: Medium H: High T: Total

Table 7.16 Regression model showing the effect of selected background characteristics of women on children ever born

Background characteristics	*Rural*			*Urban*			*Total*		
	Parameter	*SE*	*p-value*	*Parameter*	*SE*	*p-value*	*Parameter*	*SE*	*p-value*
(Constant)	1.523	0.235	0.000	1.670	0.209	0.000	1.600	0.156	0.000
Education of woman	0.009	0.020	0.642	-0.016	0.018	0.353	-0.004	0.013	0.795
Education of husband	-0.005	0.018	0.742	-0.004	0.017	0.781	-0.006	0.012	0.631
Work status	0.129	0.120	0.282	0.122	0.141	0.387	0.109	0.089	0.220
Contribution to total income	-0.119	0.072	**0.097**	-0.171	0.097	**0.078**	-0.125	0.056	**0.026**
Age at marriage	-0.001	0.010	0.840	-0.003	0.009	0.729	-0.003	0.007	0.656
Husband-wife age difference	-0.005	0.005	0.297	-0.007	0.005	0.198	-0.007	0.004	**0.081**

(Contd.)

(Contd. Table 7.16)

Background characteristics	*Rural*			*Urban*			*Total*		
	Parameter	*SE*	*p-value*	*Parameter*	*SE*	*p-value*	*Parameter*	*SE*	*p-value*
Marital duration(years)	0.149	0.008	**0.000**	0.154	0.007	**0.000**	0.151	0.005	**0.000**
Whether love marriage	0.236	0.074	**0.001**	0.041	0.067	0.540	0.141	0.050	**0.005**
Whether inter-caste / inter religious	-0.022	0.092	0.803	-0.008	0.072	0.911	-0.022	0.057	0.694
Exposure to Mass media	-0.043	0.038	0.248	-0.081	0.036	**0.024**	-0.061	0.026	**0.019**
Membership in SHG	0.039	0.043	0.352	-0.066	0.042	0.118	-0.013	0.029	0.667
Standard of living	-0.0086	0.003	**0.001**	-0.008	0.002	**0.000**	-0.008	0.002	**0.000**
Autonomy	-0.003	0.001	**0.011**	-0.004	0.001	**0.008**	-0.004	0.001	**0.000**

(a) Dependent Variable: child ever born.

The results showed that, in rural areas, women who had longer duration of marital life and women who had love marriage tended to have higher fertility than others. At the same time, women contributed more to the total family income, who had high standard of living and women who had high autonomy tended to have lower fertility than others.

In urban areas, women who had longer duration of marital duration tended to have more fertility than others. At the same time, women who contributed more to the family income, women who had more exposure to mass media, women who had high standard of living and women who had more autonomy tended to have lower fertility than others.

7.17 Effect of Various Dimentions of Women's Autonomy on Children Ever Born

The results of the regression analysis showing the effect of women's autonomy on the number of children ever born are presented in Table 7.17. In rural areas, the number of children ever born was positively affected by women's autonomy on freedom to participate in social and political activities and household decision and negatively affected by women's autonomy on sex-segregated interaction and decision about contraception and fertility. In urban areas, the number of children ever born was positively affected by women's autonomy on freedom of movement and negatively affected by autonomy of women on sex-segregated interaction, violence against women and decision about contraception and fertility. Among the overall total sample, the number of children ever born was positively affected by women's autonomy on freedom of movement, participation in social and political activities and household decisions and negatively affected by sex-segregated interaction, violence against women and decision about contraception and fertility.

The results indicate that, in rural areas, women who had more autonomy to participate in social and political activities and on household decision tended to have higher fertility than others. At the same time, women who had more autonomy on

Table 7.17 Regression model showing the effect of various dimensions of women's autonomy on children ever born

Variable	*Rural*			*Urban*			*Total*		
	Parameter	*SE*	*P-value*	*Parameter*	*SE*	*P-value*	*Parameter*	*SE*	*P-value*
(Constant)	2.479	0.227	0.000	2.454	0.170	0.000	2.484	0.137	0.000
Sex-segregated interaction	-0.0300	0.010	**0.002**	-0.0345	0.009	**0.000**	-0.0329	0.007	**0.000**
Freedom of movement	0.00735	0.005	0.128	0.0099	0.004	**0.020**	0.0081	0.003	**0.010**
Freedom of participation in Social & political, activities	0.0162	0.008	**0.037**	0.0068	0.009	0.464	0.0171	0.006	**0.003**
Financial management	0.0050	0.017	0.764	0.0079	0.016	0.614	0.0057	0.011	0.618
House hold decisions	0.0255	0.008	**0.001**	0.0089	0.008	0.235	0.0179	0.005	**0.001**
Freedom of choice	-0.0029	0.012	0.804	-0.0015	0.011	0.888	-0.0012	0.008	0.881
Violence against women	-0.0172	0.011	0.113	-0.0181	0.009	**0.041**	-0.0195	0.007	**0.005**
Decision about contraception & fertility	0.0581	0.015	**0.000**	-0.0104	0.015	**0.215**	-0.0398	0.011	**0.000**

a. Dependent Variable:-children ever born.

sex-segregated interaction and decision about contraception and fertility tended to have lower fertility than others.

In urban areas, women who had more autonomy on freedom of movement tended to have higher fertility than others. At the same time, women who had more autonomy on sex-segregated interaction, violence against women and decision about contraception and fertility tended to have lower fertility than others.

8

Women's Autonomy and Family Planning

In order to assess the influence of women's autonomy on the knowledge and adoption of family planning methods, information was collected from all the women on various aspects of family planning such as their knowledge, attitude and adoption of family planning methods. The results of the analysis of data on various aspects of family planning according to the level of women's autonomy are presented in the following sections.

8.1 Knowledge About Various Family Planning Methods

The percent distribution of women by their knowledge about various family planning methods and level of autonomy is presented in Table 8.1. In rural areas, female sterilisation was the popular method known to most of the women (96.9 per cent) followed by copper-T/IUD (80.8 per cent), male sterilization (75.5 per cent), oral pill (74.8 per cent) and condom (68.2 per cent). Rhythm and withdrawal methods were reported by only 24.9 per cent and 9.8 per cent of women respectively. It is

Table 8.1 Percent distribution of women by their knowledge of family planning methods and level of autonomy

Family planning methods	*Rural*							*Urban*						
	L-371	*M-383*	*H-446*	*T-1200*	χ^2	*DF*	*Sig*	*L-457*	*M-440*	*H-303*	*T-1200*	χ^2	*DF*	*Sig*
Female sterilization	94.3	98.4	97.8	96.9	12.250	2	**0.002**	98.0	99.8	99.3	99.0	7.345	2	**0.025**
Male sterilization	64.7	80.9	79.8	75.5	34.066	2	**0.000**	67.0	82.7	85.5	77.4	46.952	2	**0.000**
Copper T/IUD	73.3	84.3	84.1	80.8	19.600	2	**0.000**	77.2	88.4	94.4	85.7	47.881	2	**0.000**
Oral pill	65.5	77.3	80.5	74.8	25.974	2	**0.000**	69.8	80.7	89.8	78.8	44.950	2	**0.000**
Condom / Niroth	60.1	71.5	72.0	68.2	16.091	2	**0.000**	62.1	65.7	80.5	68.1	30.181	2	**0.000**
Rhythm / periodic abstinence	15.9	26.9	30.7	24.9	24.933	2	**0.000**	21.2	27.0	39.6	28.0	30.841	2	**0.000**
Withdrawal	6.7	17.7	10.5	9.8	5.878	2	**0.053**	11.6	12.3	18.2	13.5	7.599	2	**0.022**

(Contd.)

(Contd. Table 8.1)

Family planning methods	*Total*						
	L-828	*M-823*	*H-749*	*T-2400*	χ^2	*DF*	*Sig*
Female sterilization	96.4	99.1	98.4	98.0	16.917	2	0.000
Male sterilization	65.9	81.9	82.1	76.5	77.680	2	0.000
Copper T IUD	75.5	86.5	88.3	83.3	55.537	2	0.000
Oral pill	67.9	79.1	84.2	76.8	62.833	2	0.000
Condom / Niroth	61.2	68.4	75.4	68.1	36.574	2	0.000
Rhythm / periodic abstinence	18.8	27.0	34.3	26.5	48.552	2	0.000
Withdrawal	9.4	12.0	13.6	11.6	6.945	2	0.031

L: Low M: Medium H: High T: Total Sig.: Significance

Table 8.2 Percent distribution of women by current use contraception and level of autonomy

Current use of Contraception	*Rural*				*Urban*				*Total*			
	L-371	*M-383*	*H-446*	*T-1200*	*L-457*	*M-440*	*H-303*	*T-1200*	*L-828*	*M-823*	*H-749*	*T-2400*
Yes	56.1	66.8	74.7	66.4	47.5	54.1	67.3	54.9	51.3	60.0	71.7	60.7
No	43.9	33.2	25.3	33.6	52.5	45.9	32.7	45.1	48.7	40.0	28.3	39.3
Significance	χ^2= 1.455 DF – 2 P<0.000				χ^2= 29.168 DF – 2 P<0.000				χ^2= 68.581 F – 2 P<0.000			

L: Low M: Medium H: High T: Total

Figure 8.2 Current use of contraception by level of autonomy

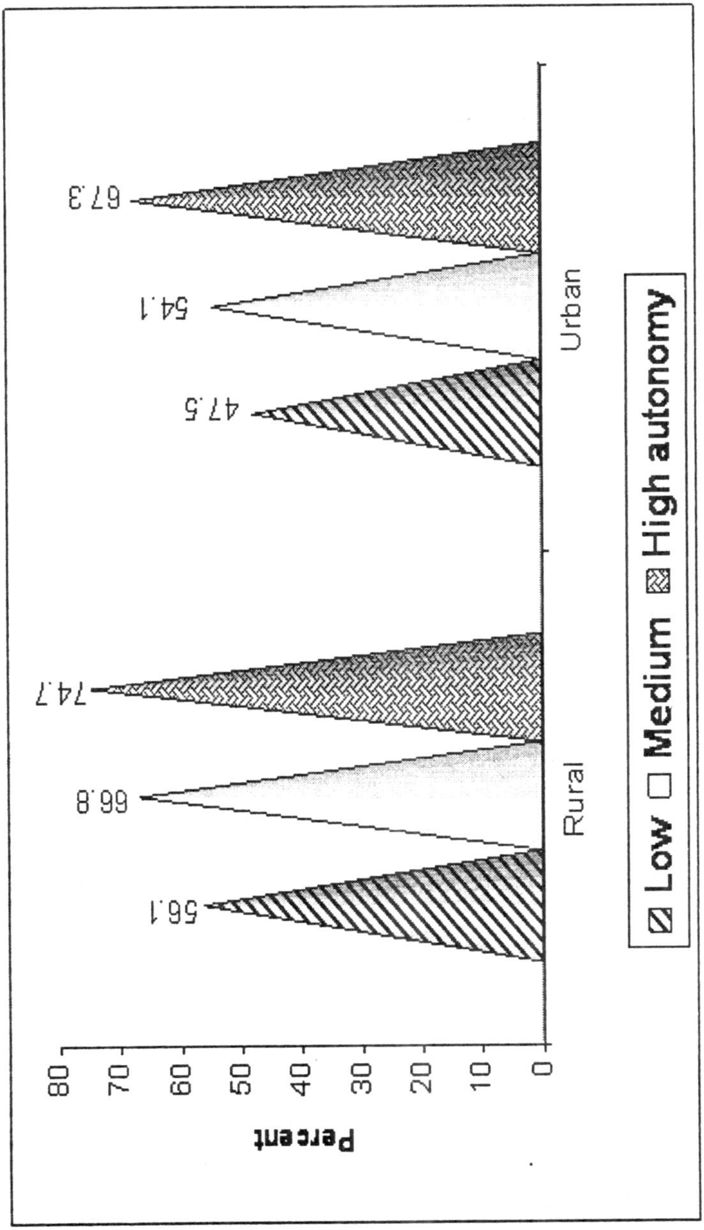

interesting to see that the knowledge of family planning methods significantly increased with autonomy.

In urban areas also, most of the women (99 per cent) were aware of female sterilization which was followed by copper-T (85.7 per cent), oral pill (78.8 per cent), male sterilization (77.4 per cent) and condom (68.1 per cent). Rhythm and withdrawal methods were reported by only 28 per cent and 13.5 per cent of women respectively. Women's autonomy showed significantly positive effect on the knowledge of women on various family planning methods.

8.2 Current Use of Contraception

The percent distribution of women by current use of contraception presented in Table 8.2 reveals that nearly two thirds of women in rural areas (66.4 per cent) and 54.9 per cent in urban areas had adopted any one of the family planning methods at the time of the interview. The adoption of family planning methods increased significantly with the autonomy of women in both rural and urban areas. It increased from 56.1 per cent for low autonomy to 74.7 per cent for high autonomy women in rural areas. In urban areas, the adoption of family planning methods increased significantly from 47.5 per cent for low autonomy to 67.3 per cent for high autonomy women. Overall, the results showed that the autonomy of women had significantly positive influence on the adoption family planning methods in both rural and urban areas.

8.3 Type of Method Adopted

The percent distribution of women by type of method adopted at the time of the interview by their autonomy status is presented in Table 8.3. Most of the adopters (around 85 per cent) in both rural and urban areas had adopted permanent methods mainly female sterilization (85 per cent in rural and 84 per cent in urban) at the time of the interview. Women's autonomy did not make much difference in the type of method adopted by women in both rural and urban areas.

Table 8.3 Percent distribution of women by type of method adopted and level of autonomy

Method	*Rural*				*Urban*				*Total*			
	L-208	*M-256*	*H-333*	*T-797*	*L-217*	*M-238*	*H-204*	*T-659*	*L-425*	*M-494*	*H-537*	*T-1456*
Female sterilization	80.8	83.2	88.0	84.6	82.9	83.2	84.3	83.5	81.9	83.2	86.6	84.1
Male sterilization	-	0.4	-	0.1	-	-	-	-	-	0.2	-	0.1
IUD	12.5	9.8	8.4	9.9	12.0	9.2	8.3	9.9	12.2	9.5	8.4	9.9
Oral pill	0.5	0.4	0.3	0.4	0.5	2.1	-	0.9	0.5	1.2	0.2	0.6
Condom	3.8	4.3	2.7	3.5	3.7	4.6	6.4	4.9	3.8	4.5	4.1	4.1
Other's	2.4	2.0	0.6	1.5	0.9	0.8	1.0	0.9	1.6	1.4	0.7	1.2
Significance	χ^2=9.671 F – 10 P<0.470				χ^2= 9.262 F – 8 P<0.321				χ^2= 12.950 F – 10 P<0.226			

L: Low M: Medium H: High T: Total

Table 8.4 Percent distribution of women by age at adoption and level of autonomy

Age at adoption (years)	*Rural*				*Urban*				*Total*			
	L-201	*M-255*	*H-338*	*T-794*	*L-228*	*M-245*	*H-211*	*T-684*	*L-429*	*M-500*	*H-549*	*T-1478*
15 – 19	6.3	4.7	3.9	4.8	2.8	1.3	2.9	2.3	4.5	3.0	3.5	3.6
20 – 24	63.5	59.0	61.6	61.2	63.6	63.6	53.4	60.5	63.5	61.2	58.5	60.9
25 – 29	30.3	36.3	34.5	34.0	33.6	35.1	53.6	37.3	32.0	35.8	38.0	35.5
Mean	22.78	22.25	23.26	23.14	22.71	22.89	23.09	22.89	22.75	23.08	23.19	23.03
Significance	$\chi^2 = 3.148$ DF-4 P<0.533				$\chi^2 = 7.398$ DF-4 P<0.116				$\chi^2 = 4.751$ DF-4 P<0.314			

L: Low M: Medium H: High T: Total

8.4 Age At The Time Of Adoption

The percent distribution of women by age at the time of adoption and level of autonomy presented in Table 8.4 reveals that women's autonomy did not make any significant difference in the age at adoption of women in both rural and urban areas. The age at the time of adoption of family planning did not vary much between rural and urban areas. The mean age at adoption was 23.14 years in rural and 22.89 years in urban areas.

8.5 Reasons For Adoption

The percent distribution of women by reasons for the adoption of family planning methods and level of autonomy is presented in Table 8.5. The main reason for the adoption of family planning methods was to limit family size as reported by 81.6 per cent of adopters in rural and 78.6 per cent of adopters in urban areas. Spacing was the next major reason reported by 15.2 per cent of adopters in rural and 19.4 per cent in urban areas. The proportion of women who had adopted family planning methods for spacing purpose decreased with increase in autonomy of women in both rural and urban areas. However, the differences were significant only in urban areas.

The proportion of women who had adopted family planning methods to limit family size increased with autonomy of women in both rural and urban areas. However, the differences were statistically significant only in urban areas.

8.6 Person Who Took Decision

The percent distribution of women by their level of autonomy and the person who took the decision to adopt family planning methods is presented in Table 8.6. Only 19.2 per cent of adopters in rural areas and 18.2 per cent of adopters in urban areas had taken decision to adopt family planning on their own. Joint decision by husband and wife was reported by 70.6 per cent of adopters in rural and 69 per cent in urban areas. Women's autonomy did not make any significant difference in the decision making process of women on the adoption of family planning methods in both rural and urban areas.

Table 8.5 Percent distribution of women by reasons for past / current use of contraception and level of autonomy

Reasons for past / current use of contraception	*Rural*				*Urban*				*Total*			
	L-220	*M-276*	*H-357*	*T-853*	*L-253*	*M-267*	*H-229*	*T-749*	*L-473*	*M-543*	*H-586*	*T-1602*
Spacing	19.1	15.9	12.3	15.2	24.9	16.9	16.2	19.4	22.2	16.4	13.8	17.2
To limit family size	77.7	81.9	83.8	81.6	70.8	81.6	83.8	78.6	74.0	81.8	83.8	80.2
Doctor's advice / Health reason	3.2	2.1	3.9	3.2	4.4	1.5	-	2.0	3.8	1.8	2.4	2.6
Significance	χ^2=8.633 DF – 6 P<0.195				χ^2=22.010 DF – 6 P<0.001				χ^2=19.238 DF – 6 P<0.004			

L: Low M: Medium H: High T: Total

Table 8.6 Percent distribution of women by person who took decision to adopt family planning method and level of autonomy

Person who took decision	*Rural*				*Urban*				*Total*			
	L-220	*M-276*	*H-357*	*T-853*	*L-253*	*M-267*	*H-229*	*T-749*	*L-473*	*M-543*	*H-586*	*T-1602*
Husband	4.1	4.7	2.2	3.5	4.7	2.2	2.6	3.2	4.4	3.5	2.4	3.4
Herself	20.0	17.0	20.4	19.2	17.8	16.5	20.5	18.2	18.8	16.8	20.5	18.7
Both	70.9	72.5	68.9	70.6	65.6	71.5	69.9	69.0	68.1	72.0	69.3	69.9
Other family members	5.0	5.8	8.4	6.7	11.9	9.7	7.0	9.6	8.7	7.7	7.8	8.1
Significance	χ^2=7.137 DF – 6 P<0.308				χ^2= 7.684 DF – 6 P<0.262				χ^2= 6.312 DF – 6 P<0.389			

L: Low M: Medium H: High T: Total

Table 8.7 Percent distribution of women by husband-wife communications about family size and level of autonomy

Husband-wife communication	*Rural*				*Urban*				*Total*			
	L-371	*M-383*	*H-446*	*T-1200*	*L-457*	*M-440*	*H-303*	*T-1200*	*L-828*	*M-823*	*H-749*	*T-2400*
Discussion about number of children												
Yes	85.7	93.2	93.3	90.9	89.7	96.8	98.0	94.4	87.9	95.1	95.2	92.7
No	14.3	6.8	6.7	9.1	10.3	3.2	2.0	5.6	12.1	4.9	4.8	7.3
	χ^2= 17.601 DF – 2 P<0.000				χ^2= 31.435 DF – 2 P<0.000				χ^2= 41.866 DF – 2 P<0.000			

(Contd.)

(Contd. Table 8.7)

Husband-wife communication	*Rural*				*Urban*				*Total*			
	L-371	*M-383*	*H-446*	*T-1200*	*L-457*	*M-440*	*H-303*	*T-1200*	*L-828*	*M-823*	*H-749*	*T-2400*
Whether Husband wants the same number												
Same number	64.4	74.9	73.5	71.2	66.7	83.2	81.5	76.5	65.7	79.3	76.8	73.8
More number	18.1	13.1	16.6	15.9	18.8	11.1	13.5	14.7	18.5	12.0	15.4	15.3
Fewer number	4.9	6.3	4.7	5.3	3.9	2.3	3.0	3.1	4.3	4.1	4.0	4.2
Don't know	12.7	5.7	5.2	7.7	10.5	3.4	2.0	5.8	11.5	4.5	3.9	6.7
Significance	χ^2= 25.391 DF – 6 P<0.000				χ^2= 50.306 DF – 6 P<0.000				χ^2= 66.035 DF – 6 P<0.000			

L: Low M: Medium H: High T: Total

Figure 8.7 Husband-wife communications about family planning and level of autonomy

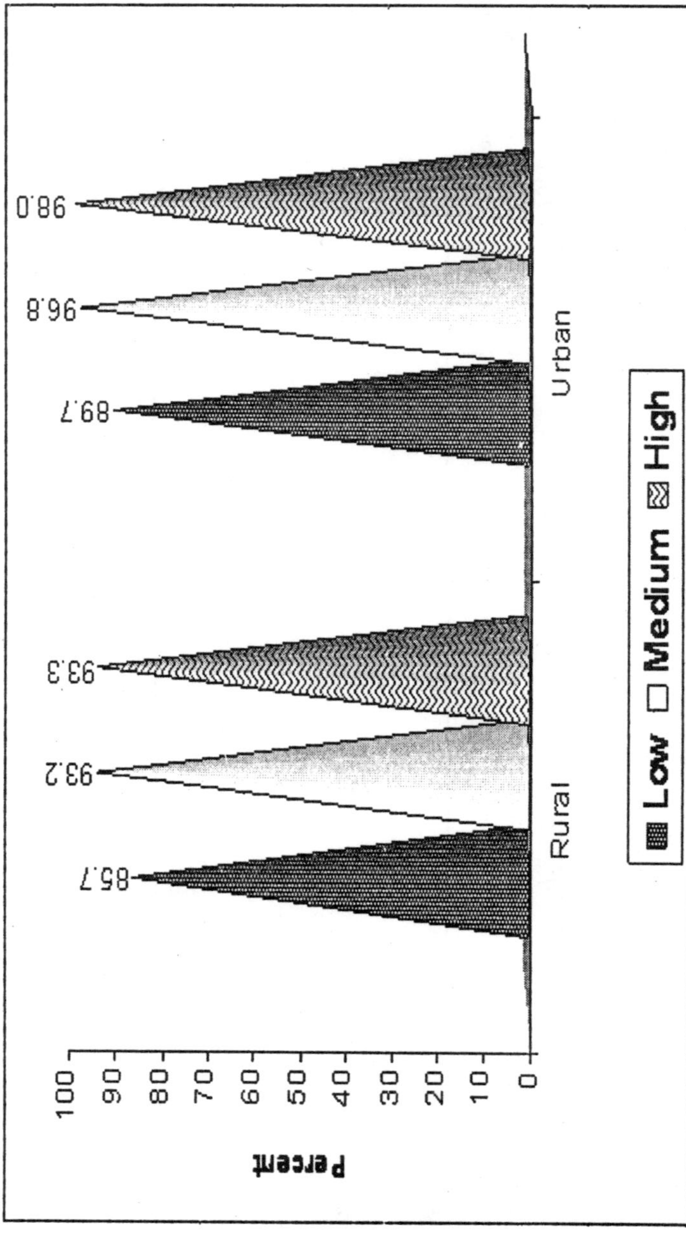

8.7 Husband-wife Communication about Family Planning and Family Size Desire

The husband-wife communication (discussion) about family planning and family size desire is expected to increase with increase in the status of women. In this study, an attempt was made to assess the husband-wife communication about family planning and family size. The results presented in Table 8.7 reveal that the proportion of women who had discussion about the number of children increased significantly with autonomy in both rural and urban areas. In rural areas, it increased from 85.7 per cent for low autonomy to 93.3 per cent for high autonomy women. In urban areas, it increased from 89.7 per cent for low autonomy to 98 per cent for high autonomy women (Figure 8.7). The women were also asked in this study whether their husband also desired to have the same number of children as they desired to have. The results showed that the number of children desired by their husband was same as that of their desire for the majority of women in both rural and urban areas (71.2 per cent in rural and 76.5 per cent in urban areas). The desire to have the same number of children by both husband and wife was significantly more among women who had medium and high level of autonomy compared to women who had low autonomy in both rural and urban areas.

9

Focus Group Discussion (FGD)

Focus Group Discussion (FGD) method was adopted in this study to collect qualitative data on various dimensions of women's autonomy and its impact on the fertility behaviour of women in both rural and urban areas. In order to get the views of the younger women and the older women, the FGDs were conducted separately for younger women aged 15-24 years and older women aged 25-29 years. In all, one FGD for younger women and one FGD for older women were conducted separately for rural and urban areas in each of the selected districts. Thus a total of 12 FGDs were conducted in all the three selected districts of Tamil Nadu.

Discussions were held on the following eight autonomy variables: sex-segregated interaction, freedom of movement, participation in social and political activities, financial management, household decisions, freedom of choice, violence against women and decision about contraception and fertility. Discussions were also held on the knowledge and adoption of family planning methods and starting, spacing and stopping of child birth. The outcome of the focus group discussions are summarized separately for rural and urban women in the following sections.

9.1 Rural Women

Younger women (age ≤ 4 years) in rural areas felt that a lot of changes had taken place in recent times in rural areas in the ability of women to take independent decision on many of their daily activities within and outside the home. They felt that they were having more autonomy on sex-segregated interaction and they need not have to wait or get permission from their husband to take food, to participate in discussion with males and engage with relatives at home. However, they still had the feeling that they could not engage with males at home in the absence of the husband. Interestingly, husbands used to share their household responsibilities, even to the extent of cooking.

Freedom of movement is still a distant factor for them and they can not move out without the permission of their husband or in-laws. The Self Help Group activities paved the way for them to move out and mingle with other women. The younger women were able to participate in social and political activities/that too because of their involvement in Self Help Group activities and the opportunities given to women to contest local body election (reservation for women). The younger women now-a-days were involved in political activities. However their political participation was mainly influenced by their husband, as reported by the women.

Important household decisions were made by husband or in-laws and the younger women were least considered in the decision making process. As they were younger in age and new to the family, they were neither consulted on any of the household matters nor their views or suggestions sought. They didn't find much hurdle in their freedom of choice like wearing dresses, hair style, voting in election, worshiping God and other personal likes. However, most of them felt that they could not refuse sex even if they were not interested at that time because of the fear that their husband might go for sex with other ladies.

Women in joint family were facing both physical and verbal abuse more often than the women in nuclear family. Most of the younger rural women complained of the drinking behaviour of their husband. Incidence of eve-teasing was reported as very low. Decision about contraception and fertility was mostly decided by their husband and in-laws and they could not take any independent decision on the adoption of family planning methods. The knowledge of younger women on family planning methods was fairly good as most of them were aware of female sterilization, oral pills, IUD and condom. Most of them preferred to have only two children of either sex. Desire for male children was very low and in fact many of the participants of the FGD had adopted female sterilization with two female children.

The results of the FGD conducted among the younger women revealed that the younger married women in rural areas had attained autonomy to a considerable extent on sex-segregated interaction, freedom of movement and freedom of choice. It is also inferred that autonomy of women is an important factor in making decisions on the adoption of family planning methods and also on the number of children. However, the small family norm was commonly accepted by all women irrespective of their autonomy status.

The opinion of older women (aged 25-29 years) in rural areas did not differ much from that of younger women on many of the autonomy factors. However, the older women were reported to be in a better position than the younger women in sex-segregated interaction, freedom of movement, freedom to participate in social and political activities, freedom of choice and violence against women. Because of their age, long marital duration and exposure to outside world, the older women were having more ability to take independent decision on many of their daily activities within and outside the home. Older women were having a fairly a good knowledge of family planning methods, spacing and importance of small family norm. Son preference was reported by only a few women and most of them wanted only two children of either sex. In fact, many of the participants of FGD had adopted permanent method of sterilization without male child. Thus, it is inferred from the Focus Group Discussions that the changes in the fertility behavior of women on starting, spacing and stopping of child birth was mainly because of the awareness of women on the difficulties in bringing up the children and aspiration for good care and education for their children. Autonomy of women also had significant effect on the adoption of family planning methods and limiting of family size with one or two children.

9.2 Urban Women

The views expressed by young and old women in the urban areas did not differ much from the views expressed by women in rural areas. Urban women reported that they were able to take independent decisions on many of their daily routine works within and outside home. They felt that women in nuclear family were enjoying more autonomy than women in joint family. They also reported that women who had love marriage and inter-caste / inter-religious marriage were enjoying more autonomy than those who had arranged and same caste marriage. There was not much variation in many of the sex-segregated interaction variables among women in rural and urban areas. The traditional habit of women taking food last was no more in existence. They were also not forced to wait until the arrival of their partners. Interaction with males was not much restricted in urban areas, if they are known persons to the family members or relatives. Otherwise, they could not participate in the discussion. Women in urban areas were having more freedom of movement. The majority of women were accompanying their husband for all social functions. Mostly, employed women were getting help from their husband for doing the household work. Engaging males in the absence of husband was not permitted as reported by all women participants.

Freedom of movement was not fully restricted for women in urban areas. They were free to move but before leaving they have to get prior permission from their husband. Going to movies and hotels were restricted by women themselves. They did not have full freedom to move fully as they liked. Returning home late in the evening after work was also not welcomed.

Women in urban areas involved in social and political activities only with full knowledge and presence of their husband. Articulation in public meetings and interacting with men / boys were highly restricted.

Regarding the financial management, earning women were able to keep their income with them and they had control over jewels brought from natal family. Mostly, the family properties were maintained by the male members. Urban women were mostly involved in household decision. Purchasing dress for themselves and other family members were mostly decided by women. Their participation was high in purchase of jewels and other household appliances. Employed women mostly involved in household decision. Women were not consulted in decision about lending / borrowing and only household budget was maintained by the women. Though women were consulted in most of the important matters, final decision was made only by the male members.

Women in urban areas were having more freedom in dressing, voting, cooking and worshiping God. They were not compelled for sex by their husband and it was mostly with mutual understanding.

Women who had husband with drinking habits had experienced both verbal and physical abuse. Illiterate women were mostly affected by domestic violence. Women in joint family system had experienced both verbal and physical abuse by their husband and in-laws more frequently than women in nuclear family system. Incidence of eve teasing was reportedly high in urban than in rural areas.

Decision about contraception and fertility was mostly decided by the couple. Women in urban areas were more aware about contraceptives and limiting of family size. The son preference was slowly weakened in urban areas. Now-a-days, many women used to adopt permanent method of family planning without male child. Timing about child birth was jointly decided by both husband and wife. Son preference was much less among educated women in urban areas. Women's autonomy was also having influence on the adoption of family planning and limiting of family size in urban areas. Irrespective of the autonomy level, all women in urban areas preferred to have only two children and a few of them preferred to stop child birth even with one child.

10

Summary and Conclusion

Women's autonomy, measured in terms of their ability to take independent decision in all spheres of their life within and outside their home, is thought to play an important role in deciding their reproductive behaviour. It is believed that women's autonomy is having significant influence on their reproductive behaviour such as age at first birth, birth interval, age at last birth, number and sex composition of children. In this context, the present study was undertaken to assess the level of women's autonomy and its effect on their reproductive behaviour in both rural and urban areas of Tamil Nadu. The study was based on a sample of 2400 married women aged 15-29 years and having at least one living child at the time of the interview. This group was chosen given the fact that most of the current child bearing occurred within this age group.

The study was carried out in three districts of Tamil Nadu viz., Kancheepuram, Thiruchirapalli and Villupuram, representing high, medium and low level of gender development (TamilNadu Human Development Report, 2003). In each district, a sample of 400 women from rural areas and 400 women from urban areas were selected using systematic random sampling procedure. Thus the total sample consisted of 1200 women from rural and 1200 women from urban areas. The selected women were interviewed at their place of residence using an interview schedule by trained research investigators. The information collected from the women covered a range of subjects which included the socio-economic, demographic and marital characteristics of the respondents, their fertility behaviour, family planning knowledge and adoption and eight different dimensions of women's autonomy variables. The different dimensions of women's autonomy examined in this study include sex-segregated interaction, freedom of movement, freedom to participate in social and political activities, financial management, household decisions, freedom of choice, violence against women and decision about contraception and fertility. The data collection work was carried out during the period from May to October 2005.

Both univariate and multivariate analysis were carried out in this study to assess the level of women's autonomy and its socio-economic, demographic determinants in both rural and urban areas of Tamil Nadu. The reproductive behaviour of women was also assessed based on the number of children ever born, age at first birth, age at last birth, birth interval and sex composition of children. The effect of women's autonomy on the reproductive behaviour of women was assessed using both bivariate and multivariate analysis. The influence of women's autonomy on family planning knowledge and use was also assessed in this study. A summary of the findings of the study is presented in the following sections.

10.1 Women's Autonomy

The salient findings of the analysis of data on the level of women's autonomy on each of the eight different dimensions by selected socio-economic, demographic and marital characteristics of the respondents and also based on the level of exposure of women to various mass media are presented in this section.

10.1.1 Sex-segregated Interaction

On a scale of 0-16, the mean autonomy score attained by women on sex-segregated interaction was 12.21 in rural (76.31 per cent) and 12.18 (76.13 per cent) in urban areas. The level of autonomy attained by women on sex-segregated interaction did not differ much between rural and urban areas. Education of women and education of husband showed significantly positive effect on women's autonomy on sex-segregated interaction in both rural and urban areas. Lower caste women (SC/ST) had significantly lower autonomy on sex-segregated interaction compared to upper caste women in urban areas. Standard of living showed significantly positive effect on women's autonomy in both rural and urban areas. Surprisingly, women involved in income earning economic activities in urban areas had significantly lower autonomy than those who were not involved in economic activities. However, women who contributed more than 25 per cent to the total family income in urban areas had more autonomy than others.

Autonomy of women on sex-segregated interaction increased with age of women in both rural and urban areas. Women who had no male child had significantly lower autonomy than women who had male child(ren) in rural areas. Women's autonomy on sex-segregated interaction significantly increased with age at marriage of women in urban areas. Though husband-wife age difference showed significant difference in the autonomy of women in urban areas, no specific pattern emerged. Women who had two or more female children and women who had three or more number of total children had significantly lower autonomy than others in both rural and urban areas. None of the marital characteristics variables showed any significant influence on the autonomy of women on sex-segregated interaction in both rural and urban areas. Women's exposure to mass media (radio, TV, movies and reading newspapers / magazines) showed significantly positive effect on women's autonomy on sex-segregated interaction in both rural and urban areas. Members of Self Help Group had significantly higher autonomy than non-members in both rural and urban areas.

10.1.2 Freedom of Movement

On a scale of 0-26, the mean autonomy score attained by women on freedom of movement was higher at 14.06 (54.08 per cent) for women in rural areas compared to 12.63 (48.58 per cent) observed for women in urban areas. An examination of the influence of various socio-economic variables on women's autonomy on freedom of movement revealed that in rural areas, women who had education up to higher secondary and above had significantly higher autonomy on freedom of movement than others. Muslim women and higher caste women (BC and others) had significantly lower autonomy on freedom of movement than others in both rural and urban areas. Women who were involved in income earning economic activities and women who contributed more than 25 per cent to the total family income had significantly higher autonomy on freedom of movement than others. Women in nuclear family had significantly higher autonomy than women in joint family in both rural and urban areas.

Age of women, age at marriage, marital duration, number of female children and total number of children were the demographic variables showing significant influence on women's autonomy on freedom of movement in both rural and urban areas. Age of women showed significantly positive effect on women's autonomy. Women who had married at ages 21 years or more had significantly lower autonomy than women who had married at ages 20 years or less. Marital duration and number of female children had significantly positive effect on women's autonomy on freedom of movement in both rural and urban areas. Women who had only one child had significantly lower autonomy than those who had two or more number of total children.

None of the marital characteristics variables showed significant effect on women's autonomy on freedom of movement in rural areas. However in urban areas, women who had love marriage and women who had inter-caste / inter-religious marriage had significantly higher autonomy on freedom of movement than others.

Exposure of women to mass media showed significantly positive effect on women's autonomy on freedom of movement in both rural and urban areas. Members of SHG also had significantly more autonomy on freedom of movement in both rural and urban areas.

10.1.3 Participation in Social and Political Activities

On a scale of 0-14, the mean score attained by women on participation in social and political activities was very low in both rural and urban areas. It was 4.24 (30.29 per cent) and 2.56 (18.29 per cent) for rural and urban women respectively. Education of women, involvement of women in income earning economic activities and contribution of women to the total family income showed significantly positive effect on freedom of women to participate in social and political activities in both rural and urban areas. Muslim women and higher caste women (BC) had significantly low autonomy on freedom of participation in both rural and urban areas. Women in nuclear family had significantly high autonomy in both rural and urban areas. Freedom of participation was significantly low for women who had low standard of living in urban areas.

Age of women and marital duration showed significantly positive effect on the autonomy of women to participate in social and political activities in both rural and urban areas. Freedom of participation was comparatively low among women who got married at ages 21 years or more compared to women married at ages 20 years or less in both rural and urban areas, but the differences are significant only in rural areas. Women who had love marriage had significantly more autonomy than women who had arranged marriage in both rural and urban areas.

Exposure to mass media and membership in SHG showed significantly positive effect on women's autonomy on freedom to participate in social and political activities in both rural and urban areas.

10.1.4 Financial Management

On a scale of 0-6, the mean score attained by women on financial management was 3.07 (51.17 per cent) in rural and 2.76 (46.0 per cent) in urban areas. Education of husband, involvement of women in income earning economic activities, percent contribution to the total family income and type of family showed significant effect on the autonomy of women on financial management in both rural and urban areas. While the education of husband showed significantly negative effect on financial management, involvement in economic activities and contribution to the total family income showed significantly positive effect on financial management in both rural and urban areas. Women in nuclear family had significantly higher autonomy on financial management than women in joint family in both rural and urban areas.

Age of women and marital duration were the demographic variables showing significantly positive effect on women's autonomy on financial management in both rural and urban areas. Women who had love marriage had significantly more autonomy on financial management in both rural and urban areas. Members of SHG also had significantly more autonomy than non-members in both rural and urban areas. Age at marriage showed significantly negative effect in rural areas. Women who had non-consanguineous marriage and women who had inter-caste / inter-religious marriage had significantly more autonomy on financial management only in urban areas.

10.1.5 Household Decisions

On a scale of 0-22, the mean autonomy score attained by women on household decisions was 11.56 (52.55 per cent) in rural and 10.81 (49.14 per cent) in urban areas. In rural areas, education of husband, religion, community, involvement in income earning economic activities, contribution to total family income and type of family were the socio-economic variables showing significant influence on women's autonomy on household decisions. Education of husband negatively associated with women's autonomy on household decisions. Christian women, SC/ST women, women involved in income earning economic activities, women who contributed more to the total family income and women in nuclear family had significantly more autonomy on household decisions than others in rural areas. In urban areas, the type of family was the only socio-economic variable showing significant influence on women's autonomy on household decisions. Women in nuclear family had significantly higher autonomy than women in joint family in urban areas.

Age of women and marital duration were the demographic variables showing significantly positive influence on women's autonomy on household decisions in both rural and urban areas. While the number of male children showed significantly positive effect on women's autonomy on household decisions in urban areas, the number of female children and total number of children showed significantly positive effect in rural areas. Women who had love marriage and women who had inter-caste /inter-religious marriage were having significantly higher autonomy on household decisions than others in both rural and urban areas. Exposure of women to mass media showed significantly positive effect only in urban areas. Membership in self help group showed significantly positive effect in both rural and urban areas.

10.1.6 Freedom of Choice

The autonomy of women on freedom of choice in their personal life style behaviour was significantly high in both rural and urban areas. On a scale of 0-16, the mean autonomy score attained by women was 14.63 (91.44 per cent) in rural and 14.22 (88.88 per cent) in urban areas. Religion and community were the socio-economic variables showing significant association with women's autonomy on freedom of choice in both rural and urban areas. Muslim women had significantly lower autonomy on freedom of choice than Hindu and Christian women in both rural and urban areas. Most backward caste women in rural areas and backward caste women in urban areas had significantly more autonomy on freedom of choice than others. Education of women and their husband showed significantly positive effect on women's autonomy on freedom of choice in urban areas.

Age at marriage showed significantly positive effect on women's autonomy on freedom of choice only in urban areas. The number of female children showed significant influence on women's autonomy in both rural and urban areas. The total number of children significantly associated with women's autonomy only in rural areas.

The overall level of women's exposure to mass media and membership in SHG showed significantly positive effect on women's autonomy on freedom of choice in both rural and urban areas.

10.1.7 Violence Against Women

The autonomy of women on violence against women was very high in both rural and urban areas. On a scale of 0-20, the mean autonomy score was 17.10 (85.50 per cent) for women in rural and 17.16 (85.80 per cent) for women in urban areas. All the socio-economic variables examined in this study showed significant association with women's autonomy on violence against women in both rural and urban areas except for religion in urban areas.

Education of women, education of husband and standard of living have showed significantly positive effect on women's autonomy in both rural and urban areas. Muslim women had significantly higher autonomy on violence against women than others in rural areas. SC/ST women had significantly lower autonomy than others in both rural and urban areas. Surprisingly, working women and women contributing more to the total family income and women living in nuclear family had significantly lower autonomy on violence against women than others in both rural and urban areas.

Age at marriage and marital duration were the demographic variables showing significant influence on women's autonomy on violence against women in both rural and urban areas. While age at marriage showed significantly positive effect, marital duration showed significantly negative effect on the autonomy of women on violence against women. Age of women, number of female children and total number of children showed significant effect on women's autonomy on violence against women in urban areas. Women aged 20-24 years had significantly lower autonomy than women aged 19 years or less and women aged 25 years or more. Women who had only one female child had significantly more autonomy than women who had no female child or women who had two or more number of female children. The total number of children showed significantly negative effect on women's autonomy on violence against women.

Women who had consanguineous marriage, women who had arranged marriage and women who had same caste marriage had significantly more autonomy on violence against women in both rural and urban areas. The overall level of women's exposure to mass media showed significantly positive effect on women's autonomy in both rural and urban areas.

10.1.8 Decision about Contraception and Fertility

The autonomy of women on decision about contraception and fertility was low in both rural and urban areas. On a scale of 0-8, the mean autonomy score was only 4.22 (52.75 per cent) for women in rural and 4.18 (52.25 per cent) for women in urban areas.

Education of women, education of husband, standard of living, involvement in income earning economic activities and contribution to the total family income were the socio-economic variables showing significant influence on women's autonomy on decision about contraception and fertility in rural areas. Education of husband and standard of living showed significantly negative effect on women's autonomy. Women involved in economic activities and women contributing more to the total family income had significantly more autonomy than others in rural areas. Education of women, standard of living and type of family were the socio-economic variables showing significant influence on the autonomy of women in urban areas. Women in nuclear family had significantly more autonomy on decision about contraception and fertility in urban areas.

While marital duration showed significantly positive influence on women's autonomy in both rural and urban areas, age of women showed significantly positive effect on women's autonomy on decision about contraception and fertility in urban areas. Women who had non-consanguineous marriage, women who had love marriage and women who had inter-caste / inter-religious marriage had significantly more autonomy than others in urban areas.

Membership in Self Help Group (SHG) showed significantly positive effect on women's autonomy on decision about contraception and fertility in both rural and urban areas.

10.1.9 Total Autonomy

The overall total autonomy score for all the eight dimensions of women's autonomy is 128. Overall, rural women had slightly more autonomy than urban women. On a scale of 0-128, the mean autonomy score attained by women in rural areas was 81.05, which is 63.32 per cent of the total expected score. In urban areas, the mean autonomy score attained by women was 76.47, which is 59.74 per cent of the total expected score.

Education of women, religion, community, involvement in economic activities, contribution to total family income and type of family were the socio-economic variables showing significant influence on women's autonomy in rural areas. Education of women, involvement of women in income earning economic activities and contribution to the total family income showed significantly positive effect on women's autonomy in rural areas. Muslim women had significantly low autonomy and MBC women had significantly high autonomy in rural areas. Women living in nuclear family had significantly higher autonomy than women living in joint family in rural areas.

Education of women, education of husband, religion, community, standard of living and type of family were the socio-economic variables showing significant effect on women's autonomy in urban areas. Education of women showed significantly positive effect on women's autonomy. Muslim women had significantly lower autonomy than Hindu and Christian women. Most backward caste women had significantly higher autonomy than others. Low standard of living women and those who were living in joint family had significantly lower autonomy than others.

Age of women, marital duration and total number of children were the demographic variables showing significant effect on women's autonomy in both rural and urban areas. Age of women and marital duration showed significantly positive effect on women's autonomy in both rural and urban areas. Women who had only two children had significantly higher autonomy than others in both rural and urban areas. Age at marriage had significantly positive effect on women's autonomy only in urban areas. Women who had love marriage had significantly higher autonomy than others in both rural and urban areas. Women who had inter-caste/ inter-religious marriage had significantly higher autonomy than others only in urban areas.

Exposure to mass media and membership in SHG had significantly positive effect on women's autonomy in both rural and urban areas.

The results of the regression analysis on the effect of various socio-economic, demographic, marital and mass media variables on women's autonomy revealed that in rural areas, women's autonomy is positively affected by education of women, work status, age at marriage, marital duration, love marriage, exposure to mass media and membership in self help. Education of husband, total number of children and standard of living had significantly negative effect on women's autonomy.

In urban areas, education of women, age at marriage, marital duration, love marriage, exposure to mass media and membership in SHG showed significantly positive effect on women's autonomy.

10.2 Women's Autonomy and Reproductive Behaviour

In this study, the reproductive behaviour of women was studied only for women who had completed their fertility at the time of the interview. It is found that out of 1200 women interviewed in rural areas 794 (66.2 per cent) reported to have completed their fertility. In urban areas, of the 1200 women interviewed 684 (57 per cent) had completed their fertility. The proportion of women who had completed their fertility increased significantly with the level of autonomy in both rural and urban areas.

The results of the analysis of data on the influence of women's autonomy on their fertility measured by mean number of children ever born showed that high autonomy women in both rural and urban areas had lower fertility than the low and medium autonomy women. However the effect of women's autonomy on fertility was more pronounced in urban than in rural areas. The fertility declined consistently with increase in autonomy in urban areas. Education of women and their husband showed significantly negative effect on fertility in both rural and urban areas. Muslim women had higher fertility than others in both rural and urban areas. Lower caste women (SC/ST) in both rural and urban areas had high fertility compared to others.

Standard of living had negative effect on fertility in both rural and urban areas. Surprisingly, women involved in income earning economic activities had higher fertility in rural areas while not much difference was observed in urban areas. Women in nuclear family had higher fertility than women in joint family in both rural and urban areas. Women's autonomy showed significantly negative effect on fertility among women in joint family in urban areas.

The mean number of children ever born increased with age in both rural and urban areas. Younger women aged 19 years or less had lower fertility than older women. While autonomy did not make any significant difference in the level of fertility in rural areas, it had significant influence on fertility in urban areas. It is observed that high autonomy women in urban areas had significantly lower fertility than others. Increase in age at marriage decrease fertility in both rural and urban areas. Women's autonomy showed significant influence on fertility among women who got married at younger ages (≤18 years) in urban areas and women married at 19-22 years in rural areas. While the husband-wife age difference did not make any difference in the level of fertility in rural areas, it had negative effect on fertility in urban areas. Women who had more number of female children (2+) had higher fertility compared to women who had more number of male children.

In rural areas, women's autonomy did not make significant difference in fertility for any of the marital characteristics variables. However in urban areas, women's autonomy had significantly negative effect on fertility among women who had consanguineous marriage, women who had married a person from the paternal side, women who had arranged marriage and women who had same caste marriage.

Exposure of women to mass media showed significantly negative effect on fertility only in urban areas. Autonomy of women showed significant influence on fertility only among women who had low level of exposure to mass media in both rural and urban areas.

Membership in SHG reduced fertility in both rural and urban areas. Though membership in SHG showed reduced effect on fertility in both rural and urban areas, the differences are statistically significant only for rural areas. High autonomy women had lower fertility among both members and non-members in both rural and urban areas.

The proportion of women who had first birth at younger ages (19 years or less) was more among women in rural areas (43.6 per cent) than among women in urban areas (33.8 per cent). Autonomy of women significantly reduced child birth at younger ages in urban areas.

The mean age at first birth was 19.94 years in rural and 20.48 years in urban areas. Autonomy of women did not make significant difference in the mean age at last birth in rural areas and it was staggering around 23 years for women at all levels of autonomy. However in urban areas, significantly higher proportion of women (66 to 67 per cent) with low or medium level of autonomy had completed their fertility by the age of 24 years compared to only 55 per cent among women who had high level of autonomy. The mean age at last birth was significantly high at 24.02 for high autonomy women compared to 23.59 years for low and 23.51 years for medium autonomy women.

Women's autonomy did not make much difference in the mean number of living children in rural areas. However, in urban areas, the mean number of living children decreased with increase in the level of autonomy. The results indicate the lower level of fertility among high autonomy women in urban areas.

Irrespective of the level of autonomy, women's desire for male child decreased in both rural and urban areas. Autonomy of women did not make significant difference in the decision of women to complete their fertility with out a male child.

The proportion of women who had at least one abortion was 19.6 per cent in rural and 17.1 per cent in urban areas. Higher proportion of high autonomy women in both rural and urban areas had experienced abortion than others. The proportion of women who had induced abortion was nearly the same (around 8 per cent) in both rural and urban areas. It was more among women who had high autonomy compared to women who had low and medium level of autonomy in both rural and urban areas.

The proportion of women who had experienced spontaneous abortion was higher in rural (12.3 per cent) than in urban areas (9.5 per cent). A higher proportion of high autonomy women had experienced spontaneous abortion than others in both rural and urban areas.

The mean duration of child bearing was 4.74 years in rural and 4.51 years in urban areas. The mean duration of child bearing years increased with women's autonomy in both rural and urban areas. However, the differences are not significant in both rural and urban areas.

The mean duration of birth interval was more than 24 months for all births in both rural and urban areas. Women's autonomy did not make significant difference in the mean duration of birth interval in both rural and urban areas.

The mean number of children died was slightly higher in rural than in urban areas. It was 0.12 per woman in rural and 0.07 per woman in urban areas. Women's autonomy did not make significant difference in the mean number of children died in rural areas whereas in urban areas, low autonomy women had experienced more child loss than medium and high autonomy women.

The results of the regression analysis showed that in rural areas, the number of children ever born was positively affected by marital duration and love marriage and negatively affected by standard of living, percent contribution to the total family income and autonomy of women. In urban areas, the number of children ever born was positively affected by marital duration and love marriage and negatively affected by percent contribution to the total family income, husband-wife age difference, exposure to mass media, standard of living and autonomy of women.

10.3 Women's Autonomy and Family Planning

Women's autonomy showed significantly positive effect on the knowledge of women on various family planning methods in both rural and urban areas. It is observed that the knowledge of women on various family planning methods increased significantly with the increase in the level of autonomy.

The adoption of family planning methods increased significantly with the autonomy of women in both rural and urban areas. In rural areas, 66.4 per cent of women had adopted any one of the family planning methods at the time of the interview. It was highest at 74.7 per cent for high autonomy women compared to 56.1 per cent for low autonomy and 66.8 per cent for medium autonomy women. In urban areas, 54.9 per cent of women had adopted any one of the family planning methods at the time of the interview. The adoption of family planning methods in urban areas increased significantly with the increase in the autonomy of women. It increased from 47.5 per cent for low autonomy to 67.3 per cent for high autonomy women. Overall, the results showed that autonomy of women had significantly positive influence on the adoption of family planning methods in both rural and urban areas. Women's autonomy did not make significant difference in the type of method adopted by women in both rural and urban areas. Most of the adopters in both rural and urban areas had adopted female sterilisation.

Women's autonomy did not make significant difference in the age at adoption of women in both rural and urban areas. The age at the time of adoption of family planning did not vary much between rural and urban areas. The mean age at adoption was 23.14 years in rural and 23.89 years in urban areas.

10.4 Conclusion

The composite index of women's autonomy derived by combining all the eight different dimensions of women's autonomy showed that the overall attainment of women's autonomy was only 61.53 per cent of the expected level for the whole sample. Surprisingly rural women attained more autonomy (63.32 per cent) than their urban counterparts (59.74). This may be due to the fact that the rural sample consisted of an equal number of women from members of self help groups. Further, it is found that among the eight dimensions of autonomy, women had attained significantly higher level of autonomy (more than 75 per cent of the expected level) only on sex-segregated interaction, freedom of choice and violence against women. The results showed that there is a long way to go to achieve the goal of empowerment of women, which is the third goal of the MGDs set forth by the United Nations to be achieved by 2015. Hence there is an urgent need to initiate special programmes for the empowerment of women.

Education of women, involvement of women in income earning economic activities, exposure of women to mass media and involvement of women in SHG activities emerged as important factors significantly influencing women's autonomy positively in both rural and urban areas. Hence programmes for the empowerment of women must focus on:

(i) Improving women's education at least up to high school level in both rural and urban areas;

(ii) Opportunities should be made available for women for involvement in income earning economic activities in both rural and urban areas;

(iii) Women should be provided more access to information, education and communication through various channels of mass media; and

(iv) Women self help group movement should be strengthened through various supportive services like training, awareness programme, liberal credit facilities, marketing support etc. Population education programmes including health and family welfare messages should be made an integral part of the programme in the SHG activities.

The second part of the study which aimed at assessing the influence of women's autonomy on their reproductive behaviour emerged with interesting findings on the relationship of women's autonomy with fertility and family planning. The findings showed that the proportion of women who had completed their fertility by the age of 29 years was more among women in rural (66.2 per cent) than among women in urban areas (57 per cent). The proportion of women who had completed their fertility by the age of 29 years increased significantly with the increase in the autonomy of women in both rural and urban areas. Thus the high autonomy women were able to take earlier decision about the number of children in both rural and urban areas.

The number of CEB among women aged 15-29 years who had completed their fertility was nearly the same (around 2.3) in both rural and urban areas. The mean number of children ever born was comparatively lower among high autonomy women than low and medium autonomy women in both rural and urban areas. Similarly, family planning knowledge and adoption were also high among high autonomy women in both rural and urban areas.

Women in both rural and urban areas started their child bearing at later ages (20 in rural and 21 in urban) and completed it by 23 years in rural and 24 years in urban areas. Most of the women in both rural and urban areas had completed their child bearing within a short span of 4-5 years.

The results of the study strongly suggest the need for the empowerment of women to attain a positive and sustainable demographic change in both rural and urban areas. The effective implementation of women empowerment programmes on a priority basis will certainly help to attain sustainable development through reduced fertility and improved reproductive health of women in India.

Annexure – I

Gender Development Index, Tamil Nadu, 2003

S. No.	*District Name*	*GDI indices*	*Level of Gender Development*
1.	Chennai	0.766	**High** ($\geq$ **0.7)**
2.	**Kancheepuram**	**0.710**	
3.	Kanniyakumari	0.708	
4.	Thoothukudi	0.703	
5.	Coimbatore	0.697	**Medium (0.6 to 0.69)**
6.	Nilgiris	0.686	
7.	**Thiruchirapalli**	**0.671**	
8.	Madurai	0.661	
9.	Tirunelveli	0.656	
10.	Erode	0.656	
11.	Vellore	0.655	
12.	Nagapattinam	0.652	
13.	Thiruvallur	0.651	
14.	Virdhunagar	0.649	
15.	Cuddalore	0.643	
16.	Karur	0.641	

(Contd.)

(Contd.Annexure - I)

S. No.	*District Name*	*GDI indices*	*Level of Gender Development*
17.	Dindigul	0.638	
18.	Sivagangai	0.635	
19.	Tiruvarur	0.633	
20.	Namakkal	0.631	
21.	Thanjavur	0.629	
22.	Theni	0.628	
23.	Ramanathapuram	0.626	
24.	Salem	0.625	
25.	Pudukottai	0.615	
26.	Thiruvannamalai	0.608	
27.	Perambalur	0.592	
28.	**Villupuram**	**0.582**	**Low (<0.6)**
29.	Dharmapuri	0.582	

Source: Tamil Nadu Human Development Report, 2003, Govt. of Tamil Nadu

Annexure - II

Women Autonomy Score

I. Sex –Segregated Interaction (SSI)

Sl. No	*Indicators*	*Score*
1	Taking meals	
	Take lastly	0
	Depends	1
	Take together...........................	2
2	Presence in the same room when husband is discussing with male members.	
	Never	0
	Sometimes...............................	1
	Always....................................	2
3	Participation in discussions with male members	
	Never	0
	Sometimes...............................	1
	Always....................................	2
4	Accompany husband for social functions	
	Never	0
	Sometimes...............................	1
	Always....................................	2

(Contd.)

(Contd.Annexure - II)

Sl. No	*Indicators*	*Score*
5	Husband helps in routine household works like collection of water, fuel and fodder etc.	
	Never	0
	Sometimes................................	1
	Always.....................................	2
6	Getting adequate quantity of food	
	Never	0
	Sometimes................................	1
	Always.....................................	2
7	Getting adequate nutritious food	
	Never	0
	Sometimes................................	1
	Always.....................................	2
8	Engaging relatives/friends at home in the absence of husband	
	Never	0
	Sometimes................................	1
	Always.....................................	2

Total Score (I) : Minimum: 0 Maximum: 16

II. Freedom of movement

Sl. No	*Indicators*	*Score*
1.	Going to shopping alone	
	Never	0
	Sometimes................................	1
	Always.....................................	2
2.	Going to shopping with friends/ neighbours	
	Never	0
	Sometimes................................	1
	Always.....................................	2

(Contd.)

(Contd.Annexure - II)

Sl. No	*Indicators*	*Score*
3.	Going to movies alone	
	Never	0
	Sometimes................................	1
	Always....................................	2
4.	Going to function/parties alone	
	Never	0
	Sometimes................................	1
	Always....................................	2
5.	Attending village/community functions alone	
	Never	0
	Sometimes................................	1
	Always....................................	2
6.	Visiting friends home alone	
	Never	0
	Sometimes................................	1
	Always....................................	2
7.	Visiting parents/relatives house alone	
	Never	0
	Sometimes................................	1
	Always....................................	2
8.	Attending religious festivals alone	
	Never	0
	Sometimes................................	1
	Always....................................	2
9.	Going to hospital alone	
	Never	0
	Sometimes................................	1
	Always....................................	2
10.	Going to temple alone	
	Never	0
	Sometimes................................	1
	Always....................................	2
11.	Going to hotel alone	
	Never	0
	Sometimes................................	1
	Always....................................	2
12.	Going out of villages/town alone	
	Never	0
	Sometimes................................	1
	Always....................................	2

(Contd.)

(Contd.Annexure - II)

Sl. No	*Indicators*	*Score*
13.	Scolding for returning home at late evening	
	Never	0
	Sometimes................................	1
	Always......................................	2

Total Score (II) : Minimum: 0 Maximum: 26

III. Freedom to Participate in Social and Political Activities

Sl. No	*Indicators*	*Score*
1	Taking part in club/women's group activities	
	Never	0
	Sometimes................................	1
	Always......................................	2
2	Taking part in election activities	
	Never	0
	Sometimes................................	1
	Always......................................	2
3	Taking part in Panchayat activities	
	Never	0
	Sometimes................................	1
	Always......................................	2
4	Taking part in community welfare activities/ meetings	
	Never	0
	Sometimes................................	1
	Always......................................	2
5	Articulation in public meetings	
	Never	0
	Sometimes................................	1
	Always......................................	2
6	Interaction with men/boys	
	Never	0
	Sometimes................................	1
	Always......................................	2

(Contd.)

(Contd.Annexure - II)

Sl. No	*Indicators*	*Score*
7	Membership in local Institution	
	Never	0
	Sometimes................................	1
	Always......................................	2

Total Score (III): Minimum: 0 Maximum: 14

IV. Financial Management

Sl. No	*Indicators*	*Score*
1	Maintaining family income	
	Husband/Others........................	0
	Both...	1
	Herself.....................................	2
2	Control over jewels brought from natal family	
	Husband/Others........................	0
	Both...	1
	Herself.....................................	2
3	Maintaining family property	
	Husband/Others........................	0
	Both...	1
	Herself.....................................	2

Total Score (IV): Minimum: 0 Maximum: 06

V. Household Decisions

Sl. No	*Indicators*	*Score*
1	Purchase of major household items (e.g. Furniture's, appliances, bicycle etc)	
	Husband/Others........................	0
	Both...	1
	Herself.....................................	2
2	Purchase of dress for herself/for family members	
	Husband/Others........................	0
	Both...	1
	Herself.....................................	2

(Contd.)

(Contd.Annexure - II)

Sl. No	*Indicators*	*Score*
3	Decision about purchase of property/jewels etc.	
	Husband/Others........................	0
	Both...	1
	Herself.....................................	2
4	Decision about lending/borrowing	
	Husband/Others........................	0
	Both...	1
	Herself.....................................	2
5	Decision about household budget	
	Husband/Others........................	0
	Both...	1
	Herself.....................................	2
6	Decision about children's education	
	Husband/Others........................	0
	Both...	1
	Herself.....................................	2
7	Decision about children's marriage	
	Husband/Others........................	0
	Both...	1
	Herself.....................................	2
8	Decision about performing/attending function/ceremonies	
	Husband/Others........................	0
	Both...	1
	Herself.....................................	2
9	Decision about inviting and engaging guests at home	
	Husband/Others........................	0
	Both...	1
	Herself.....................................	2
10	Consultation in making important family decisions	
	Never	0
	Sometimes................................	1
	Always.....................................	2
11	Weightage given for her views/suggestions	
	Never	0
	Sometimes................................	1
	Always.....................................	2

Total Score (V): Minimum: 0 Maximum: 22

VI. Freedom of Choice

Sl. No	*Indicators*	*Score*
1.	Wearing dresses of her choice	
	Does not allow...........................	0
	Allows some times......................	1
	Always allows............................	2
2.	Hair style of her choice	
	Does not allow...........................	0
	Allows some times......................	1
	Always allows............................	2
3.	Voting in election as she likes	
	Does not allow...........................	0
	Allows some times......................	1
	Always allows............................	2
4.	Freedom to decide the timing of sex with husband	
	Does not allow...........................	0
	Allows some times......................	1
	Always allows............................	2
5.	Freedom to cook the food items according to her choice	
	Does not allow...........................	0
	Allows some times......................	1
	Always allows............................	2
6.	Freedom to talk with neighbours	
	Does not allow...........................	0
	Allows some times......................	1
	Always allows............................	2
7.	Freedom to use household appliances like radio, TV, telephone etc. as she likes	
	Does not allow...........................	0
	Allows some times......................	1
	Always allows............................	2
8.	Freedom to worship the God of her choice	
	Does not allow...........................	0
	Allows some times......................	1
	Always allows............................	2

Total Score (VI): Minimum: 0 Maximum: 16

VII. Violence Against Women

Sl. No	*Indicators*	*Score*
1	Experience of verbal abuse from husband	
	Never	0
	Sometimes..................................	1
	Always......................................	2
2	Experience of verbal abuse from in-laws	
	Never	0
	Sometimes..................................	1
	Always......................................	2
3	Experience of any physical abuse by husband	
	Never	0
	Sometimes..................................	1
	Always......................................	2
4	Experience of any physical abuse by in-laws	
	Never	0
	Sometimes..................................	1
	Always......................................	2
5	Ill-treatment at home by husband	
	Never	0
	Sometimes..................................	1
	Always......................................	2
6	Ill-treatment at home by in-laws/others members of family	
	Never	0
	Sometimes..................................	1
	Always......................................	2
7	Drinking habit of husband	
	Never	0
	Sometimes..................................	1
	Always......................................	2
8	Harassment from family members/husband	
	Never	0
	Sometimes..................................	1
	Always......................................	2

(Contd.)

(Contd. Table)

Sl. No	*Indicators*	*Score*
9	Intimidation by any of the family members	
	Never	0
	Sometimes.................................	1
	Always.....................................	2
10	Incidence of eve teasing	
	Never	0
	Sometimes.................................	1
	Always.....................................	2

Total Score (VII): Minimum: 0 Maximum: 20

VIII. Decision about Contraception and Fertility

Sl. No	*Indicators*	*Score*
1	Decision about timing of child birth	
	Husband/Others........................	0
	Both..	1
	Herself.....................................	2
2	Decision about number of children	
	Husband/Others........................	0
	Both..	1
	Herself.....................................	2
3	Decision about adoption of family planning method	
	Husband/Others.....................	0
	Both.....................................	1
	Herself..................................	2
4	Decision about sex composition of children	
	Husband/Others........................	0
	Both..	1
	Herself.....................................	2

Total Score (VIII): Minimum: 0 Maximum: 08

Total autonomy score (I to VIII) - 128

On the basis of total score attained by each woman, the autonomy status of woman was classified into three groups as:

(a) Low autonomy: If the total score was 73 or less (. 33.3 percentile).

(b) Medium autonomy: If the total score was between 74 and 86 (>33.3 and .66.6 percentiles).

(c) High autonomy: If the total score was 87 or more (> 66.6 percentile).

Annexure – III

Standard of Living Index (SLI)

Sl. No	*Household Items / Housing Characteristics*	*Score*
1	Clock/Watch	1
2	Fan	1
3	Bicycle	1
4	Pressure Cooker	1
5	Table/Chair	1
6	Mattress	1
7	Sewing Machine	2
8	Radio/Transistor/ Tape Recorder	2
9	VCR/VCP/VCD/DVD	2
10	Cooking Gas	2
11	Phone	2
12	Mixie	2
13	Grinder	2
14	Moped	2
15	Cot / bed	2
16	Refrigerator	3
17	Television	3
18	Sofa Set	3
19	Washing Machine	3
20	Air condition	4
21	Bore well alone	4
22	Bore well with motor pump	5
23	Motor Cycle/ Scooter	5
24	Car	6

(Contd.)

(Contd. Annexure - III)

Sl. No	*Household Items / Housing Characteristics*	*Score*
25	Type of house	
	Hut	1
	Katcha	2
	Pucca	3
26	Ownership	
	Own	1
	Rented	0
27	Toilet facilities	
	Yes	1
	No	0
	Total Score	65

The total score varied from a low of 0 to a maximum of 65. On the basis of total score, women were grouped into three categories of standard of living as:

a. Low SLI : 21 or less

b. Medium SLI : 22 - 42

c. High SLI : 43 or more

Annexure – IV

Mass Media Index (Score)

Sl. No	*Indicators*	*Score*
1	Watch television once a week	
	Yes	1
	No	0
2	Listen to radio once a week	
	Yes	1
	No	0
3	Going to cinema once a month	
	Yes	1
	No	0
4	Reading newspapers / magazine	
	Yes	1
	No	0

Minimum score – 0

Maximum score – 4

Mass Media Index

No exposure to mass media – 0

Low exposure to mass media – 1 to 2

High exposure to mass media – 3 to 4

Bibliography

Abadian S. 1996. 'Women's autonomy and its impact on fertility'. WORLD DEVELOPMENT. 1996 Dec; 24(12) : 1793-809.

Al Riyami A and Afifi M. 2003. 'Women empowerment and marital fertility in Oman'. J Egypt Public Health Assoc. 2003; 78 (1-2) : 55-72.

Al Riyami A; Afifi M and Mabry RM. 2004. 'Women's autonomy, education and employment in Oman and their influence on contraceptive use'. Reproductive Health Matters. 2004 May; 12 (23) : 144-154.

Basu A.M. 1992. "Culture, the status of women and Demographic Behaviour", Oxford, Clarendon press.

Beijing documents. 1995. 'The agenda for women's Empowerment'. *Populi,* 22:8, December 1995.

Bhagyalakshmi. J. 2004. 'Women's Empowerment: Miles to go'. *Yojana*, 48, pp. 38-41.

Bhatt KK. 2000. 'Women's autonomy among Rajasthani migrants in Mumbai'. Mumbai, India, International Institute for Population Sciences, 2000 April 18. [7] p.

Bloom SS; Wypij D and Das Gupta. M. 2001. 'Dimensions of women's autonomy and the influence on maternal health care utilization in a north Indian city'. Demography. 2001 Feb;38(1):67-78.

Cairo, 1994. 'International conference on Population and Development (ICPD)', Cairo, Egypt.

Cleland J; Kamal N and Sloggett A. 1996. 'Links between fertility regulation and the schooling and autonomy of women in Bangladesh'. In: Girls' schooling, women's autonomy and fertility change in South Asia, edited by Roger Jeffery and Alaka M. Basu. New Delhi, India, Sage Publications, 1996. : 205-17.

Das Gupta M; Lee S; Uberoi P; Wang D and Wang L. 2000. 'State policies and women's autonomy in China, the Republic of Korea and India 1950-2000: lessons from contrasting experiences'. Washington, D.C., World Bank, Development Research Group / Poverty Reduction and Economic Management Network, 2000 Dec. 46 p. Policy Research Report on Gender and Development Working Paper Series No. 16. http://www.worldbank.org/gender/prr/wp16.pdf

Dey D and Bhavsar S. 2002. 'Women's empowerment and its relevance to fertility and child mortality: an analysis based on NFHS-2, Gujarat data'. Presented at the 25th Annual Conference of the Indian Association for the Study of Population, International Institute for Population Sciences, Mumbai, India, February 11-13, 2002. 18 p.

Dey. A.S. 2002. 'Measurement of women's empowerment: problems and prospectives'. Presented at the 25th Annual Conference of the Indian Association for the Study of Population, International Institute for Population Sciences, Mumbai, India, February 11-13, 2002. 11 p.

Drovandi S and Salvini S. 2004. 'Women's autonomy and demographic behaviour'. Population Review. 2004; 43 (2) : [31] p.

Dyson, Tim and Moore, M (1983). "On Kinship structure, Female autonomy and demographic behaviour", Population and Development Review, Vol. 9, No. 1. pp. 35-60

Geneva. 1996. 'Forty-ninth World Health Assembly, Geneva'. 20-25 May, WHA 49.12 WHO global strategy for occupational health for all.

Greenspan A. 1994. 'Culture influences demographic behavior: evidence from India'. Asia Pac Pop Policy. 1994 Mar; (28):1-4.

Gupta VM and Sen P. 2002. 'Women empowerment'. Indian Journal of Public Health. 2002 Jan-Mar; 46 (1) : 22-27.

Hadi A; Nath SR and Chowdhury AM. 1997. 'Credit programme, women's autonomy and reproductive behaviour: evidence from BRAC villages, Bangladesh'. In: Comparative perspectives on fertility transition in South Asia. Based on the seminar organized by the Committee on Fertility and Family Planning of the International Union for the Scientific Study of Population (IUSSP) and the Population Council, Islamabad, Rawalpindi / Islamabad, 17-19 December 1996. Papers. Volume I. Liege, Belgium, International Union for the Scientific Study of Population [IUSSP], [1997] :15 p.

Hindin MJ. 2000. 'Women's autonomy, women's status and fertility-related behavior in Zimbabwe'. Population Research and Policy Review. 2000 Jun ; 19 (3) : 255-82.

Hogan. D.P., Berhanu. B and Hailemariam A. 1999. 'Household organization, women's autonomy and contraceptive behavior in southern Ethiopia'. Studies in Family Planning. 1999 Dec ; 30 (4) : 302-14.

Hussain R. 2001. 'The effect of marriage preferences on women's autonomy: a case study'. In: Pakistan's population issues in the 21st century. Conference proceedings Oct 24th - 26th, 2000, Karachi, [compiled by] Population Association of Pakistan. Islamabad, Pakistan, Population Association of Pakistan, 2001. :117-33.

Jeffery R and Basu AM. 1996. 'Girls' schooling, women's autonomy and fertility change in South Asia'. New Delhi, India, Sage Publications, 1996. 339 p.

Jejeebhoy SJ. 1991. "Women's status and fertility: Successive Cross-Cultural Evidence from Tamil Nadu, India" studies in family planning 22(4), pp. 217-230

Jejeebhoy SJ and Sathar ZA. 2001. 'Women's autonomy in India and Pakistan: the influence of religion and region'. Population and Development Review. 2001 Dec; 27(4):687-712.

Jejeebhoy SJ. 1997. 'Women's autonomy and reproductive behaviour in India: linkages and influence of socio-cultural context'. In: Comparative perspectives on fertility transition in South Asia. Based on the seminar organized by the Committee on Fertility and Family Planning of the International Union for the Scientific Study of Population (IUSSP) and the Population Council, Islamabad, Rawalpindi / Islamabad, 17-19 December 1996. Papers. Volume I. Liege, Belgium, International Union for the Scientific Study of Population [IUSSP], [1997]. :20, [7] p. 3.

Kishor S. 1995. 'Three faces of women's autonomy in Egypt: are they painted with the same brush?' [Unpublished] 1995. Presented at the Annual Meeting of the Population Association of America, San Francisco, California, April 6-8, 1995. 30, [14] p.

Manisha Gangwar and Nita Kandekar, 2004. 'Empowerment status of rural women: Insights from dairy cooperatives'. *Social change,* 34:1, pp.112-125.

Mason KO. 1997. 'How family position influences married women's autonomy and power in five Asian countries'. Honolulu, Hawaii, East-West Center, 1997 May. 20 p. East-West Center Working Papers. Population Series No. 89.

Meenakshi Joshi. 2004. 'Empowering Rural Women through Watershed Project'. *Kurukshetra*, 52:9, pp. 19 -24.

National Family Health Survey India (NFHS-2) 1998-99 Tamil Nadu, India.

Naushin Mahmood and Durr-E-Nayab. 1998. 'Gender Dimensions of Demographic Change in Pakistan'. The Pakistan Development Review. Vol 37. issue 4. pp. 705-725

Nawar L. 1995. 'Women's autonomy and gender roles in Egyptian families: implications for family planning and reproductive health'. In: CDC 25th Annual Seminar, 1995, [compiled by] Cairo Demographic Center. Cairo, Egypt, Cairo Demographic Center, 1996. :173-209. Cairo Demographic Center Research Monograph Series No. 25.

Neidell S.G, 1998. 'Women's Empowerment as a public problem': A case study of the 1994 International conference population Research and policy Review, Volume 1, No. 3, pp. 247-264 (14).

NFHS. 1998-99. 'National Family Health Survey India (NFHS) 1998-99, Tamil Nadu, India.

Panda PK. 1994. 'Household poverty, women's autonomy and reproductive behaviour: linkages in a rural setting in Orissa, India'. In: Women, poverty and demographic change. Based on the seminar organized by the IUSSP Committee on Gender and Population in collaboration with El Colegio de Mexico, the Mexican Society of Demography (SOMEDE), the National Population Council (CONAPO) and the State Population Council of Oaxaca, Mexico, 25-28 October 1994. Papers. Liege, Belgium, International Union for the Scientific Study of Population [IUSSP], 1994. :14 p.

Population Briefs. 1995. 'Gender inequalities and demographic behavior.' Population Briefs. 1995 Jan;1(1):6.

Population Briefs. 1999. 'Women's Autonomy necessary for fertility decline?' Population Briefs. 1999 Dec; 5 (4):4.

Population Briefs. 1999. Title: Is women's autonomy necessary for fertility decline? POPLINE Document Number: 166632, Population Briefs, 1999 Dec; 5(4):4.

Ramachandran V. 2002. 'Fertility and women's autonomy'. Seminar. 2002 Mar; (511):76-80.

Roy TK and Niranjan S. 2002. 'Empowerment of women in India: indicators and its evidence'. [Unpublished] 2002. Presented at the 25th Annual Conference of the Indian Association for the Study of Population, International Institute for Population Sciences, Mumbai, India, February 11-13, 2002. 12 p.

Sathar ZA and Kazi S. 2000. 'Women's autonomy in the context of rural Pakistan. Pakistan Development Review. 2000 Summer;39(2):89-110.

Sathar ZA; Kazi S and Zaidi S. 1996. 'Women autonomy and the onset of fertility change in Pakistan: the significance of gender inequality across communities'. [Unpublished] 1996. Presented at the Annual Meeting of the Population Association of America, New Orleans, Louisiana, May 9-11, 1996. 27 p.

Senthil Vadivoo. K and Sekar. V. 2004. 'Self-Help Group – A moment for women', *Kisan world,* 31:7, pp. 13-14.

Sharma, S.L. 2000. 'Empowerment without Antagonism: A Case for Reformulation of Women's Empowerment Approach'. *Sociological bulletin*, 49, pp. 19-39.

Shastri VD. 2002. 'Measuring and analyzing women's empowerment / autonomy: a cross state comparative study based on National Family Health Survey-2'. Presented at the 25th Annual Conference of the Indian Association for the Study of Population, International Institute for Population Sciences, Mumbai, India, February 11-13, 2002. [14] p.

Smita Mishra Panda. 2000. 'Women's Empowerment through NGO Interventions: A frame work for assessment'. *Social change issues and perspectives*, 30:3 & 4, pp. 44 – 63.

Sthapit S. 1999. 'Gender, autonomy and women's reproductive health: Manmaiju, Kathmandu, Nepal'. Bangkok, Thailand, Asian Institute of Technology, School of Environment, Resources and Development, 1999 Aug. xii, 123 p.

Sulaja S. 2002. 'Social development and empowerment of women in south Indian states'. Presented at the 25th

Annual Conference of the Indian Association for the Study of Population, International Institute for Population Sciences, Mumbai, India, February 11-13, 2002. [7] p.

TamilNadu Human Development Report. 2003. 'Government of TamilNadu, India'.

United Nations. 1987. 'Female autonomy and fertility: an overview of the situation in South Asia'. Asia Pac Popul J. 1987 Dec;2(4):43-52.

United Nations. 1993. 'World Conference on Human Rights'. General Assembly, United Nations, A/CONF.157/23.

United Nations. 1995. 'Women's Education and Fertility Behaviour' A case study of Rural Maharashtra, India", U.N. New York.

United Nations. 1995. 'Fourth World Conference on Women'. Beijing Declaration (4-15 September, 1995).

United Nations. 1998. 'Global Population. The Facts of Life'. United Nations, 2, p. 1999.

United Nations. 2005. 'UN Millennium Development Goals'. World summit United Nations Headquarters, NY.

Vienna. 1993. 'World conference on Human rights'. Vienna declaration and programme of Action, 14-25 June. General Assembly, United Nations A/CONF 157/23.

Visaria, L. 1993. "Female Autonomy and Fertility Behaviour: An Exploration of Gujarat Data In: International Union for the scientific study of Population (IUSSP)," proceedings of the International Population conference, Montreal Vol. IV international Union for the scientific study of population liege.

Index

Index

Z